COMING APART
AT THE
SEAMS

COMING APART
AT THE
SEAMS

HOW BASEBALL OWNERS, PLAYERS, AND TELEVISION EXECUTIVES HAVE LED OUR NATIONAL PASTIME TO THE BRINK OF DISASTER

JACK SANDS AND PETER GAMMONS

MACMILLAN PUBLISHING COMPANY
New York

MAXWELL MACMILLAN CANADA
Toronto

MAXWELL MACMILLAN INTERNATIONAL
New York   Oxford   Singapore   Sydney

To ARRIA,
teammate for twenty years who has never once filed for arbitration, declared Free Agency or demanded to renegotiate our contract.

J. S.

Copyright © 1993 by Jack Sands and Peter Gammons

Macmillan Publishing Company　　Maxwell Macmillan Canada, Inc.
866 Third Avenue　　　　　　　　1200 Eglinton Avenue East
New York, NY 10022　　　　　　　Suite 200
　　　　　　　　　　　　　　　　Don Mills, Ontario M3C 3N1

Macmillan Publishing Company is part of the Maxwell Communication Group of Companies.

Library of Congress Cataloging-in-Publication Data
Sands, Jack.
　　Coming apart at the seams : how baseball owners, players,
and television executives led our national pastime to the brink of
disaster/Jack Sands and Peter Gammons.
　　　　p.　　　cm.
　　Includes index.
　　ISBN 0-02-542411-4
　　1. Baseball—Economic aspects—United States.　2. Baseball—United
States—Organization and administration.　I. Gammons, Peter.
II. Title.
GV880.S26　1993　　　　　　　92-34157　CIP
338.4'7796357'64—dc20

Macmillan books are available at special discounts for bulk purchases for sales promotions, premiums, fund-raising, or educational use. For details, contact:

Special Sales Director
Macmillan Publishing Company
866 Third Avenue
New York, NY 10022

Designed by Michael Mendelsohn

10　9　8　7　6　5　4　3　2　1

Printed in the United States of America

"Baseball must be a great game
to survive the fools who run it.
No business in the world has ever
made more money with poorer management.
It can survive anything."

—Bill Terry, *Player and Manager*,
on retiring from baseball in 1941

CONTENTS

ACKNOWLEDGMENTS

If the manuscript for this book had been turned in when it was due much of the most recent events that are shaping baseball's future would not have been reported. I would like to first thank our agent, Jay Acton, for finding the right editor who understands that baseball, and those who write about it, are not conscious of a clock. To Rick Wolff, the editor at Macmillan who allowed the clock to run, both Peter and I owe you our gratitude. I now know why the Cleveland Indians hired you as their team psychologist. You listen, encourage, and counsel equally well. Finally, without Gretchen McGill's assistance the manuscript would still not be completed. Thanks for being part of the team.

J. S.

CAST OF CHARACTERS

THE COMMISSIONER'S OFFICE
Bowie Kuhn
Peter Ueberroth
Bart Giamatti
Fay Vincent

THE OWNERS
Peter O'Malley
Bud Selig
Jerry Reinsdorf
Eddie Einhorn
Bill Giles
George Steinbrenner
Ted Turner

THE PLAYER RELATIONS COMMITTEE
Lee MacPhail
Barry Rona
Richard Ravitch

THE PLAYERS ASSOCIATION
Marvin Miller
Donald Fehr

THE INDEPENDENT ARBITRATOR
George Nicolau

THE AGENTS
Jerry Kapstein
Dick Moss

Tom Reich
Dennis Gilbert
Scott Boras

THE COMMISSIONER'S OFFICE

Bowie Kuhn: Baseball's commissioner from 1969 to 1984, during which time the owners lost control over the players. Some saw him as a Jimmy Stewart character, in dark suits and striped ties, resembling a wonderful grandfather. Some saw him as a stuffed shirt. Others felt in the end that, after he'd risen from being the National League's lawyer to become a compromise selection when General William Eckert turned out to be a disaster, he was like Richard Nixon, willing to do anything to retain his office.

Peter Ueberroth: The Machiavellian pragmatist who was exactly what the owners wanted to succeed Kuhn; but when they got caught price-fixing salaries and had to fork over $10 million apiece, they claimed it was all his doing and that what they really wanted was a traditional baseball idealist. He ran the Los Angeles Olympics for profit and without gridlock, and he tried to so organize baseball. He was the boss. When Lee MacPhail and the Player Relations Committee settled the 1985 strike, they wouldn't tell Ueberroth where they were meeting, but he still managed to take credit for the settlement. He quit before his five-year contract was to expire in 1989.

Bart Giamatti: The Philosopher King who died in office less than one year after succeeding Ueberroth. The former president of Yale University, he was a brilliant Renaissance scholar, a romanticist who walked across the Yale campus in a Red Sox hat and wrote odes to the beauty of the game and the evils of the designated hitter. He was also a classic conservative, a comrade of Robert Bork, who attracted the owners because he broke the unions at Yale.

Fay Vincent: Giamatti's close friend and confidant, who tried to carry his predecessor's romantic ties with the game when he was chosen to serve out Giamatti's term. He faced several problems not the least of which was that he didn't have the ingratiating political savvy or inherent leadership skills necessary for an impossible job. His prior experiences of working for a federal bureaucracy (the Securities and Exchange Commission) and an international conglomerate (Coca-Cola) did not prepare him for the task of overseeing twenty-eight teams with separate economic self-interests. His attempt to use the media to rally public support around him only hastened his removal from the most difficult job in sports.

The Owners

Peter O'Malley: Son of Walter O'Malley, who took the Brooklyn Dodgers and major league baseball west of the Mississippi. He looks like the chairman of a Brahmin bank, loves the ballet, theatre, and the arts, and is a dedicated social benefactor; but, like his father, he loves money—hence the nickname, Peter O'Money. Where his father had the passion for politics of a Boss Tweed, Peter refused to get his fingernails dirty in baseball politics until he realized that the O'Malley name was no longer synonymous with power.

Bud Selig: Everyone's next-door neighbor. He inherited his father's automobile dealership, then successfully led the fight to bring baseball back to Milwaukee after the Braves left. He constantly fought the small-market fight to save baseball for Milwaukee when no one else likely would have tried. Politics—he's a social liberal and fiscal conservative right out of the Paul Tsongas school—is his first love; not only is he active in Wisconsin politics, but he is the number one political power and broker in baseball. The night he interviewed Giamatti for the commissioner's job, they walked the streets of New York waxing about the game until 4:00 A.M.

Jerry Reinsdorf: A brilliant, blunt businessman from Brooklyn who is a born dealmaker. He made millions in real estate syndications, then structured similar partnership deals consisting primarily of other people's money to buy the White Sox and Bulls. A baseball mogul who knows "what makes sense for me," he believes that sports franchises go through cycles like real estate. He's a classic entrepreneur who, unlike his good friend Selig, knows no romanticism when it comes to dollars.

Eddie Einhorn: Reinsdorf's law school classmate and partner. With his background in producing sporting events for television, Einhorn knows more about the medium that controls baseball's financial future than anyone else in the game. Also the most "streetwise" of all the owners, he considers himself an outsider with the traditional baseball establishment.

Bill Giles: Led syndicate that bought the Philadelphia Phillies from the Carpenter family in 1982. He is the son of a former National League president, Warren Giles, and was raised to be in baseball. As director of public relations for the Houston Astros, he ran the first electronic scoreboard and caused a stink in Houston by insulting umpires and opposing players alike. He has never shaken the PR mold, and has always been swayed by public reaction—he once called a press conference to announce that he wasn't firing his manager because of the negative response to the leaked news that he was firing him. He's sympathetic to Einhorn's maverick ideas, but with his upbringing, Giles is also sensitive to old-line National League views.

George Steinbrenner: The man who was BORN ON THE FOURTH OF JULY! and lives for the limelight. He came from Cleveland as chairman of American Shipbuilding, and from the time he bought the Yankees from CBS in 1973, he was smitten by the "New York is bigger and better" disease. He once fired all his telephone operators at American Shipbuilding because he didn't get an answer at 4:57 P.M. He had an operator fired at the Sheraton-Boston because she fouled up a message. He fired PR directors, managers, general managers . . . and then paid them double because he felt bad. One of his partners once said, "There is nothing more limited than being a limited partner in Steinbrenner's partnership."

Ted Turner: After buying the Atlanta Braves in 1976, he tried to promote baseball in a region fanatically devoted to football. He became more successful selling his team to other parts of the country as filler programming for his ever-growing cable network. When he was actively sailing 12-meter yachts, one of his crew members said, "If everyone else in the race tacked away from the shore, he tacked into shore, so he either won or sat becalmed." The characteristic that made him an America's Cup champion also made him *Time* magazine's 1991 Man of the Year for his creation of an incredible media empire: He loves living on the edge.

THE PLAYER RELATIONS COMMITTEE

Lee MacPhail: The grand uncle of baseball. Generation Two of baseball's most distinguished three-generation family, but unlike Larry MacPhail, his electric father, Lee was a solid pragmatist who ran clubs, was American League president, served as chairman of the Player Relations Committee, and never lost an ounce of anyone's respect because he was, above all else, forever honest.

Barry Rona: Succeeded Lee MacPhail as chairman of the Player Relations Committee and was fired on the eve of the 1990 labor negotiations after years of losing clashes with the Players Association. He then tried to become an agent, but the Players Union denied him certification because of the clubs' refusal to waive their prior attorney/client confidentiality privilege with him.

Richard Ravitch: A multimillionaire who was an unsuccessful candidate for mayor of New York City in 1989, Ravitch was hired in 1991 by the owners as a message to both Commissioner Vincent and the Major League Baseball Players Association. The owners were preparing for an all-out war on the union and Ravitch would have more power—and a larger salary—than the commissioner.

THE PLAYERS ASSOCIATION

Marvin Miller: The classic Upton Sinclair laborite, after working for the steelworkers union, he was brought to baseball in 1966 by a few rebel players—including future Congressman Jim Bunning—to create and head the Players Association. He did it on a shoestring, fighting and contesting ownership at every turn, and between logic, brass, and an adept ability to control the media, he completely turned baseball around.

Donald Fehr: A Midwestern lawyer who represented the players in their successful challenge to the reserve clause in 1976, he was hired to replace the flamboyant, Eastern Dick Moss as counsel for the Players Association, and was then promoted to executive director when Miller's successor, Ken Moffett, was fired by the players. He was never as brilliant a media manipulator as Miller was, but he is the master of outrage and as honest and true to the cause of keeping the playing fields level as Miller. Like the union's first leader, suspicion keeps Fehr ever alert. As one owner once said, "All we have to fear is Fehr himself."

THE INDEPENDENT ARBITRATOR

George Nicolau: Baseball's permanent arbitrator who in 1988 found the owners guilty of acting in concert to hold down the players' salaries. A lawyer in his late sixties, Nicolau lost his left leg while navigating a B-17 bomber over Germany during World War II. Nicolau became baseball's permanent arbitrator in September 1986, after the owners fired Tom Roberts, his predecessor.

THE AGENTS

Jerry Kapstein: He was the first big-time agent, rising from his family's office in Providence to gather the first load of powerful players when free agency struck in the seventies. He once believed that his phone had been tapped by Oakland A's owner Charles O. Finley. Then when Kapstein moved to San Diego he became an eccentric recluse, so media-shy that if someone called him, he would pick up the phone, not answer, and wait for the other party to speak; if it were someone he didn't want to talk to, he hung up. He later married Linda Kroc, stepdaughter of the McDonald's czar who owned the Padres; became president of the Padres; was decertified as an agent by the Association; engineered the club's sale; and then, when Kroc first divorced him and then had him fired, he dropped out of baseball. He and Kroc recently remarried.

Dick Moss: Marvin Miller's right-hand man throughout the early battles with the owners. He quit to become an agent and quickly acquired many household names as clients, such as Nolan Ryan, and Andre Dawson. Moss has been less of a force in the industry over the last few years, as he has worked with outsiders to develop a new league to challenge major league baseball.

Tom Reich: Out of Pittsburgh, he originally represented Latin and black players, and built a considerable practice. He is outspoken, brilliant, sometimes outrageous, and one of the prime maverick dealmakers in the business. On more than one occasion New York sportwriters have reported that George Steinbrenner cannot say no to any free agent represented by Reich.

Dennis Gilbert: Known as Go-Go, he was a former minor league ballplayer and scout who made a killing in insurance for Hollywood stars. When his friend, former Red Sox star Tony Conigliaro, had a stroke and could no longer run the Beverly Hills Sports Council, Gilbert took it over. By the nineties Gilbert had built a huge practice with Jose Canseco, Bobby Bonilla, Barry Bonds, Danny Tartabull, and many other big names. Other agents tried to show that Gilbert bought his clients, but nothing was ever proven, and Go-Go drives through Beverly Hills in his Rolls-Royce with the license "GO GO 17." (Yes, 17 was his number in the Boston farm system.)

Scott Boras: Former minor league player who for many club officials has replaced Dick Moss as the most disliked agent. Boras single-handedly changed the minor league draft process by convincing top draft picks that the signing bonuses paid to high school and college players has not kept pace with the salaries paid to major league players. Several clubs now refuse to draft players who they suspect have retained Boras as their "family advisor."

ORGANIZATIONS

MAJOR LEAGUE BASEBALL
The twenty-eight clubs that make up the American and National leagues.

MAJOR LEAGUE BASEBALL PLAYER RELATIONS COMMITTEE, INC.
Referred to as the Player Relations Committee (PRC), it is responsible for negotiating the collective bargaining agreement with the players's union on behalf of the owners.

EXECUTIVE COUNCIL
A committee composed of the commissioner of baseball, the president of each of the major leagues, and eight club members, four from each league. In the absence of a commissioner, the Executive Council is the governing body of Major League Baseball.

OWNERSHIP COMMITTEE
A committee made up of owners from both leagues responsible for interviewing and making recommendations regarding all prospective new owners of existing and expansion franchises.

MAJOR LEAGUE BASEBALL PLAYERS ASSOCIATION
The players union, headed up by an executive director. It is responsible for negotiating all work-related matters on behalf of the players with the Player Relations Committee.

NATIONAL ASSOCIATION OF PROFESSIONAL BASEBALL LEAGUES
The governing body of the minor leagues.

AGREEMENTS

MAJOR LEAGUE AGREEMENT

Agreement between the American and National League clubs, first executed on January 12, 1921. The Major League Agreement, along with its accompanying rules, is the governing constitution for major league baseball.

BASIC AGREEMENT

The collective bargaining agreement between the American and National leagues and the Major League Baseball Players Association.

PROFESSIONAL BASEBALL AGREEMENT AND RULES

The agreement between the American and National League clubs and the National Association of Professional Baseball Leagues regarding all matters that involve the minor leagues.

PLAYER DEVELOPMENT AGREEMENT

The agreement between each major league club and its minor league affiliates that covers the working conditions between the parent major league club and its affiliates.

UNIFORM PLAYER'S CONTRACT

The standard-form contract each major league player signs that covers all work-related conditions with his major league club. Except for the issue of compensation above the minimum salary, every player in the major leagues signs the same Uniform Player's Contract.

Thinking to get at once
all the gold the goose could give,
he killed it and opened it
only to find—nothing.
  —Aesop
  "The Goose with the Golden Eggs"

PROLOGUE

FENWAY PARK, OCTOBER 1990

Dwight Evans, the veteran Red Sox designated hitter, waited in the on-deck circle for one last at bat. His team, three outs away from clinching the 1990 American League East title, was clinging to a 3–1 lead over the Chicago White Sox with one out in the bottom of the eighth inning.

The irony of it all was not lost on Evans. The White Sox had been scheduled to open the 1990 season in Fenway. Instead, the three-game series had been tacked on at the end. There had been no spring training in 1990 because the owners had locked the players out of the camps until a new collective-bargaining agreement was reached, and as a result the teams' opening series had been postponed from April to October.

Bent on one knee, Evans casually looked up at the new glass-enclosed "600 Club" above home plate, where the noise of typewriters used to cascade down from the old press box. Waiters were scurrying up and down the plush aisles delivering catered meals and choice California wines to the club members, who were separated from the rank and file by their air-conditioned, pneumatically sealed playpen. For a moment, Evans wasn't sure who was in the fishbowl—the uniformed players below or the suited spectators above.

With his eyes now transfixed on the pitcher, Evans allowed his mind to wander to another time. His eighteen seasons with the Red Sox had gone by fast, with no old friends remaining on the current Boston team to share the memories with. In the early years Carl Yastrzemski, Boston's great Hall of Famer, had been like a protective older brother, advising his young teammate on how to carry himself both on and off the field. On more than one occasion

1

they had sat in the empty stands with their paternalistic owner, Tom Yawkey, discussing for hours the most minute details of the prior day's game.

Back then there was an accepted apprenticeship that every player went through when he first made it to the big leagues. Even the young wives listened patiently to the "dos" and "don'ts" handed out by the veterans' spouses. Not now. Now the younger women resent the older wives whose husbands take up precious playing time from theirs. Playing time translates into days of service. Days of service add up to years of service. Three years of service means having arbitration rights and being three years closer to free agency. "When is Dwight going to retire?" a young player's wife asked Susan Evans as she watched her husband from the wives' section behind home plate.

Little did Evans know in 1973, when the American League adopted the rule allowing a designated hitter to bat in place of a pitcher, that seventeen years later he would be one of its biggest fans. A rookie when the "experiment" was introduced, Evans was better known for his prowess with the glove than with the bat. For over a decade between 1975 and 1986 he had established himself as the premier defensive outfielder in the game, winning eight Gold Gloves, symbolic of defensive excellence, while patrolling the toughest right field in the major leagues. But in the middle of the 1990 season the pain in his lower back had prevented him from taking his customary position in right field. And the additional at bats were precious to an aging ballplayer approaching 400 home runs and 1,500 runs batted in for his career.

A few feet away, Carlton Fisk, the Chicago catcher, surveyed the scene from his familiar position behind home plate. Deliberate as always, he briefly glanced at the screen above the left field wall where the most famous hit of his career had disappeared against a full autumn moon fifteen years before, abruptly ending the sixth game of the 1975 World Series, a game considered by many to be the most dramatic ever played. Slowly pivoting his head 180 degrees, he focused on the visitors' bullpen in right field, where in the eleventh inning on that same night a young Dwight Evans had reached over his head, robbed the

Reds' Joe Morgan of a home run, and then turned and doubled Ken Griffey off first base, allowing Fisk the opportunity to win the game in the bottom of the twelfth inning. Sparky Anderson, the Cincinnati manager at the time, had called Evans's catch the greatest he had ever seen.

Halfway between the Green Monster, the affectionate name by which Boston's left-field wall is known, and the bullpen stood the huge, state-of-the-art television scoreboard. Besides providing up-to-the-minute statistics on the batter at the plate, the newly in-stalled scoreboard was incessantly transmitting commercial messages that shattered the stillness of the crisp New England fall evening. Fifteen years before, as both Fisk and Evans remem-bered, Yawkey had resisted any commercial intrusions on his little park in the Fens. The crowded luxury boxes hanging out over the first and third baselines were another reminder of the recent changes to the smallest and most revered of all major league ballparks. How many more structural changes could it stand be-fore Boston's filled-in Back Bay shifted and claimed it for itself?

Satchel Paige, the great pitcher from the defunct Negro Leagues, once said, "Don't look back—something might be gaining on you." Fisk is a devout follower of the Gospel according to St. Paige. Squatting in his stance, Fisk's knees ached, and surgery had already been booked for the off-season on both. One more game. But the pain had been worth it. He had caught against Johnny Bench only once, and he had upstaged the Hall of Famer, even though the Reds had won the 1975 World Series. Now he had Bench's record as well. Early in the 1990 season Fisk had passed Bench by setting the major league record for home runs by a catcher. As with Evans, 400 home runs were within his sight, as well as Bob Boone's major league record for games caught.

Same place, another time, Fisk reminisced as he allowed him-self a momentary reflection on past glories and long-since-retired teammates he had shared with Evans. Slowly, he raised himself out of his crouch, placed his mask over his head, and walked out to the mound to give instructions to the young pitcher who, barely half his age, waited patiently for his orders.

Fisk's internal time clock was set to mirror the pace of the game he plays. Every move, every decision, and every confrontation in Fisk's mind requires careful analysis before commitment to action. As the players waited in suspended animation, Fisk returned to his position. A made-to-order double play ended the inning. But more than an inning had closed in the record books. Dwight Evans realized that unless the visitors rallied in the top of the ninth he probably would never get another chance in a regular-season game to wear the only uniform he had put on for eighteen years.

No active player had worn only one team's uniform longer and, except for George Brett and Robin Yount, it's doubtful that anyone will match his service to one club in the future. Certainly financial security is no longer a driving force for a player to stay in the game for twenty years. Likewise, clubs would rather see aging veterans, with their high salaries, retire and hawk their memorabilia on the card show circuit and television's Home Shopping Network. Boston had expressed no interest in exercising its option to bring back Evans for the 1991 season.

The opposing players rushed off the field without so much as a glance at the veteran who stood dispassionately, bat in hand, refusing to accept the finality of his career as a member of the Boston Red Sox. The noise from the scoreboard was deafening as a commercial jingle competed with the organist for the crowd's attention while the television sets in the luxury boxes broadcast a different message to a nonattentive audience. The fans below hurried to the concession stands for one last purchase.

Wiping the sweat from his brow, the umpire lifted his mask and walked away, leaving two tired warriors standing alone at home plate. No words were spoken. The admiration each held for the other required no verbal acknowledgment. Suddenly, not because he had remembered his last at bat in the same uniform ten years before, or because of their shared excellence on that fateful night in 1975, but out of respect for a former teammate who'd known the game when it was just a game, forty-two-year-old Carlton Fisk grabbed thirty-nine-year-old Dwight Evans as he turned to the dugout, and embraced him. It was over, and they both knew it.

Oh, there would be a few more games to play, but the game they learned as young boys growing up in California and New

England was now overshadowed by a much more avaricious one being fought in the towers on Park Avenue. Catching and hitting a ball had made them far wealthier than they had ever imagined. But the feeling of emptiness was equally unexpected. The joy of playing—of competing on the field—would last a lifetime. The rest they would just as soon forget.

O'HARE HYATT, DECEMBER 1990

The 1990 World Series ended with the sudden sweep of the mighty Oakland A's by the underdog Cincinnati Reds. The competition on the field was over, but the major confrontations that had overshadowed the Reds' victory were just beginning.

Two months later at the baseball winter meetings, the owners of the twenty-six major league clubs were turning in all directions to regain control over a simple game that had become a complex business. The first challenge to their old way of doing things hit them harder than the subzero temperature outside the hotel. "This is what we settled for?" one owner yelled in disbelief. Scared that if left to the arbitrators the fines would have been even worse, the clubs reluctantly agreed to pay the players $280 million. That was the sum awarded to the players by two arbitrators who had ruled during the 1990 season that owners had illegally conspired to hold down salaries between 1986 and 1989.

George Bush, Jr. was sweating profusely. The Secret Service agents looked out of place in the health club at the Hyatt while they watched the president's son attack the computerized exercise bike.

"Ueberroth told us when we bought the Texas Rangers that the collusion business wasn't our problem. Now we are expected to chip in ten million dollars toward the settlement. Hey, we didn't take part in it. Now we are being told that we might have to give players to the two new National League clubs in 1993, but that the American League clubs might not get a part of the money that Miami and Denver are paying to join the majors. We were led to believe that the expansion revenues would be shared with us too. We're a small-market team. There is no way we can survive in this climate." The revolutions on his bike increased dramatically. Bush's face was red, owing more to his anger and frustration than to his physical workout.

One owner, Jerry Reinsdorf of the Chicago White Sox, at least saw a silver lining in the collusion settlement. "The players will fall all over each other trying to divide up the two hundred eighty million. The union now has a bigger challenge to its unity than we ever presented."

Peter Ueberroth, tan and fit as always, was far removed from the snow squalls that engulfed the Chicago Hyatt and the baseball barons hovering inside. Commuting between Los Angeles and Hawaii after his recent purchase of Hawaiian Airlines, baseball's commissioner during the embattled 1980s scoffed at the owners' settlement. "They were stupid. As usual, the owners overpaid. Besides, they should have taken the decisions to court. They probably would have won and owed the players nothing."

Having lost yet another battle with the players, the owners turned their attention toward the minor leagues in hopes of expanding their control over a group of businessmen whom they felt had become too successful at the major leagues' expense. The lobby at the Hyatt seemed like a ghost town compared to most winter meetings. Missing were the minor league executives. The current agreement between the major leagues and the minor leagues had expired. But instead of joining the minor league executives at the scheduled site—Los Angeles—the major league owners held their own meeting in Chicago.

Sitting in his Rhode Island office, Ben Mendor, like the majority of minor league owners, had experienced little, if any, prosperity since he'd bought his club, the Pawtucket Red Sox, thirteen years before. But the escalating value of major league franchises had caused a ripple effect throughout the minors. He now held a lucrative asset, unless the doomsayers were correct with their prediction that the deflation of the 1990s will hit the sport. The majors were now expecting Mendor and his colleagues to pick up more of the expenses associated with his ball club, while sharing a percentage of his revenues with them. If not, the majors had a simple solution: We'll shut you down, take our players away, and start our own minor league cooperatives in Arizona and Florida, they warned. "The situation is a nightmare," Mendor explained.

High above the Avenue of the Americas at CBS's Manhattan headquarters, the network's chairman, Larry Tisch, was furious over the staggering red ink that continued to spread. Tisch announced that televising baseball had been a major mistake. Neal Pilson, head of sports for CBS, remembered the day he had helped to pry baseball away from NBC. The year 1990 was supposed to be the crowning moment in his career. Instead, his gamble had cost his network over $100 million in losses that year. And the contract with Major League Baseball still had three years to run.

Sure the recession had hurt. And a World Series sweep by one small market (Cincinnati) over another (Oakland) had been disastrous. But there was no way to hide the obvious: CBS had greatly overpaid for the rights to broadcast major league baseball. Pilson decided to approach his old law school classmate, Commissioner Fay Vincent, and ask for relief on the contract. After all, weren't they partners? But by the end of the winter meetings, the owners had already spent $230 million of their new riches on signing free agents and were in no mood to give any of it back to their television partner.

Meanwhile, back in Chicago, Al Rosen, the general manager of the San Francisco Giants, thought he had seen it all. A terrific player in the early 1950s with the Cleveland Indians, he had worked with several clubs over the last twenty years. But even serving as president of the New York Yankees—where George Steinbrenner's signings of free agents had become an annual event rivaling the opening of a major Broadway musical—had not prepared Rosen for the media circus that suddenly engulfed him. As usual, Rosen was impeccably dressed and distinguished-looking, his close-cropped hair as white as the snow outside. But the anger in his voice was apparent as he faced the horde of reporters and television lights that surrounded the small platform he was standing on in the makeshift pressroom in the Hyatt's basement. The Giants had just signed three free agents—Bud Black, Dave Righetti, and Willie McGee—for a total of $33 million, and Rosen was announcing the terms of the contracts.

"Gentlemen, for one hundred years we couldn't find a way to destroy the game," he said, "but now we have found the key." Rosen defended the signings as a necessity for his club to stay competitive in a small market whose loyalty was divided between the Giants and the A's. His anger was directed toward the spiraling free market system that had forced him to pay the huge salaries.

In the back of the room, another general manager turned to a rival and laughed sarcastically. "Al writes the most checks and then holds a press conference to announce he has just played a key role in killing baseball. This is some business." His listener didn't laugh. One of the players had been from his team.

George Steinbrenner got wind of the Righetti signing from his home in Tampa. Righetti had been the Yankees' premier reliever for several years. Steinbrenner, however, did not blame his former employee, Al Rosen. He was instead incensed at Commissioner Fay Vincent, who had recently banished Steinbrenner from running the New York Yankees because of his relationship with a known gambler. "If I was still in charge, Righetti would still be a Yankee," Steinbrenner exclaimed.

Across town from Steinbrenner's office, Frank Morsani sat in an empty Tampa showroom explaining to his creditors why baseball had forced him into bankruptcy. "For ten years we were promised a franchise. We had the opportunity to buy both the Oakland A's and the Texas Rangers, but we backed down in order to allow local businesses to keep the franchises from moving. We even sold back our interest in the Minnesota Twins at no profit to Carl Pohlad so the Twins could stay in Minnesota. Instead, we waited for an expansion franchise that was promised to us by both Bowie Kuhn and Peter Ueberroth."

Morsani's dream was to bring major league baseball to Florida. For ten years he had actively pursued his goal while leaving much of the day-to-day operations of his car dealerships to others. His dream had turned into a nightmare. Florida was indeed awarded an expansion franchise. But it went to Miami's Wayne Huizenga, principal owner of Blockbuster Video.

The three-member expansion committee had recommended the Miami application over several others, including Tampa's. Douglas Danforth, chairman of the board of the Pittsburgh Pirates, was the head of the National League Expansion Committee. His close friend and president of the Pirates, Carl Barger, is a board member of Blockbuster Video. Soon after the announcement, Barger left the Pirates to take the same position with the Miami club. Another member of the committee, John McMullen, owner of the Houston Astros, happens to own an interest in Affiliated Regional Communications, which owns 49% of the Sunshine Network. Soon after the Marlins were granted a major league franchise, the Sunshine Network was awarded the lucrative cable contract with the Miami expansion team. Morsani announced that he was suing Major League Baseball.

Back at the Hyatt, the owners were dividing into different committees to figure out what to do next. Their lieutenants, the various general managers, shuffled around the lobby, talking to each other, to members of the press, and, mostly, to player's agents. Many of the general managers, like Tom Grieve of the Texas Rangers, had orders to keep their wallets in their pockets. But building a club the old-fashioned way—through trades and the farm system—had given way to the quick-fix approach that Rosen and the Giants were using. Grieve sat with his manager, Bobby Valentine, and surveyed the other diners in the hotel's restaurant. "It must be nice," Grieve smiled at Valentine with a shake of his head toward John Schuerholz, his counterpart with the Atlanta Braves. Schuerholz had just filled two gaping holes in his infield by signing two free agents, Sid Bream and Terry Pendleton, whose prior teams were located in small markets. Pendleton would go on to win the National League batting title and MVP award while leading Atlanta to its first World Series. Grieve thought about his own superstar, Ruben Sierra. Which big-city team would shower him with millions in two years?

* * *

As the club owners bickered among themselves in Chicago, a bitter old man sat in his New York apartment finishing the last chapter of his autobiography. His name unknown to Sierra and the majority of millionaires who had arrived in the majors after his retirement, Marvin Miller looked out at the cold East River. The union he had created had offered him a token stipend and a small, windowless cubicle to write its history. Insulted by the offer, he was instead writing of the split in the Players Association between young and veteran players over the riches created largely through his efforts, efforts which neither group appreciated.

Six months later, five people would show up at a bookstore outside of Boston to hear Miller speak while several hundred waited at a neighboring suburban shopping mall for a Red Sox utility outfielder to appear to sign autographs. No one from either the Red Sox or the Oakland A's, in town for a three-day series with Boston, would bother to call or visit Miller. The occasion marked the twenty-fifth anniversary of the Major League Baseball Players Association. Miller had taken a group of subservient players making $19,000 a year on average in 1967 and transformed them into the highest-paid, most organized union in the history of labor. The average player was earning close to $1 million when Miller spoke to his small audience of curious book browsers.

Reggie Jackson, in Boston to broadcast the games back to California, looked around the Oakland locker room. "Man, the young players just don't understand what the union has won for them over the years. They want it all now. They don't know, they don't even care about the game's history. They all think they are entitled to whatever they can get." Jackson reminded himself to call Miller when he returned to New York.

Not everyone at the Hyatt was in a foul mood. Agent Scott Boras, his blond hair combed straight back in typical California style, was enjoying himself. Having represented the last three number one players in the June draft, he had persuaded Brien Taylor's mother to let him be their "family advisor." Taylor was a young pitching phenom from North Carolina who was expected to be drafted in the first round by the New York Yankees. Boras had rapidly become the owners' most disliked agent in the business. Boras had found a niche and capitalized on it. A former minor league player who never made it to the majors, the young attorney had solicited promising high school players and quickly educated their families on the art of using the threat of going to college. That threat gave the prospect the leverage to extract record-setting signing bonuses from clubs that would lose the rights to the player if he entered college instead. Since only one in ten minor leaguers ever make it to the majors, Boras was selling a simple message: Get as much money as you can while you have the hammer. The owners were incensed. Plans were being made to change the draft. Boras was planning to add his lawsuit to the growing list.

Late at night, several agents were sitting around the lobby bar toasting each other on the daily signings they had orchestrated. As usual, Alan Meersand, another West Coast agent, was angry. Meersand doesn't trust most other agents. He is convinced that they are trying to steal his clients, and this evening he was more on edge than usual. Tom Grieve had rejected his proposal for a contract for Steve Buechele, the Rangers' starting third baseman. An arbitration confrontation seemed inevitable. The confrontation came sooner than anticipated.

John McAdams, the Rangers' outside counsel, wandered by with a drink in hand and casually sat down uninvited next to Meersand. In his best Fort Worth drawl, McAdams turned to Meersand and said, "Well, Jew boy, I guess I'll be beating your ass in arbitration this year." Meersand jumped to his feet. "I don't have to take that kind of crap from you," he announced as he rushed across the crowded lobby to find Grieve. Meersand told the Rangers general manager that if he didn't get an immediate written apology from the club, the Jewish Anti-Defamation League would be apprised of the comments made by an attorney representing the President of the United States's son. The apology never came. As with many agents disliked by clubs, the Rangers got rid of Meersand by getting rid of his client: They simply traded Buechele to the Pirates.

The next night, Eddie Einhorn, an owner of the Chicago White Sox, opted for the sauerkraut booth instead of the sushi bar at the annual banquet. "Its only a matter of time." His eyes fixed on the group of Japanese businessmen across the room. "So many clubs are spending themselves out of existence. We'll be forced to let the Japanese buy in. They'll then dictate where their club can play. They won't care about the local communities, only about protecting their investment. Eventually, one will move his franchise without league approval and sue when the move is blocked. We'll have an Al Davis scenario in baseball. We'll probably lose our antitrust exemption over it." The sauerkraut was not going down well. The lawsuits surrounding the National Football League when Al Davis relocated the Oakland Raiders to Los Angeles seemed strictly minor league compared to baseball's impending clashes.

The lawyers in the commissioner's office had their hands full. Now the commissioner himself was being sued. George Steinbrenner's partners felt that Fay Vincent's personal vendetta against the Yankee's principal owner had illegally expanded to include them. Several of the other owners were hoping that Vincent would lose. The commissioner suddenly felt ill and stayed home in New York, avoiding the angry baseball tycoons who gathered in Chicago. Instead, he sent his lieutenant, Deputy Commissioner Stephen Greenberg, to read his prepared remarks. The assembled throng of major league gentry found nothing to cheer about as Greenberg left the podium and exited the hall.

How did a simple game get so out of control?

Bill Terry, who played for the New York Giants in the 1930s, was only referring to the owners when he made his pronouncement in 1941 about the resiliency of baseball. Today, the men who run the game come from both the owners' and the players' camps, and baseball may very well not survive the greed that holds the national pastime captive. No one—player, owner, or fan—seems to enjoy the game anymore. The simple confrontation between a pitcher and a batter is today far less significant than confrontations over huge sums of money. The press writes of it daily and the fans know that monetary considerations, more than astute skill evaluations, will determine who wins in the end each fall.

Bill ("Spaceman") Lee saw it coming before most anyone else did. A Red Sox pitcher in the early 1970s, Lee was famous for his irreverent views on baseball, politics, and everything else on the planet Earth. Lee started the seventh game of the 1975 World Series. The following spring the Red Sox traded his best friend on the club, Bernie Carbo, to Milwaukee, after Carbo threatened to become one of the game's first free agents. But Lee instinctively knew that the players' newfound freedom would forever change the way clubs dealt with players. On hearing that Carbo was traded, Lee yelled out: "Send lawyers, guns, and money. The shit has hit the fan!"

Some twenty years before his inevitable date in Cooperstown, Carlton Fisk, along with his former teammate Dwight Evans, was there in 1976 when the owners started to lose control over their monopoly. But the real battles for economic control, shrouded in moral overtones, started ten years later. Baseball will never be the same. The battle for control continues today between the commissioner's office, the owners, the players, the agents, and the networks, with the future of what was once a leisurely pastime hanging in the balance. And like an old ball that has been smacked around once too often, major league baseball is quickly coming apart at the seams.

PART I
PAST SKIRMISHES

CHAPTER ONE

BEER WARS AND OTHER FAMILY FEUDS

SOUTH FLORIDA EXPOSITION CENTER, OCTOBER 2000

"This is all an *ex-minor-leaguer-turned-commissioner could ask for,"* Mario Cuomo said as he walked behind the batting cage in the South Florida Exposition Center. *"A seventh game, two great pitchers, two great teams, and weather so beautiful that the roof is open."*

It was the afternoon of October 28, 2000. In a couple of hours, the Florida Marlins would start their ace, twenty-six-year-old Jesus Martinez, against thirty-year-old Steve Avery, the veteran ace of the White Sox, a matchup of twenty-game winners, the first time that the starters in the All-Star Game had also both started the seventh game of the World Series.

Cuomo was in a particularly good mood. At the morning meeting of baseball's board of directors, the thirty-two owners and one player on the board, as well as baseball CEO Michael Eisner had given glowing reports on the state of the game. Eisner, former chairman of Disney, was hired by baseball when Disney merged with Sony in 1997. Japanese League representatives had reported that ad rates and licensing revenues promised an all-time-high profit for the ensuing Sony U.S.-Japan Summit Series, no matter whether the Marlins or White Sox won, principally because the Tokyo Giants had one of the greatest seasons in the history of the Japanese Central League.

Vancouver Pacifics owner Shinichiro Torii, who had recently inherited the Suntory liquor fortune, claimed that next spring's 2001 International

Series in Brisbane had already been sold to more than twice as many international television outlets as the 1997 games in Seoul.

"T-shirts in Tehran, jackets in Jakarta, and royalties in Riga," player board member Shaun Green, an Angels outfielder, had cracked during the meeting. "What happened to the good old days?"

As he walked near the cage, Cuomo smiled just thinking about Yankees owner George Steinbrenner's reply to Green. "What you miss is former Milwaukee owner Bud Selig saying, 'Gentlemen, this is in . . . SAN . . . ity,' " Steinbrenner had said.

This was Cuomo's third World Series as commissioner. He understood his role. After all the game's strikes, lockouts, and turmoil in the 1990s, the role of baseball commissioner had been clearly defined so that henceforth there would be none of the delusions that the office had brought out of its previous occupants, who had thought the job somehow was a mix of being pope, talk-show caller, and chairman of the Foreign Relations Committee.

Finally, when all the lawyers lost their voices in the mid-nineties, the players stopped litigating, the owners stopped thinking the union wouldn't hold together, and both sides figured out that since they're all in this thing together, a real partnership was able to be forged. And in time the real power game evolved, in the form of a board made up of the owners and a player representative, with a chosen CEO. The commissioner, chosen by both the owners and players, then became the game's goodwill ambassador, watchdog, and judge of the moral and ethical "best interests of the game." Most of the job was fun. "It's like being Prince Charles without the paparazzi," Cuomo liked to say. He got to put Pete Rose and Shoeless Joe Jackson in the Hall of Fame and to dedicate Havana's spectacular Fidel Castro Stadium, and he continually gets the last laugh on George Bush over the bloody '92 election that Cuomo had shrewdly ducked out of. Actually, one month after taking office in September 1998, Cuomo had had to deliver the Commissioner's Trophy for winning the World Series to Texas owner George Bush, with his proud father looking on.

This had also been a memorable postseason, especially since the White Sox had clinched the final wild-card playoff berth on the last day of the season and were trying to become the first third-place team ever to win a World Series. Vancouver won the American League West, Boston the East. Texas actually finished with a better record than Boston and got the first wild-card position, but the battle for the final wild-card spot came down to Chicago and Oakland and was decided on the final day when the White Sox won and the A's lost. The White Sox upset the heavily favored Pacifics, the Rangers defeated the Red Sox, and in the American League Championship Series veteran Frank Thomas and twenty-six-year-old superstar catcher Ryan Luzinski each hit three homers and fifty-two-year-old Charlie Hough won the seventh game as Chicago—which finished only 85–69—won its first pennant in forty years.

Florida and the St. Louis Cardinals rolled through the regular season, but each had unexpected problems in the first round of the playoffs. The Marlins lost the first two games of their series to Houston. They trailed 4–2 in the bottom of the ninth of Game Three. But back-to-back one-out homers by aging superstars Jose Canseco and Omar Linares tied the game. The Marlins won it in the 11th inning on a David Segui double, then swept the final two games, 3–1 and 4–0, behind the pitching of Martinez and Tavo Alvarez. St. Louis won the Western Division, but also had to go to five games—and get three homers from National League MVP Dmitri Young—to defeat Connecticut, which had beaten the crosstown rival New York (New Jersey) Mets three straight over the final weekend to clinch its wild-card position. Florida then beat the Cardinals in six thrilling games, winning the final game 7–6 in 13 innings when star right fielder Rondell White tripled home Robbie Alomar.

So even before he got a seventh game of the World Series, Cuomo knew this was a heckuva lot better than balancing state budgets or campaigning for president. The Baseball Channel, which was run out of Major League Baseball Productions, Inc., had had a fantastic year, from Moline to Moscow. All the realignment and expansion had settled. The Mets had been the first franchise to relocate, moving to New Jersey in 1995. Then, when Quebec had seceded first from Canada and then from the U.N., the Expos had moved north of New Haven, Connecticut, two years after the Mets moved to New Jersey and Pittsburgh finally gave up and moved to Charlotte in conjunction with the 1997 expansion and realignment.

As had so often been the case in baseball history, when the owners

*didn't get what they wanted, they instead got what they needed. After
the industry was shut down in 1994 and the players and owners came
to an agreement on sharing the revenues and being run by a board of
directors that, like Chrysler's, included a member of the Union, former
Houston minority owner David LeFevre (with agent Dick Moss's help)
started The Baseball League in 1995. They opened the eight-team league,
got national television contracts with SportsChannel America and Disney—which had its own team in Orlando—and acquired players, first
by signing a few available free agents, then by raiding the minor leagues
and colleges.*

*As Branch Rickey's Continental League in the late fifties had forced
the original 1961–62 four-team expansion, so baseball had to react and
again expand. Vancouver, with its booming post–Hong Kong flavor and
dynamic owner Torii, became an immediate success. Torii signed a
dozen of the Baseball League players who had become free agents via the
new league—including stars like pitchers Todd Van Poppel and Frankie
Rodriguez and outfielders Al Shirley and J. J. Johnson—as well as luring players from Australia, Korea, and Taiwan. Florida, which finished
fourth in its initial season (1993), also signed fifteen of the former Baseball League players, including White, Alvarez, and Martinez.*

*The two leagues then finally aligned into two eight-team divisions. The
clubs played fourteen games against each of their divisional opponents, six
with each club from the other division, and four two-game interleague
series. The divisions thus were broken down to:*

AMERICAN LEAGUE

East	West
Boston	Seattle
New York	Minnesota
Baltimore	Kansas City
Chicago	Phoenix
Cleveland	Oakland
Detroit	California
Toronto	Vancouver
Milwaukee	Texas

NATIONAL LEAGUE

East	West
Connecticut	Chicago
New York (New Jersey)	St. Louis
Philadelphia	Los Angeles
St. Petersburg	San Diego
Charlotte	Houston
Miami	San Francisco Bay
Cincinnati	(San Jose)
Atlanta	Sacramento
	Denver

As the electronic media with its immediate reporting had replaced the print media at most sporting events, there were two dozen newspapers still covering the World Series. While the beat writers lamented the changes to the national pastime, Cuomo was quick to remind the reporters and Baseball Channel studio host Bob Costas that three of the Series games had been played outdoors in Chicago. Thirteen clubs already played in domed stadiums, including new ones built in New Jersey, West Haven, Connecticut, and Detroit, and ground had been broken for a two-stadium complex with a sliding roof for baseball, football, and the 2016 Olympics in Boston's Forest Hills section (with the final step the moving of the famous Left Field Wall from the Fens to the new park). "I remember sitting in Shea Stadium freezing during the '73 World Series," Cuomo told some reporters at the cage. "Those were the good old days?"

" 'Good' and 'old' are relative terms," said the graying but no less cynical Boston columnist Dan Shaughnessy. " In my mind, newspaper strikes are the good old days. At least we had them to strike, and you had them to state something more substantial then a seven-second soundbite. For the commissioner, the good old days were when you had the designated hitter controversy." (The DH was abolished as part of the settlement of the '94 Basic Agreement.)

Cuomo laughed, then was pulled away for a picture with the two managers, Chicago's Chico Walker and Florida's thirty-two-year-old player-manager, Roberto Alomar. "There will be a day when Caracas,

Mexico City, San Juan, and Havana are in the big leagues, too,'' Alomar told him. *"Maybe I'll pull off the triple crown in the next six months— win the World Series, beat Japan, then lead Puerto Rico to the International Cup next spring. How would that be?''*

"How about the All-Star Game?'' asked Cuomo.

"Can I pick myself?''

"Robbie,'' interjected Walker, the local-boy-made-good manager of the White Sox. *"You're thirty-two, you've got more than a hundred million dollars, and you're going to the Hall of Fame. Don't you relax?''*

"I'm afraid of losing. I'll relax when I die.''

"Better than listening to Orrin Hatch debate Ted Kennedy,'' thought Cuomo. And so was the game.

Avery, who had signed with Chicago as a free agent for $27.5 million over three years (plus 5 percent of the pay-per-view fees every time he pitched) before the '99 season and had gone 17–10 and 21–8 for the White Sox, shut out the Marlins over the first five innings. Martinez, whose older brothers each had starred for the Dodgers but who signed with Orlando in The Baseball League in '95 to free himself from the minor league reserve system, allowed only a fifth-inning run that scored when Thomas doubled and Linares let a ground ball through his legs at third base. In the bottom of the sixth Alomar had to make a crucial decision. With two outs and nobody on against Avery, Alomar's brother Sandy singled and shortstop Victor Mesa walked. Roberto Alomar figured he had his whole bullpen available, so he sent up Segui, who singled into right-center to tie the game.

Inning after inning, situation after situation, the game wove to the 10th. In the bottom of the seventh, White Sox center fielder Deion Sanders had made a spectacular catch to save a run, and then he'd singled in the top of the eighth, stolen second, and scored on Luzinski's single for a 2–1 lead. But Canseco, the thirty-eight-year-old local hero, had homered leading off the bottom of the ninth to tie it.

In the 10th, Luzinski singled in Chicago second baseman Calvin Murray to give Chicago a 3–2 lead. But against White Sox ace closer Don Peters in the bottom of the inning, Alomar singled. So did Rondell White. Linares, Cuba's greatest star before the gates were opened in 1994 (after Cuba's baseball team won the 1992 Olympics and Castro had no other assets to sell), then ripped a double into the left field corner to tie the game at 3–3. The game and the Series ended when Canseco lifted a fly ball to *center to score White and bring Miami and the Caribbean their first World Series. Blockbuster Video and Miami owner Wayne Huizenga instantly shipped "The Official World Series Highlights Video" to his ten thousand stores worldwide.*

So baseball began the 21st century. "It seems as if baseball has been through four centuries in the last twenty-five years," White Sox owner Jerry Reinsdorf told his executive vice president, Tony LaRussa. Indeed, one era ended with the 1975 World Series. The next began when arbitrator Peter Seitz unlocked the door that had barred players from becoming free agents. That era ended when Peter Ueberroth took over in September 1984. Four years later arbitrators Thomas Roberts and George Nicolau ruled that the owners had closed the door and were guilty of collusion and restraint of trade and owed $280 million to the players in damages. Then came the turbulent nineties, the owners' lockout and the change to the way baseball became by the year 2000.

"The 1975–84 period was simply the awakening," Cuomo told Reinsdorf. "With Ueberroth, baseball finally began to reckon with reality: After 100 years of being run as a game, you guys finally realized it had to be run like a business. It just took another decade to figure out how to do it."

DODGER STADIUM, JANUARY 1984

Peter O'Malley was angry, and Dodger Stadium, the world's biggest saloon west of the Mississippi, was about to have its Budweiser taps shut off.

For twenty-five years, Walter O'Malley and then his son, Peter, had been the sport's top power brokers. The senior O'Malley had recognized the green pastures of the West Coast long before his rivals, and had moved his Brooklyn club to Los Angeles in 1958. Of course, he was smart enough to realize that he needed a playing partner west of St. Louis, so he persuaded the Giants to move to San Francisco at the same time.

If he had been born fifty years earlier, Walter O'Malley would have been behind closed doors at Tammany Hall. He was rough-hewn, broad, and outwardly tough, always chewing on his cigar. One had the sense that this man knew where all the bodies were buried. He also had the vision to see that without a new, domed stadium in Brooklyn, the future was California—Los Angeles, to be precise. O'Malley understood what fans wanted and what they needed—and how to satisfy those needs for a profit. He later denied that when he originally got the Chavez Ravine land for a dollar—and built a ballpark that thirty years after its construction was still state-of-the-art—he tried to build it without water fountains so that thirst would translate into concession dollars, but the story was, at worst, apocryphal.

O'Malley knew that owning a baseball club meant that you are a part of the entertainment business, and that your product should be packaged, marketed, and sold as a family outing in a spotless environment. Los Angeles, the entertainment capital of the world, was made for baseball; and Walter O'Malley and the Dodgers were perfect for Southern California. The Dodgers had become the model team for the industry, both at the gate and on the field. By leaving New York for the sunny skies of Southern California, the O'Malleys and the Dodgers also left the shadows of their most hated rivals: the New York Yankees. They, and not the Yankees, had become the envy of the other clubs. Former Cubs owner Phil Wrigley was not the first or the last to turn to Walter O'Malley and ask, "Well, Walter, what do I think on this issue?"

In the mid 1960s a Wall Street lawyer, Bowie Kuhn, served as the assistant National League counsel. His job, according to Marvin Miller, the founder of the Major League Baseball Players Association, was to be a messenger boy for Walter O'Malley during negotiations between the players and the owners over various collective-bargaining issues. Miller soon realized that whether O'Malley was present or not his advice was always sought, and that more often than not Kuhn was his mouthpiece.

In 1968 William D. Eckert was fired as baseball's fourth commissioner. After several heated meetings, the owners could not agree on a successor. "Who do we want as commissioner, Walter?" they pleaded. "Kuhn, of course," O'Malley replied. His man in place at the top, the transplanted Brooklynite then turned the presidency of the Dodgers over to his son.

Peter is a tall, stilted, reserved gentleman with parted, slickened hair and wire-rimmed glasses whose presence is reminiscent of Gregory Peck in *To Kill a Mockingbird*. Where his father was a tough businessman who clawed his way to the top, Peter has always had more affinity for the arts and society than the baseball business, although he has never lost the O'Malley touch for making money. Where Walter did it himself, Peter has always been smart enough to hire the right people to make things work—profitably—while trying to adhere to the Dean Acheson ideal to "do the right thing" and to continue the lead of Branch Rickey, the club's former president, in making the Dodgers pioneers in minority rights issues. With Peter, there's always the sense that in twenty minutes he has to leave for a board meeting of the UCLA Medical Center.

What a glorious fifteen years it had been for the Dodgers! Four National League pennants, a World Series win over—who else?—the Yankees, and often, from 1978 onward yearly attendance of over three million. No other team in either league could match those numbers. Peter O'Malley sat on the owners' Long-Range Planning Committee, the Player Relations Committee, and the most powerful of them all—the Executive Committee. And when O'Malley spoke, Kuhn listened (or as the late New York writer Red Smith once said, "When O'Malley sends out for coffee, Bowie asks, 'One lump or two?' ").

Kuhn was one of those guys who played tennis stiff-backed. Honest, sincere, earnest, and controlled, he was a gentleman lawyer who should have handled widows' estates. He would have been dandy on the board of St. Andrew's School, but in a business that needed an Edward Bennett Williams, Kuhn was uncomfortable with the tough politics, and in the last year of his reign, he clung to his office and to Bud Selig's coattails as if he were trying to hold on to a twenty-year partnership with a firm that had decided to go in a different, younger direction.

Other owners were not as enamored of Kuhn as O'Malley was. August A. Busch, Jr.—variously known as Auggie or Gussie—had had plenty of success with his brewery and his baseball club—the St. Louis Cardinals—over the years. The Cardinals have won ten

World Series in their history, including a victory over Selig's Brewers in the "Suds Series" in 1982, and they emerged as the Dodgers' chief National League rival on the field since the Dodgers had replaced the Redbirds as the westernmost club in 1958. But even though people were buying beer and baseball tickets to the Cardinals, Auggie Busch, a hard-liner in union matters with his employees at Budweiser, was incensed by the string of victories that the Players Association was winning. Gussie Busch had convinced the Supreme Court in 1969 to uphold baseball's antitrust exemption so that he could trade a player (Curt Flood) whenever and to whomever he liked, regardless of whether that player was under contract for the next year or not. But since 1976 he had seen his victory disappear through arbitration decisions and collective-bargaining agreements. In Busch's mind, Kuhn's leadership in this area was a complete failure.

Anheuser-Busch, the owner of the St. Louis Cardinals, views the baseball team as a marketing arm for the brewery. In St. Louis, the traditional seventh-inning stretch and singing of "Take Me Out to the Ball Game" was replaced by the sight and sound of clapping to the Budweiser jingle, while Gussie waved to the crowd from a Clydesdale-pulled wagon that circled the outfield. What's good for Bud is good for the Cardinals. And, as one of the largest television advertisers of sporting events, Anheuser-Busch and its crusty old chairman got people's attention when they wanted changes.

Kuhn possessed no marketing acumen. Indeed, the marketing arm of major league baseball was a separate corporation, generating relatively small annual dividends for the clubs. If salaries were going to continue to escalate, Busch, the Budweiser King, pronounced, "We've got to find new ways of increasing our revenues." Rising labor costs and stagnant revenue increases alone would have sealed Kuhn's fate with Busch. But probably more damning was his allegiance to the O'Malleys, which their chief National League rival found intolerable. Yes, Kuhn had to go, and Busch found enough agreeable partners to lead the ouster.

Realizing that Kuhn's fate was sealed, O'Malley changed his brand of beer. Budweiser was out at Dodger Stadium and Miller (beer, not Marvin) was in. Naturally, Busch retaliated by pulling

Budweiser advertising from O'Malley's park. And, of course, Kuhn was history, as well as the O'Malley influence over the other owners.

Busch's allies came from a group of old hard-liners and Young Turks who had recently bought into baseball. Miller and the union's success from 1976 to 1981 convinced several owners that their days in the sun were over. While the Wrigley family in Chicago and the Carpenters in Philadelphia could have survived financially and would have actually made more money by holding on to their franchises, they both sold out in 1981.

It took the Phillies ninety-seven years to win their first World Championship in 1980. But they didn't get to enjoy it for long. The 1981 season was interrupted by a mid-season strike on June 11 that lasted some fifty days and wiped out a third of the season's playing schedule. The Carpenter family had had enough.

"This isn't any fun anymore. It's absurd. I am not going to be a part of a business where I am forced to pay a player a ridiculous sum of money because some joker in Atlanta or New York overpays his players," Ruly Carpenter said in frustration as he sold his club to a partnership headed up by his former marketing director, Bill Giles. The Carpenters had owned the Phillies for almost forty years. And for thirty-five years, they alone had decided who would play for them each season, and for how much. To them, the past represented baseball's Golden Era, and they wanted no part of its future.

Giles, on the other hand, having never been accustomed to buying and trading employees at his own whim, did not share the Carpenters' disdain for the way the game was changing off the field. Giles represented both the past and the future and had the inside track on the Phillies when the Carpenters announced that the club was up for sale.

Ironically, had it not been for free agency, the Phillies might have gone without their World Championship even after ninety-seven years. A key member of the Phillies' 1980 World Championship team was Pete Rose. After the 1978 season, Rose had become a free agent and was actively pursued by many clubs. The Rose dog and pony show, orchestrated brilliantly by his agent, would have inspired the admiration of P. T. Barnum. As Rose crisscrossed the country on a private jet, he left behind a marketing tape on his achievements with each club that lusted after his services. Along the way, he would hold daily press conferences in each city to announce how excited he was about the possibility of playing for the hometown team and to make public the supposed additional inducements that were being presented to him by that city's club. At each stop the reports of the riches thrown at his feet grew. Knowing his keen interest in gambling and horses, Daniel Galbreath, the owner of the Pittsburgh Pirates and the Darby Dan Stables, supposedly offered him a couple of thoroughbreds if he would play for the Bucs. Not to be outdone, Gussie Busch countered with a beer distributorship. By the time the road trip hit the South, it was reported that Ted Turner was waiting with a chunk of stock in a television station.

Rose's last stop was Philadelphia. Giles convinced Ruly Carpenter that the Phillies needed Rose's bat and leadership to get them over the top. As important, Giles was certain that in the process, Rose would break a few more league records while a Phillie that would parlay into a box office bonanza for the club. Carpenter, however, was unwilling to meet Rose's asking price. So Giles contacted WPHL, the television station that held the local rights to the club. Would WPHL be willing to increase its guaranteed-rights fees to the club if the Phillies signed Rose? WPHL gladly wrote the check that allowed the Phillies to sign Rose. Giles later estimated that the Phillies' revenue increased by at least $2.5 million a year with the Rose signing. Unlike the Carpenters, Giles liked and understood this game. "We are all partners—the owners, the players, and the networks. It is just a question of figuring out who gets what piece of the pie," Giles remarked.

Bill grew up in Cincinnati, where his father, Warren Giles, had been president of the Cincinnati Reds until 1951, when he was elected president of the National League. The senior Giles ran the National League for eighteen years. Bill worked his way up through several organizations until he was running the business side of the Phillies for the Carpenter family. His strength lay in promotions and marketing, and when he put the syndicate together to purchase the club he used all his skills to land a financial heavyweight to anchor his package: Taft Broadcasting of Cincinnati. Giles had seen the light, and it originated from a hand-held camcorder.

The emerging cable television industry was desperate for programming, and local baseball's television rights were about to escalate. Taft Broadcasting saw the opportunity to control these rights by direct ownership, and therefore gave Giles the money he needed to buy the club. But Giles and Taft Broadcasting were not the first of the new breed. Ted Turner had bought the Atlanta Braves in 1975 to provide programming for his national cable network, WTBS. Turner was the first to see the potential of sports programming on cable television. It was at about the same time that labor costs began to escalate.

Ted Turner was a maverick from the start. Dubbed the "Mouth of the South," he became an immediate pain in the sides of the old families that had controlled baseball for generations. Brash, outspoken, and irreverent, Turner, like that fictional Atlantan Rhett Butler, didn't give a damn what others thought of him. A world-class sailor, he'd won the America's Cup, to the chagrin of the yachtsmen who staged the race.

If there is one august body that took itself more seriously than the Barons of Baseball, it is the New York Yacht Club. For over one hundred years, the New York Yacht Club had kept the America's Cup trophy in its headquarters. Once very four years, it would be brought out and presented, amid much pomp and circumstance, to the winning skipper. Needless to say, the Lord High Commanders were not amused at the award ceremony when Turner, champagne bottle in hand, slid out of his chair and disappeared under the dais.

On another occasion, Turner was trying to figure out how to give a motivational speech to his team, which was, as usual, mired in last place at the All-Star break. Instead, he flew the players up to Rhode Island, crammed them on a motor boat, and had them watch him sail around Nantucket Bay for the day. "Just so the boys can see what it takes to be a champion," he explained.

It was only appropriate that Ted Turner signed Andy Messer-

smith to a Braves contract after Messersmith opened the flood-
gates of free agency in 1976. Little did Messersmith know when he
signed and received jersey No. 17 that stitched above the number
would be the word "CHANNEL", a blatant reference to WTBS,
Turner's flagship station. Turner definitely was before his time,
but there was no way that Bowie Kuhn was going to let him use
a player's back to advertise his television station.

The following season, Turner created even more of a ruckus by
firing his manager, putting on a uniform, and managing the team
from the dugout. He did have a point, though—he certainly could
not have done any worse than the guy he'd fired. The press had
a field day with this. Defensive over comments that his knowledge
of the game was suspect, he replied, "Sure, I know what a ground-
rule double is. I'm not stupid. The only stupid thing I did was buy
this franchise." Of course, Kuhn fined him for conduct "unbe-
coming an owner."

Turner, like his Yankee rival up north, George Steinbrenner,
was turning the other owners on their heads, and prior owners
over in their graves. Arriving in baseball along with free agency in
1976, Turner seized the opportunity to promote his television station across the country to the emerging cable audience. He gave
his WTBS programming away to cable companies for nothing. He
correctly figured out that advertising income to WTBS would increase as the number of viewers grew. Since he offered his programming for free, local cable operators were only too willing to
pass it on to their subscribers as part of a basic package.

As a result, households all around the country were picking up
Atlanta Braves games, at the expense of local teams that charged
for their telecasts. Adding insult to injury, Turner took some of the
additional ad revenues he was generating from his large subscription base and used it to buy free agents. While free agency provided him a market to buy the players, more often than not,
unfortunately for Atlanta fans, he bought the wrong players.
"Well," he rationalized after paying millions for a broken-down
pitcher who immediately went on the disabled list, "at my stupidest, I was never as stupid as the Boston Red Sox." Or as con-
troversial as George Steinbrenner.

*   *   *

At an owners' meeting about ten years ago, nearly one hundred members of the media hovered in the hallway of a Boston hotel awaiting word on the fate of Bowie Kuhn. The door to the meeting room opened, a voice shouted "STEINBRENNER," and the entire horde began a stampede for the Yankees owner. A TV camera inadvertently hit the head of a reporter, who fell in front of the herd, and in the shoving for position, a New York newspaperman slugged a woman TV reporter, all to hear Steinbrenner say he had no news, in five hundred words or more.

This is what George Steinbrenner lives for. He is the King of the Back Page, the sports lead for the three New York tabloids. After being exiled from baseball by Commissioner Fay Vincent, he made the front page of the *New York Post*. "I Shall Return . . . George Says N.Y. Wants Him Back," the headline read, accompanied by a picture of The Boss in sunglasses and adjacent headlines about the Rev. Al Sharpton and Mother Teresa. Steinbrenner's presence is that of a door being blown open by the wind, his sound that of a loud crash.

In the early years of free agency, Steinbrenner and the New York Yankees had more success in their shopping than Turner did. In 1977 they signed Reggie Jackson, and proceeded to win two World Championships. By then, the genie was out of the bottle and the old-timers, like the Carpenters, wanted out.

The Carpenters were not the only old-line baseball family to sell out in 1981. William Wrigley had purchased the Chicago Cubs in 1921 and the family had held on to the club for sixty years. The Wrigleys knew how to make gum, but like the Carpenters, they lost their taste for baseball when player salaries got too large for them to chew. A major corporation, the Chicago Tribune, was more than willing to meet Wrigley's price. The parent company for WGN (one of the largest national cable television companies in the United States), the Tribune saw the Chicago Cubs as a perfect source of programming for its cable outlet, particularly over the summer months when the networks primarily showed reruns. The dramatic growth of WTBS and its Braves affiliation, naturally, was not lost on the Tribune.

The sale of the Phillies by the Carpenter family and of the Chicago Cubs by the Wrigley family in 1981 were perfect examples of the changes that were rapidly occurring in the makeup of the ownership of major league clubs in the early 1980s. The days of family-and-business-owned baseball clubs were over. The new breed of owners were either entrepreneurs backed by a syndicate of investors or a Fortune 500 corporation interested in a club for promotional and marketing value to enhance the corporation's primary business.

Besides the Wrigleys and the Carpenters, who sold of their own volition, two mavericks were forced to sell because of the changing economics of the game. Charlie Finley—he of the orange balls and mules in the outfield—sold what was left of the Oakland A's to the Haas family, who own Levi Strauss blue jeans. Bill Veeck, the consummate promoter, folded his tent and sold out to a syndicate led by real estate syndicator Jerry Reinsdorf and television mogul Eddie Einhorn. Other clubs, including the New York Mets, Seattle Mariners, Texas Rangers, and Baltimore Orioles, also changed hands during this time. Soon, three more—the Cleveland Indians, San Francisco Giants, and Pittsburgh Pirates—were on the verge of moving or selling. Baseball then said good-bye to its most colorful and ridiculed owner, Calvin Griffith of the Minnesota Twins.

If the Carpenters and Wrigleys were a throwback to an earlier age, Griffith was absolutely a dinosaur. His adopted father, Clark, purchased the Washington Senators in 1920, and after forty years of ineptitude—which gave rise to the often-quoted phrase, "First in war, first in peace, and last in the American League"—Calvin Griffith moved the Washington franchise to Minnesota in 1960.

"I'll tell you why we came to Minnesota," he bluntly told a businessman's luncheon in 1978. "It was when I found out you only had fifteen thousand blacks here. Black people don't go to ball games, but they'll fill up a wrassling ring and put up such a chant they'll scare you to death. . . . We came here because you've got good, hardworking white people here."

Calvin Griffith was always viewed as a character from a television sitcom, wise enough to make a buck out of the game under the old pre-Messersmith Decision system, but a small-town boss who ran a family business. He had brothers, sisters, cousins, and a son on the payroll, but the important friends he kept in high places were pure baseball men who knew that Calvin could always break even if they came up with the players. But as the game became more electronic and the economics more complex and even penurious, Minnesotans began to react to the constant loss of stars like Larry Hisle and Bert Blyleven who signed elsewhere for more money. In 1979, Griffith tried to lowball his seven-time batting champion, Rod Carew, who had become a free agent at the end of the 1978 season. Soon thereafter, Carew, a Panamanian black, signed a five-year contract with Gene Autry and the Angels, and said as he left town, "I won't be a nigger on his plantation anymore. I will not ever sign another contract with this organization. I don't care how much money or how many options Calvin Griffith offers me. . . . The days of Kunta Kinte are over. . . . He respects nobody and expects nobody to respect him."

When Griffith's son, Clark (named after his grandfather), tried to modernize his father's thinking and signed some of their bigger-name players (Roy Smalley, Butch Wynegar) over his father's objections, it caused such a family rift that father and son didn't speak for several years.

By 1984, there was no way that Calvin Griffith could survive under the new economic system. Griffith had sold a minority interest in the club to a group of Florida businessmen, led by Frank Morsani, who, along with Griffith, wanted to move the franchise to Tampa. Only the lease on the new Minneapolis Metrodome stood in their way. Griffith tried to get out of the lease through an escape clause which would let the team pull up roots and move if the paid attendance did not reach a certain level. But to keep the team in Minneapolis, a variety of public and private groups, including the Minnesota Vikings, chipped in to buy the tickets.

"This is some way to do business," said Griffith as he looked around at the sparse crowd of 6,300 fans on hand to witness an 8–7 loss to Toronto in May of 1984. A few minutes before, it had been announced over the loudspeakers that the paid attendance was almost 52,000.

Griffith did not know who he despised more, Marvin Miller or George Steinbrenner. But he knew that it was time to get out, so he sold the club to Minnesota banker Carl Pohlad, who kept the team in Minnesota.

The clubs were quickly falling into different camps. Some, like Peter O'Malley and the Dodgers, were holdovers from the 1970s. Others, like the Atlanta Braves and the Chicago Cubs, were viewed as little more than programming fillers for the parent cable companies. Still others, like the St. Louis Cardinals, were held as promotional and marketing outlets for their parent owners.

The battle lines hardened. On one side were the superstation teams, such as the Atlanta Braves, the New York Mets, and the Chicago Cubs. On the other were the smaller teams, like the Pittsburgh Pirates and Milwaukee Brewers, who were trying to develop their own cable networks, without much success.

It wasn't just the superstation teams that were bidding for players. Other owners, like "the singing cowboy," Gene Autry, desperately wanted a World Series championship and were prepared to spend on the open market to improve their chances. Even if he had wanted to, Calvin Griffith could not have competed with these tycoons.

A new order was shaping up, and each time a club sold for a new record price, the stakes got higher. What had once been hobbies for wealthy sportsmen to indulge in were now something more than expensive toys: Ball clubs had become small businesses worth anywhere from $30 million to $100 million, with all the inherent problems. And unlike sons and daughters, partners and stockholders expected an annual accounting.

The new owners were not satisfied with the status quo or the old way of doing business. By 1984, they were a disgruntled lot. In addition, football had passed them by as the most popular professional sport with the public. More important, the national television contract reflected this. And on the horizon, three personalities in high-tops—Magic Johnson, Larry Bird, and Michael Jordan—were more appealing to a younger, hip market than Mike Schmidt, Pete Rose, and Steve Garvey, whose appeal depended on the daily market value of their Topps trading cards.

In hindsight, it is easy to see why Gussie Busch was able to put together a coalition of owners to force Kuhn out. If the commissioner couldn't stop the various factions from fighting each other, what chance did he have of leading them to a victory over the players? For sixty-five years, baseball had been run by a federal judge, a politician, a sportswriter, a general, and, finally, a lawyer. After Bowie Kuhn, Gussie Busch was tired of lawyers. Find a businessman instead, he shouted. The search committee went out looking.

CHAPTER TWO

PETER THE GREAT COMES DOWN FROM OLYMPUS

PEBBLE BEACH, CALIFORNIA, FEBRUARY 1984

T he luck of the Irish and the influence of the O'Malleys were not shared by Horace Stoneham and his Giants up the Coast. In fact, they probably would have been better off if they had stayed in New York. The club almost did return East, when Stoneham negotiated its sale to a Canadian brewery in 1976 that planned to move it to Toronto. But Robert Lurie, a local real estate magnate, was persuaded to buy the club and keep the Giants in San Francisco. In return, Toronto was given an expansion club, the Blue Jays. Unfortunately for Lurie, the Giants more often than not played themselves out of contention by the All-Star break each year. Also, their stadium, Candlestick Park, located next to the bay, has always been a dreary, cold, and windy place to watch a ballgame. Jerry Reuss, former Dodgers pitcher and now an ESPN broadcaster, once said, "This wouldn't be such a bad place to play if it wasn't for that wind. I guess that's like saying hell wouldn't be such a bad place if it wasn't so hot." And Reuss once pitched a no-hitter there.

Attendance continued to dwindle, until it sank below the fan support that the Giants had suffered during their last years in New York. With a club mired in last price, a long-term lease on a municipal facility that he would rather not have been playing in, and a fan base quickly being usurped by the upstart Oakland A's across the bay, Lurie grasped for any life preserver he could find. First, he put the Giants up for sale. Then he lined up a golf match down the coast at Pebble Beach. But Lurie had more on his mind than a round of golf. He was hoping that his opponent Peter Ueberroth, head of the Los Angeles Olympic Organizing Committee, would join him for lunch with a car dealer who, like Lurie, owned a baseball club in a small market and had something else to sell besides cars. Bob Lurie was convinced that Ueberroth should replace Bowie Kuhn as commissioner of baseball, and he wanted the chairman of the search committee, Milwaukee Brewers' owner Bud Selig, to meet him firsthand.

Allan H. ("Bud") Selig had become by far the most liked and respected owner in baseball. Appearing younger than someone approaching his sixtieth birthday, Selig has spent his entire life in Milwaukee and is a pillar of the community, serving on many charitable boards while running his family's automobile business. He became the Milwaukee Braves' largest public stockholder in 1963, and when the Braves moved to Atlanta, he actively sought another major league franchise for Milwaukee. On April 1, 1970, a Seattle bankruptcy court awarded the Seattle franchise to Selig and his group of investors. A man of tremendous energy, Selig immediately took a leadership role among the owners, who mostly viewed their teams as diversions from their other pursuits.

Selig has always downplayed his power, saying that he really doesn't make any decisions. He just happens to have a passionate interest in keeping the various ownership factions loosely united, and he will work the phones day and night to make sure differing viewpoints are heard. He was the obvious choice to find a successor to Bowie Kuhn.

Soon Selig was chairman of just about everything: the committee that negotiates with the players; the commit that reviews ownership disputes; the committee that decides whether the majors should expand; and the committee to find a new commissioner.

Bud never wanted the commissioner's job himself, despite prodding from other owners. His first choice, Bart Giamatti, president of Yale University, had his hands full with a bitter workers' strike and stayed in New Haven. Besides, Giamatti had always said that the only baseball job he ever really wanted was to be president of the American League so he could continue to root for his hometown team, the Boston Red Sox. The only other viable candidate, a relatively unknown White House aide, James Baker, had other plans. So, as head of the panel in charge of finding a successor to Bowie Kuhn, Selig offered the job of commissioner of major league baseball to *Time* magazine's 1984 Man of the Year, Peter Victor Ueberroth.

Central casting could not have found a better choice. In 1984 the Games of Summer—the 1984 Olympics, held in Los Angeles—had completely overshadowed the Boys of Summer. Not only had Ueberroth turned the ultimate work stoppage—the Russian boycott—into a home field advantage, but there were reports of record-breaking crowds, multimillion-dollar corporate sponsorships, and the largest TV package in Olympic history, all orchestrated under his leadership, and none of which were lost on Bud Selig.

One's first impression on meeting Ueberroth is the same now as it was when Selig first was introduced to him. He looked like a water polo player, which he was. His hair was neat, bleached by the sun and chlorine, his nose slightly ajar from an elbow illplaced. He talked, then and now, in direct, halting, well-planned sentences. His public speaking told a lot about him: He would begin each talk by reading a list of the eight or ten issues he wished to address, then go from index card to index card with a Teutonic clarification of each issue. Because he was so dispassionate and so menued, he was not a dynamic speaker; however, his style made it clear that this man was, above all else, a manager.

Ueberroth initially turned down Selig's offer, under the pretense that he did not want to commit himself to any other endeavor until the conclusion of the Summer Olympic Games. More important, he viewed the baseball commissioner's office as little more than a public relations arm for the various owners—in particular, the Los Angeles Dodgers' Peter O'Malley.

"It's not properly structure to be an effective position," Ueberroth informed Selig's committee. Convinced that they needed a strong administrator with a proven record, and one from the business community, Selig's committee persuaded the other owners to basically give Ueberroth all the power he wanted, as well as a reporting date after the Summer Olympics. For the first time in history, the commissioner was given the additional title of chief executive officer, symbolized by the power to levy fines of up to $250,000 against clubs. Another key to Ueberroth's decision to take the job was the change in the number of votes needed to elect the commissioner. The old requirement of a three-fourths majority was scuttled in favor of only a simple majority of team votes. A year later, Ueberroth bluntly stated what his goal had been during the negotiations surrounding his appointment: "If you are trying to accomplish something, you should control as much of the environment as you can."

The irony of the changes in the commissioner's powers was not lost on Ueberroth's predecessor. Bowie Kuhn's reelection bid was blocked by five of the National League's twelve owners, and that led to Ueberroth's appointment. Kuhn was viewed by many of his employers as being an ineffective figurehead who came across to the public as a stuffed shirt, and they figured a tough, no-nonsense, "can-do" executive was needed. By being forced out, Kuhn rationalized, he had helped strengthen the office he couldn't hold on to. "I don't know if 'sacrificial lamb' is the right terminology, but the issue of my remaining in office was the vehicle for the reforms and restructuring of the office that I had said were necessary all along."

Ueberroth disagreed with Kuhn's assessment that the job description, and not the man, made the difference. "That wasn't true," Ueberroth countered. "The changes were more window dressing than substance. I took the job because I felt I could do something about the problems facing baseball. I hoped to restore its traditional values. Baseball is a very important part of the fabric of our country."

Elected on March 3, 1984, for a term commencing October 1, 1984, the new commissioner quickly outlined his agenda. "The game lacks economic viability," he said after his selection. "I have studied the financial condition of baseball now, and it is not viable. It loses an awful lot of money, and if anything loses a lot of money for an extended period of time, it finally damages itself."

Between his election in March and the World Series in October, Ueberroth made a quick study of the business of baseball. "The problem with baseball is that it has been taken over by lawyers. Bowie has never run a company in his life. Over the years he has stacked the commissioner's office with other lawyers. Naturally, the Major League Baseball Players Association, under Marvin Miller's reign, followed suit. The umpires felt they needed representation, so they went and hired lawyers too. I have discovered in my short time here that everything is done by confrontation. Well, that is going to change." The question left unanswered was whether the change would be for the better or for the worse.

Believing that authority is 20 percent given and 80 percent taken, Ueberroth disbanded the various owners' committees set up by Kuhn, brought the marketing arm of Major League Baseball in-house under the commissioner's control, and grasped for the other 80 percent that the owners were reluctant to part with. Ueberroth was far too busy at first to take his eye off the fiscal ball; but when he did, he soon became afflicted by what several owners refer to as "commissioneritis."

Judge Kenesaw Mountain Landis was the first commissioner of baseball. Landis was hired in 1920 to restore the public's confidence in the game's integrity after eight players on the White Sox admitted that they had known of a fix to throw the 1919 World Series. Out of the uproar over "the Black Sox Scandal," the commissioner was empowered to make decisions he deemed appropriate "in the best interests of baseball"—a vague, broad definition of powers.

Landis, like Ueberroth later, knew how to assume authority he did not possess. In 1941 he was outraged when he heard that the owner of the Boston Braves planned to build a dog track around the playing field, install pari-mutuel betting, and put on races when the Braves were out of town. "Get rid of that fellow!" he barked to another National League owner. "Go back there and tell him I don't give a damn how he gets out—that's up to him—but let him understand that he better get out in a hurry if he doesn't want to be thrown out."

Judge Landis, who viewed his position as commissioner solely as a watchdog, did not make many friends in baseball. He had no vision of the game's future, only a commitment to keep it clean. He opposed the creation of farm systems, as well as the racial integration of organized baseball. But the games were played without further scandal during his reign and he stayed on as commissioner longer than anyone has since, until his death in 1944. Appropriately, one year later, Jackie Robinson became the first black player to sign a major league contract.

Albert ("Happy") Chandler, Ford Frick, and William Eckert, the three commissioners who followed Judge Landis, are but a footnote in the history of baseball. Their legacies are forgotten, because basically there were none to remember. After being replaced by Frick, Chandler sized up his successor's contributions as follows: "There was a vacancy when I left, and the owners decided to continue it. Frick's sleep was not as long as Rip van Winkle's, but it was equally deep."

Los Angeles Times columnist Jim Murray came to Frick's defense (sort of): "Ford Frick isn't the worst commissioner in baseball history, but he's in the photo. I make him no worse than place. He could get up in the last few strides, but I don't think anybody can catch Happy Chandler at the wire. He has too long a lead."

Bowie Kuhn probably would have suffered the same reputation if not for the rise of the Major League Baseball Players Association, and in particular its executive director, Marvin Miller. Kuhn's tenure as commissioner was marked by general malaise and stagnation. But Kuhn, with his legal background, was enamored of his role as the final arbiter on issues that affected "the integrity of the game." Kuhn basically left the office with no enduring legacy, except for his unwitting role in the growth of the players' union. As Marvin Miller has stated on many occasions, if Bowie had not existed, the Players Association would have had to invent him. He was the perfect foil for Miller, who orchestrated the union's string of shutout victories in labor negotiations during Kuhn's tenure.

Even Miller, the owners' chief adversary, agrees with the "commissioneritis" theory. "There must be something around that commissioner's desk," Miller told Bob Ryan of the *Boston Globe*. "They enter the job as an ordinary individual and very quickly acquire delusions. They become, in their minds, czars who wish to control everything and who feel there are no laws to restrain them."

At first, Ueberroth was so busy consolidating power and developing a new marketing agenda that he was not afflicted by commissioneritis. But it didn't take long. Soon after taking office in October 1984, Ueberroth moved quickly to show his employers— the twenty-six owners who had hired him as their CEO—that he had acquired mystical powers that placed him above the fray. "My responsibility is not to the owners or the players, it is to the game overall—which includes the players, the umpires, the fans. It is to institution called Baseball. I have an accountability to all parts of baseball, but in the sense of a boss, the commissioner doesn't have one. It's the national pastime—it belongs to the public in a real sense." Bowie Kuhn, or even Judge Landis, could not have said it better, and the press ate it up.

Barely two weeks into his new job, Ueberroth found the perfect opportunity to exert his power on a public stage. The umpires went on strike just before the commencement of the playoffs. "In the best interests of baseball," Ueberroth quickly settled the strike, basically by giving them most of what they wanted. Predictably, the umpires were ecstatic, and most of the owners irate. "Hopefully, the independent posture displayed by the commissioner in this case will help insure labor peace in baseball in the years ahead," Richie Phillips, the union's negotiator, said. Little did he know, however, that all prior labor-management confrontations would seem pale compared to the all-out war that would break out during Ueberroth's reign one year later.

In his first press conference in October, Ueberroth stated that the most urgent problems facing him were to resolve the conflicts among various owners, to control the television superstations, and to reverse the financial losses being suffered by many clubs. Conspicuous by their absence were any reference to the pending

collective-bargaining negotiations or any mention of labor confrontations. The new commissioner had already figured out where
the real power in baseball was located, and he wanted a closer
look. Sometime between October and the December winter meetings, Ueberroth bought Marvin Miller lunch.

Ueberroth knew all about the importance of the star system.
The success of the Olympics had been as much attributable to
Mary Lou Retton's smile and vaulting ability as it was to his organizational skills. It is one thing for the Russians not to show up;
it is another for 650 baseball players to go on strike. If he was going
to sell baseball to Madison Avenue, he wanted to make sure he
could deliver the product, uninterrupted by "technical difficulties." Why had "technical difficulties" caused problems in the
past? Ueberroth wanted to know. Miller was only too happy to
explain. The education process was a quick one.

By the time he reached Houston for the winter meetings in
December of 1984, Ueberroth was thoroughly versed in the history of the collective-bargaining negotiations that had taken place
between the clubs and the players since the inception of free
agency in 1975. The Olympic Games had shown that he was a
master at marketing a product and increasing revenue, and he was
certain he would succeed in multiplying by severalfold the gross
revenues of the baseball industry. But first he needed to convince
the players that the overall financial health of the sport was in
trouble, that they were partners with the owners, and that therefore it was in their best interests to work together with the owners
to enlarge the pie and their share of it. His game plan was in place
when he arrived at Houston. He would use the public platform of
the winter meetings to downplay the friction that existed between
the players and the owners, by holding himself out as the independent arbitrator who would bring the parties together, increase
revenues, get costs under control, and fulfill Richie Phillips's
hoped-for prophecy.

Superstations, not labor conflicts, are the biggest problem facing major league baseball, he told the owners in Houston. Furthermore, while baseball's financial problems were serious, he
said, they were not as critical as some owners had suggested.
Having now chastised some of the owners for making profits at

the expense of the others, and having downplayed the supposed financial crisis that existed within baseball, Ueberroth announced to the national press that his number one priority as the new commissioner was to establish "unity" between the owners and the players. He concluded his speech by informing everyone that he was going to leave the owners' meetings in Houston and join the Players Association meetings in Las Vegas. After all, as commissioner of everyone, he reasoned, shouldn't he spend as much time at the players' meetings as he had spent at the owners'?

Donald Fehr, Miller's successor, didn't buy it. "He's the new kid on the block. He works for the owners; they hired him. He can meet with a couple of players if he wants to, but not on collective-bargaining issues."

Despite Fehr's skepticism toward his intentions, Ueberroth went to Las Vegas and met with Fehr and the association's executive board. Actually, his grand entrance was met with typical indifference by the players. Many were more interested in playing golf and working on their tans. For the first time, Ueberroth realized the strength of the union and its distrust of management. But since he had come to play and not to fold, he laid his cards on the table. He informed the players that they shouldn't believe the owners' plea of poverty and again reminded them of his independence, as he represented "all of baseball and not just the owners." After he left, Fehr told the executive board that Ueberroth would do justice to any Las Vegas high roller and warned that no one should buy into his bluff.

The year 1984 came to a close with Ueberroth batting 1.000 in his new job. Playoffs began on time because he gave the umpires what they wanted; new licensing agreements at $1 million a pop were dramatically increasing marketing revenues to the clubs; he had become the first commissioner to attend a Players Association board meeting; and he had found the hot topic for his commissioneritis: drugs. Peter Victor Ueberroth had a plan to save not only baseball, but the country as well, from drug use.

"We always felt that Ubie was just passing through—a momentary pause between opportunities," one owner stated. "But we assumed he wanted to be the president of the United States—or at least governor of California. It never occurred to anyone that he wanted to be the drug czar."

Before the 1984 Olympics, Ueberroth had been concerned over the possibility of a drug scandal during the Games. Eastern bloc weight lifters were definite candidates for drug testing. As a result, Ueberroth had instituted tough testing policies during the Olympics. He was anxious to apply the same policies to baseball and to clean up the sport. The FBI convinced him that the problem was even worse than he had imagined.

"Organized crime is involved, and they are using women to get the players hooked. Many players aren't buying cocaine; they are getting it for free from girls at bars," Ueberroth confided to a visitor in his office. "The mob is looking for a hook into the players so that they can fix games." Ueberroth was not going to have another Black Sox scandal under his administration. He was convinced that Donald Fehr and the association's founder and outside consultant, Marvin Miller, would go along with his plans. He met several times with Fehr to get the association to accept more testing. To him, this was not a question to be resolved in collective bargaining; it was simply the right and prudent thing to do.

Fehr saw it differently. If Ueberroth wanted to change the Drug Policy Agreement between the clubs and players, he would have to take it up in collective bargaining. Grandstanding for the press about drug abuse throughout the country was not going to persuade the association to change its position.

Ueberroth was a persuasive man who was not accustomed to being rebuked, especially on a stance that was so fundamentally right in his mind. If the players would not cooperate on this issue, what chance did he have of convincing them that the clubs needed their cooperation in structuring a new financial partnership for the future? At that moment he realized that the owners had lost control of their game and that it was up to him to show them how to get it back.

At first, he really thought he could be above the fray. But as long as the commissioner is hired solely by the owners and can be fired by them, the union will view him as being in the enemy's camp. Ueberroth now understand this. He also understood why the players had come out ahead in every collective-bargaining agreement. It was a lot easier for Marvin Miller to keep the players united than it was for the owners to act in their collective best interests. "A group of owners couldn't even agree what to have for breakfast," he was fond of saying. Ueberroth knew what he had to do.

If they had hired him to give them a kick in the rear, he would oblige. But first he had to teach them how to take advantage of their antitrust exemption and to act as a cartel. A cartel shares information. The Yankees should not compete off the field against the Brewers, or the Dodgers, or any team, Ueberroth felt. George Steinbrenner, Bud Selig, and Peter O'Malley had to be shown that they were partners first and rivals second. The owners needed shock therapy to get their books in order. Since he was responsible for increasing their revenues, it would also be his job to show them how to control their expenses.

To get the owners united, he would embarrass them into sub-mission. This time there would be no breaking from the ranks. Ueberroth would make sure of that.

CHAPTER THREE

THE OLD WAR-HORSE IS PUT OUT TO PASTURE

$\bigoplus$

SPRING TRAINING, 1984

I t was time to quit. For fifteen years Marvin Miller had been the most potent man in baseball. By 1982 he had created the most powerful union in sports, if not in all of America. The Major League Baseball Players Association had the best pension, medical benefits, and working conditions of any labor organization in the country. The average salary in baseball was over $240,000, and every player had the right to negotiate his own individual contract. He had orchestrated the longest work stoppage in professional sports history, fifty days, and the players had clearly emerged the winners, as they had in all prior collective-bargaining agreements under his leadership. Finally, Bowie Kuhn was on his way out, so it was only fitting that Miller could even beat his old adversary out the door. Kuhn was being forced out; Miller was retiring on his own terms.

One was always aware of Marvin's right hand, because so many management people who refused to accept the reality of the union made cheap, tasteless jokes about it. A birth defect had left Miller with only partial use of his right arm. Miller never was a man of physical presence, for he was short and slight and obviously lacked the businessman's power handshake. He brushed his gray hair straight back, accentuating the sharp features of his face, his dark eyebrows, and his pencil-thin mustache. But when he opened his mouth, he had all the presence of a William Jennings

Bryan with a New York accent. His deep, resounding voice, with its educated Eastern coating, could skip from philosophy to data to dogma with transfixing skill. When he wanted to make his point about the owners, he punctuated his argument with a unique, sneering laugh that made anyone listening say to himself, "You know, Marvin is right—the owners *are* blunderers, bandits, and thieves."

A search committee of players selected Ken Moffett to succeed Miller. Moffett had been the federal mediator during the 1980–81 baseball negotiations and had become friendly with several of the players. Miller was retained as a consultant to educate Moffett on the history of prior labor negotiations and to offer his advice as needed. Theirs was a match that was doomed from the start.

Miller had built the position of executive director of the Players Association to resemble its counterpart in a typical labor organization. The executive director, according to Miller, has two basic responsibilities—first, through collective bargaining, to seek additional benefits for his members, whether they be pension improvements, salary increases, or other fringe benefits; and secondly, to insure that the rights earned by the membership are not violated. Moffett, on the other hand, with his background in mediation, rejected Miller's view that his role should be solely that of an advocate for the players.

Perhaps because there were no immediate collective-bargaining battles on the horizon, or because he wanted to establish his own imprint on the office, Moffett took a conciliatory approach toward the owners. The long 1981 strike had left both sides bitter. Moffett, with a more casual style than Miller's, was going to bring the parties back together. He would have had more success getting Humpty-Dumpty back on the wall.

Miller had worked to build a strong union by preaching that for close to one hundred years the players had been manipulated, used, and discarded without the basic rights granted by the Constitution to other workers. He made sure his message was understood by all the players at his annual visits to spring training camps. Miller knew how to get the players' attention: Besides his annual

State of the Union address, he would hand out individual licensing royalty checks to each player. Companies, such as Topps Chewing Gum, must pay the union for the right to merchandise products with the players' likenesses on it. The money is then passed on to the players based on their prior year's days of service.

The timing of the distributions was obvious. Handing out money always insures a positive reaction from an audience, and the players would listen a little bit more intently to what Miller had to say. The licensing checks were also a reminder to the players that the union leadership was working on their behalf to develop new sources of income beyond the royalties from baseball cards. Miller's greatest fear was that the players, who were now earning far more than they ever imagined, would grow complacent and forget the past. A true laborite, Miller was convinced that sixteen years of hard-earned gains could be reversed in a heartbeat if the players became tired of the battle.

Along the way, Miller trained some lieutenants to keep the troops in line. Until Miller came along, clubs could prohibit players from having any outside representation. Collective bargaining changed that, and the first agent probably appeared before the ink was dry on the agreement. From the beginning, the profession of agent has drawn comparisons to the titles of Clint Eastwood's spaghetti westerns: *The Good, the Bad and the Ugly; For a Few Dollars More;* and, of course, every owner's favorite, *Hang 'Em High.* Most agents see themselves as the central character in these films, the loner with no name. Just a hired gun, who comes into town, protects his clients, and rides out.

This hired-gun mentality often leads many agents to boast of the "groundbreaking" size of a contract they have just negotiated—a notch on their gun—to publicize their skills and bring in more business.

The union is quick to remind, however, that through collective bargaining it has the sole right to negotiate players' work benefits and that only with the union's blessing are agents allowed to exist. The message is clear: In return for providing salary data on all players to anyone who represents a player, and for allowing agents to negotiate individual contracts, the union expects the agent to toe the line. And the line is heavy with antimanagement rhetoric.

For years the union leadership has steered players away from some agents and toward others who are more adversarial.

Miller often criticized the industry he helped spawn, but the top agents have been very successful in taking tools provided to them by the association and ratcheting up players' salaries by hundreds of millions of dollars since 1976. As advance scouts for the union, agents have also kept the association well apprised of clubs' tactics to regain control over their players.

Anyone can be an agent. There are no professional standards. In the early years of the union only the most senior veteran on a club relied on outside representation. Now, it is rare for a player at the Class A level to be unrepresented, and most of the top high school prospects have "family representation." The education process starts long before a young hitter faces his first major league curveball.

The fifty-day strike in 1981 marked the high point of Marvin Miller's tenure as director of the Major League Baseball Players Association. The union held strong, and refused to give back what had been negotiated in 1976—namely, free agency.

No sooner had Miller introduced the new director to the players' executive committee than he knew that the search committee had found the wrong person. With a union more united than ever in its mistrust of management, Moffett announced, "No one ever wins a strike."

Ken Moffett's term started on January 2, 1983, and lasted less than one year—he was fired on November 23, 1983. Moffett was basically a nice fellow who didn't seem to work very hard, and with his background tended to see things in shades of gray instead of black and white. After one too many conciliatory speeches addressed toward management, Moffett's fate was sealed. Following Miller would not have been easy for any new director; following him with no agenda and a pro-management stance on many issues, including drug testing, was tantamount to a death wish.

Miller agreed to return on an interim basis. To find a permanent successor, the players then looked within the association and chose their general counsel, Donald Fehr. It was the appropriate choice. As a young labor attorney in 1975, Fehr was assigned by his Kansas City law firm to work with the Players Association during its federal case that upheld Peter Seitz's ruling and led to free agency. Seitz had ruled that the clubs' right to retain the services of a player for one more year after his contract expired because of the option clause in his contract means just that: The option to re-sign the player for just one more year and not in perpetuity as the clubs argued. The next year Fehr was hired as the union's general counsel when Dick Moss left to become an agent. He had been through the most recent battles with Miller and was on the same philosophical page.

Fehr has been aptly described as a pit bull. He has a scrubbed, evangelical approach that turns the slightest owner-player issue into a breach of the Constitution, but what makes him so effective is not only his paralegal eloquence, but his sincerity. Miller could finally retire, knowing that the union would stay on the course he had charted for it.

Moffett didn't leave quietly. He sued the union for breach of contract and remarked, "It's ironic that the one thing the players look for is a guaranteed contract. The association pushed for that. But that's not the case if you *work* for the association." Several months later, still upset by his dismissal, Moffett went public with statements regarding drug usage by major league players.

The epidemic of drug abuse throughout the country had hit baseball as well. The players and the owners had been working on a joint drug policy, but the stumbling block was the issue of mandatory testing. Moffett's comment to the *New York Times* that "some player representatives felt that there were four or five on the average on their club who used drugs" did not help the players' stance, and Fehr was incensed.

"How does he know?"

Moffett countered that his source was the FBI. Even more astounding, Moffett had been told that Whitey Herzog, the manager of the St. Louis Cardinals, said that the FBI had taken photos in the Cardinals clubhouse and in the bullpen showing players using cocaine during a game.

Moffett's allegations and the fact that three members of the Kansas City Royals—Willie Wilson, Jerry Martin, and Willie Aikens—were

serving time in a federal penitentiary on drug charges turned public sentiment against the Players Association's position on drug
testing.

When the three Royals were released in early 1984, they found
themselves in the eye of a storm. They had become the first players in the history of baseball to serve time for drug convictions. As
convicted felons, they had to deal with the public scrutiny that
awaited their release.

Willie Wilson had kicked the habit on his own. It had made
him sick to his stomach and taken his appetite away. "I like to
eat," he explained. "The highs no longer outweighed the lows,
so I stopped."

The press, and especially the commissioner's office, wanted to
know more than just why and when he quit. Bowie Kuhn wanted
Wilson to reveal everything about his drinking and smoking habits. Said Wilson: "I didn't even drink or smoke before I started
playing baseball. It really started to get to me after the 1980 World
Series."

Wilson could not understand that the more success he enjoyed
the more criticism would be directed to him. The 1980 season
should have been the most enjoyable of his short professional
career. He led the American League in hits, runs, and triples and
batted .326 in helping the Royals win the American League pennant. Unfortunately, he also set a major league record by striking
out twelve times as the Royals lost to the Philadelphia Phillies in
the World Series. "There was so much negative stuff and I must
have heard the ['How many K's are there in Wilson? Twelve'] joke
thousands of times."

Unfortunately, as Wilson's career flourished, so did the jokes
and resentment. In 1982 he won the American League batting
title, but was held out of the starting lineup the last day of the
season to protect his lead over Robin Yount. Wilson wanted to
play; the club convinced him otherwise. During the off-season he
was painted as a coward who'd cravenly ducked Yount's coura-
geous challenge. The boos started.

"I used the cocaine to forget. It helped me forget, not only
about the bad stuff but about everything. There were so many

demands on my time. Fans wanted your time, teammates wanted your time, the media wanted your time, your family wanted your time, and your friends wanted your time. Nobody could seem to understand that sometimes you need time to yourself. It caused a lot of pressure," he told the assembled press after he was released from prison. Welcome to Spring Training, 1984.

The irony of it all was not lost in Wilson. He'd licked his habit in 1983 on his own. A former teammate, in town for a series against the Royals, had pestered him for the name and telephone number of an acquaintance who had gotten Wilson hooked on the white powder at a party during the off-season. Turning down the Seattle player's request, Wilson finally agreed to call the dealer himself and give him the player's name and hotel number—"Just so this guy wouldn't bug me anymore." The dealer's phone lines were being tapped on a drug bust, and Wilson, Aikens, and Martin who'd contacted him also, were caught in the web. Wilson was convicted and sentenced to one year in prison, not for possession, or selling, or distribution, but for attempting to possess cocaine, "a Schedule II narcotic drug/controlled substance." The player who was actually seeking the drug was never caught or fined. The United States attorney prosecuting the case recommended to the judge that in consideration of Wilson's cooperation in the case he be put on probation and spend time in the community educating kids on the evils of drugs.

Fourteen years earlier, Marvin Miller and Donald Fehr had won their greatest victory in a federal court in Kansas City. On October 13, 1983, Willie Wilson and his teammates left a courthouse in the same town with entirely different emotions, as the judge ignored the federal attorney's recommendations and sentenced the players to one year in prison.

"You occupy a special place in our society. It carries with it special obligations," the judge said.

Of the thousands of drug arrests and convictions throughout the United States in 1983, no other individuals served a day in prison on a charge of attempting to possess illegal drugs.

Wilson, along with Martin and Aikens, served three months in prison and was released early for good behavior. However, before he could earn a living again, he had to get his job back. The lame-duck commissioner, Bowie Kuhn, was waiting to exert his commissioneritis.

"These players have each acknowledged an awareness and understanding of baseball's prohibition regarding the possession and use of illegal drugs. Their actions have clearly violated this prohibition. It is beyond question that their activities have proven detrimental to the best interests of the Kansas City Royals and of baseball. The game's integrity and the public's confidence in it are jeopardized. Accordingly, I have determined that Willie Wilson, Jerry Martin, and Willie Aikens should be suspended without pay for one year, effective immediately."

There was only one small detail Kuhn left out. Wilson had not been caught either possessing or using drugs. The commissioner was using Wilson's cooperation with the government and admission of prior use to prevent him from earning a living. Baseball had just changed the Bill of Rights. According to Bowie Kuhn, commissioneritis takes precedence over the right against self-incrimination.

The Players Association, of course, immediately filed a grievance against Bowie Kuhn, and the arbitrator sided with the union, overturning Wilson's suspension.

"For the integrity of the game—that's what the commissioner said he suspended us for," Wilson said. "I don't know if I agree with that. And the judge, he said he sent me to prison not for the crime, but because I was a bad role model. Well, I didn't ask to be a role model—but enough of that; I don't want to say any of the wrong things. The judge gave me three months to think about it. I didn't think he had to give me that long, but the judge did his job. And now I think the commissioner thinks he needs to help us out a little more."

Wilson left the press conference and spring training with one last thought: "I would like everyone to know that, as ballplayers, we're just human beings, not gods. It is a simple game we play and I am not awed by the hitting, fielding, and running I do, because I've been doing it since I was a little kid. We've got problems just like everybody else."

Shortly thereafter, the first joint agreement dealing with drug use was reached between the Players Association and the owners. But it did not include mandatory or random drug testing. In essence, the Joint Drug Policy Agreement dealt only with the ramifications if a player was caught using drugs. The players agreed with the agreement, because they knew the clubs too well. While publicly all the clubs took a tough stance on drug usage, no one wanted to be involved in any way in confronting his own players, and without random testing, there was little chance that any player would be caught. The program did serve a public relations purpose, however. Since it dealt with the issue of the commissioner's right to discipline once a player was caught, baseball would at least avoid one black eye. It's bad enough for the public to find out that players are using drugs; it is worse for the players to escape punishment.

Ueberroth had to know that he couldn't control the players on this issue. But he also knew where the winds of public opinion were blowing from, and saw that the Joint Drug Policy Agreement had no teeth without mandatory testing. He therefore announced that commencing in 1985 there would be mandatory testing throughout the minor leagues, which are not covered by the Collective Bargaining Agreement, as well as in all front offices in baseball. The strategy was obvious; since he had no real power over the major league players, he was going to exert his powers over everyone else. For Ueberroth, the public relations fallout for him would be a home run.

"It is imperative that we rid baseball of drug abuse—for the sake of our youth, who look to baseball for role models, and also for the future of our country. Someone somewhere has to say 'Enough is enough' to drugs. And I've done that."

The new commissioner's grand plan to eliminate drugs from baseball through mandatory testing received a lot of attention from the press. Phillies manager John Felske wasn't as receptive. "You mean I have to take a drug test and the players won't? I don't understand that."

Felske's confusion was understandable. After all, he had only played in the major leagues for fifty-four games, and his career ended in 1973, three years before the pendulum really started to swing in the players' favor. If there was going to be a new drug

policy affecting the players, it would have to be negotiated with
the union. Peter Ueberroth knew this. But he also knew that a
grand jury in Pittsburgh was considering indictments against several players for possession of cocaine. Public sentiment was clearly
on his side, and perhaps he could make Leland MacPhail's last job
in baseball a little easier.

CHAPTER FOUR

THE BLUEPRINT FOR BATTLE

350 PARK AVENUE, NEW YORK CITY, FEBRUARY 1985

In an industry renowned for its "old-boy network," Lee MacPhail is the ultimate old boy. He was born into a famous baseball family, the son of Larry MacPhail, ran the Orioles, the Yankees, the American League, and the Player Relations Committee (PRC), and at one point was virtually the most powerful insider in the game; yet he is never slick—in fact, he is always a tad rumpled—and when he engages in conversation, his head often bows in self-deprecation. He is, however, a direct-contact person whose eyes flash seriousness, and the fact that he always pauses and swallows after being asked a question or offered a challenge attests to his honesty and thoughtfulness.

The Player Relations Committee is the negotiating arm of the clubs with the players. Every four years it gets a new chairman, because the current leader is always fired by a frustrated group of owners convinced that the inmates have just taken over the asylum. Both Ueberroth and his employers were more optimistic on the eve of the 1985 negotiations. First of all, Marvin Miller had finally retired, undefeated and unscored-on. Also, in the two prior negotiations, MacPhail had emerged as the one representative from the owners' side who was able to effect a settlement.

"Baseball is sick. It can't get well by taking a couple of sugar-coated pills and maintaining the status quo. Baseball must take a

57

deep breath and revise its whole operation," MacPhail emphatically stated. Several clubs were in the red, several more were threatening to move, and yet most of the owners were complacent. MacPhail knew what was to blame. "The revenue from television is the anesthetic that has put the club owners to sleep," he remarked. MacPhail was convinced that if the owners continued to depend on television revenues to bail them out of their fiscal mess, they would be attending their own funeral. "The game will be at the mercy of a fickle, push-button audience. When this happens, baseball will be through." In 1984, Lee MacPhail agreed with these dire predictions that his father had made twenty-seven years earlier in 1958.

Larry MacPhail operated three major league clubs—the Cincinnati Reds (1933–1937), Brooklyn Dodgers (1938–1942), and New York Yankees (1945–1947). All three clubs saw their attendance rise under his regime and both New York franchises won pennants with MacPhail at the helm. But Larry MacPhail is primarily remembered for being the first baseball executive to bring night games and television to baseball. The senior MacPhail saw the immediate benefits from his experiment with television, but he was concerned by the declining attendance that followed.

Television was in its infancy, but already its impact had dramatically changed the course of baseball. During the 1950s nearly a third of the major league clubs moved, attendance fell dramatically, and more than half of the minor leagues went out of business. While more and more fans were staying home and casually following baseball on television, a more fundamental reason was to blame for baseball's decline: Major league baseball was primarily being played in decaying ballparks in Eastern inner cities.

MacPhail's solution was to open up the country to expansion and promote the live gate. He was a visionary on two counts, but his son hoped that he would be proven wrong on a third.

At first, Larry MacPhail's suggestions fell on deaf ears. As usual, it took a threat from the outside to change things. A rival major league, the Continental League, emerged. Its strategy was to bring major league baseball to the outposts ignored by the existing league.

Faced with a real challenge to its monopoly, baseball expanded westward and southward during the 1960s and 1970s, bringing about a renaissance (as well as the construction of new municipal parks), as MacPhail had predicted. He was also subsequently proven right in his advocacy of the creation of four divisions, in the belief that "a series between the East and West champions of each league would increase rather than diminish interest in the World Series."

But once baseball was brought into the living room, its financial future was directly tied to the studio. Larry MacPhail speculated that "instead of being a sport, baseball will be in the entertainment business, in competition with movies, giveaway shows, wrestling, and theatricals—and baseball will be putting on the poorest show."

Baseball, of course, had long competed for a share of the entertainment dollar. After all, Boston Red Sox owner Harry Frazee sold George Herman Ruth to the Yankees so he could finance his play *No, No, Nanette.* The Babe's act lasted longer than the play. And as any fan of the movie *Bull Durham* knows, to escape the minors is to make it to "the Show." How to package and sell "the Show" in the future was not Lee MacPhail's immediate concern or area of expertise. Besides, Lee MacPhail was retiring at the end of 1985. It would be up to Peter Ueberroth, with all of his marketing skills, to prove Larry MacPhail wrong. The problems Lee MacPhail faced had not existed for his father. The senior MacPhail never had to worry about the entertainers, just how to get more people into the tent.

Free agency. For ten years every player had thought about it. "When do I get to choose where I want to play?" "When will clubs start bidding for my services?" Likewise, every owner had publicly cursed the term. "We are spending ourselves out of existence." "We can't afford to pay these high salaries." But George Brett, the great star of the Kansas City Royals, summed it up best: "Hey, I didn't put a gun to anyone's head. If they can't afford to pay me what they're paying me, they wouldn't."

The great fear of owners was that free agency would allow the wealthier clubs to buy up all the top players, only a few clubs would be competitive, and attendance would drop dramatically. The exact opposite occurred. In the ten years since the seventh game of the 1975 World Series, major league attendance had risen, and salaries and franchise values with it. No one team dominated the World Series as the Yankees had done in the "good old days." During those ten years the following clubs won the World Series: the Cincinnati Reds; the New York Yankees; the Pittsburgh Pirates; the Philadelphia Phillies; the Los Angeles Dodgers; the St. Louis Cardinals; the Baltimore Orioles; and the Detroit Tigers. What had changed was who was in control.

Before the advent of free agency, the clubs had viewed each other as partners who, like puppeteers, pulled all the strings. After 1976, the economics of the free market began to come into play. The supply side (players) was too tempting for the demand side (owners) to pass up. Fearful that the system would work too well, clubs began to sign up their top players to long-term contracts so they wouldn't pack up their bags and move elsewhere. In 1981 the owners turned to the players, and in essence said, "Save us from ourselves." Sure, every club would have liked to have a Reggie Jackson, but no team wanted to be the one that lost a Reggie Jackson's services. So the owners asked the players to agree to a form of compensation. If a club loses a player to another team they proposed that the acquiring team be forced to give the free agent's original team a player off its roster. This did not sound like a free market. "Sure, you can sign Reggie Jackson—just give me Mike Schmidt in return."

The players, of course, rejected equal compensation, being well aware of the chilling effect it would have on free agency. Lee MacPhail had spent fifty hot days in New York in the summer of 1981 witnessing the players' resolve on this issue. He was not going to force it again in 1985.

If the clubs disliked free agency, they absolutely got sick over the mention of salary arbitration. The concept of salary arbitration actually preceded the birth of free agency, but it did not take on its true importance until the dramatic rise in players' salaries through free agency. When first introduced, all players had the right to submit their salary negotiations to binding arbitration after playing two years in the major leagues. To encourage settlement, the arbitrator was forced to pick either the club's or the player's figure. However, key criteria in salary arbitration were the salaries of other players with comparable statistics. As the open market drove the salaries of free agents upward, other players with similar or better statistics were able to gain sizable increases through salary arbitration. As one owner exclaimed, "Players don't lose in arbitration; it's only a matter of how much of a raise they get."

The owners' major complaint about the arbitration system was expressed by Bud Selig. "If I want to overpay my shortstop, that's my stupidity; but why should I have to pay my shortstop relative to what some idiot in New York pays his!" Without the arbitration process, however, clubs would be able to dictate salaries for six years, at which point a player could finally jump to another team. Lee MacPhail knew that the players were not going to restrict their right to become free agents. But he sensed less resistance toward a change in the arbitration process.

As salaries continued to rise, player turnover increased as well. Since the owners had a complete hammer for the first three years of a player's career, and a partial one for the next three, younger players were being rushed to the majors at a far greater rate than in the past. As a result, less than 50 percent of the players in 1985 had been members of the union during the strike in 1981. Those who were around in 1981 were mostly all beyond their arbitration years as well, having played three years or more. MacPhail sensed the first real schism in the player ranks. The veterans did not want to strike over the question of arbitration rights for young players.

MacPhail was also ready to play his trump card. In all prior negotiations, Miller had always opened the talks by asking the owners if they were going to make proposals based on their "ability to pay." The owners had each time avoided Miller's trap. Under federal rules, if an employer makes its "ability to pay" an issue, then the union has the right to review management's financial statements. Since the owners never pleaded financial hardship, the union always used this admission to their advantage. "The clubs' ability to pay is not an issue," Miller would announce to the press at the commencement of every negotiating period. If money wasn't the issue, then what was? Miller would leave the answer to that question for the owners.

MacPhail assumed correctly that the owners would again want to keep their books closed. He knew he stood as much of a chance of getting Gussie Busch to send his financials to Peter O'Malley as persuading Busch to share them with Marvin Miller. But this time he could prove that eighteen clubs were losing money. And with that realization, it all started to make sense to him. Maybe he couldn't force the owners to share their private finances with each other, but someone else could. His plan began to hatch.

The hard-liners were getting militant. "The players should get rid of Miller and Fehr," John McMullen, the outspoken owner of the Houston Astros, told the press. O'Malley and the Dodgers unilaterally started to put drug clauses in the individual contracts of some of their players, contrary to provisions of the Joint Drug Policy Agreement between the owners and players. The owners wanted rollbacks and the players wanted a bigger share of the pie. The 1981 strike was looking like a minor temblor compared to the major earthquake that loomed on the immediate horizon.

MacPhail was ready to open up the books. But he needed help. As expected, the owners, and particularly John McMullen, said "No way." MacPhail laid his plan out to Ueberroth. It was an opportunity too good for the commissioner to pass up. It had taken him a few months, but he was finally ready to seize total control. On February 26, 1985, Ueberroth announced to the owners that if they would not voluntarily hand over their financials to the Players Association, he would order them to do so. He also announced that there would be no more quarterly regional meetings of the owners, and no more meetings of the owners' Executive Council. He had the owners in his hip pocket, public support for his position on mandatory drug testing, and the players back on their heels for the first time.

MacPhail and Ueberroth then started their "good cop-bad cop" routine on the players. While MacPhail proposed a new payroll plan based on the National Basketball Association's revolutionary salary-cap formula, Ueberroth met with the players around the country and told them not to worry about the salary plan. On

August 6, the players walked. Two days later a compromise was reached and MacPhail was able to tack another year on the requirement for arbitration eligibility. Preventing younger players from going to arbitration until their third year meant not only substantial savings to the industry, but getting back partial control over these newer players.

Opening the books didn't have much of an impact on the players. They suggested that there were really "two sets of books" and that the numbers "had been cooked." But whether they were cooked or not it sure got the reaction from the owners that Ueberroth had hoped for. "I didn't realize I had lost so much money," flabbergasted Oakland A's owner Walter Haas blurted out.

"I've been the stupidest," the Braves' Ted Turner announced.

With Lee MacPhail's and the PRC's assistance, Ueberroth was going to educate the owners in the art of seizing control. Barry Rona, a legal counsel to the PRC, was named to replace MacPhail, who resigned one week after negotiating a new Basic Agreement between the owners and players.

"And so my baseball career finally came to an end. Before leaving, I wrote the clubs urging them to accomplish on their own, by their own individual financial discipline, the fiscal responsibility necessary to keep baseball viable. Surprisingly, in some areas, they seem to have heeded my advice," Lee MacPhail stated in his autobiography.

MacPhail's advice to the owners was simple: "Just say no to free agency." It was left up to Peter Ueberroth, with Barry Rona's help, to make sure the owners kicked the habit.

CHAPTER FIVE

THE BIG CHILL

$\bigcirc$

1985–1989

Messersmith went south and Reggie went north. Some players packed their bags, while others stayed put. A few even signed with their hometown teams. Some were bargains, others were busts. The length of their contracts were as short as one year or as long as ten. Some clubs were active shoppers; others never bought. From its beginnings through 1984, the free agent market always opened for business soon after the last out of the World Series. Each off-season took on a life of its own and the hot stove league was always well stocked with speculation over imminent free-agent signings. The year 1984 had been a fairly typical one. Forty-six players had filed for free agency and twenty-six had changed teams. And then it stopped. Cold turkey.

The thirty-two players who went to the market after the 1985 season were in for a surprise. By the time spring training came around, twenty-eight had re-signed with their old clubs, having received either no offers or none better from other teams. Only four moved on, and their former clubs made it clear that they had had no interest in re-signing them anyway.

The Players Association immediately filed a grievance, arguing that the system had been rigged against the players.

Under the Basic Agreement between the clubs and players, any grievance between the parties is determined by a three-member arbitration panel. However, since both the clubs and players pick one arbitrator each, for all practical purposes there is only one independent arbitrator on the panel, who serves as the chairman. Also, either the players or the owners can fire the independent arbitrator at the conclusion of his decision on a matter before the panel.

After a ruling an another matter that went in favor of the players, the owners gave Tom Roberts, the independent arbitrator, notice that he was fired. This was done during the hearings regarding the players' contention that the free market had been rigged. So even before a ruling could be made on this key grievance, the players filed another grievance, arguing that Roberts could not be dismissed quite so soon. Only in baseball.

George Nicolau was chosen as the new independent arbitrator, and he quickly ruled that Roberts should be allowed to rule on the collusion case. The owners reluctantly presented their arguments.

"These were all individually made, rational, independent decisions," Barry Rona, as spokesman for the owners, contended. There was no conspiracy, and there was no violation of the Collective Bargaining Agreement, the clubs protested.

If it hadn't been for Sandy Koufax and Don Drysdale, the clubs might have gotten away with it.

Long before free agency, Sandy Koufax, the best pitcher of his day, had used the only leverage he had to try to get a better contract from the Los Angeles Dodgers: He announced that he would not report to spring training unless he got a better deal. The number two pitcher on the staff (and quite possibly in all of baseball), Don Drysdale, was nobody's fool. If he also stayed out, he realized, the Dodgers would really be in a bind. So Koufax and Drysdale announced that they were acting in tandem and would not report to spring training unless they got better deals (it was reported that the hitters around the league took up a collection to match any offer that the Dodgers would make in order to keep the talented duo from reporting). Koufax and Drysdale finally got their money, but the clubs, concerned by the precedent, sought the inclusion of a clause in the Basic Agreement to prevent players in the future from joining forces to negotiate better terms. The players agreed to the inclusion as long as it was a "two-way street" and applied as well to the clubs. It was agreed that all negotiations with free agents should be of an individual nature, and that neither players nor clubs would "act in concert."

Free agency certainly had a dramatic effect on baseball's economic structure. The average salary in 1976 was $51,501. The next year it rose nearly 50 percent to $76,066. By 1980, the average salary had nearly doubled, to $143,756. By 1984, it had reached $329,408. Before free agency there were no multiyear contracts—why give a multiyear contract, owners reasoned, when you own the player's service in perpetuity? Between 1976 and 1984 at least eleven reentry free agents annually signed contracts with guaranteed terms of three years or more. In some cases, contracts were guaranteed for up to five years; and the contract of Dave Winfield, who went from the San Diego Padres to the New York Yankees, was guaranteed for ten.

The competition in the marketplace was so fierce that when a "superstar" player reached the stage where he could file as a free agent, he usually signed with a new club. To keep their key players from leaving town, clubs attempted to sign them up before they could leave. In each of the years 1977 through 1984, at least twenty-one players who were not free agents signed contracts with their clubs for a guaranteed term of three years or more. The players had no reason to expect that the 1985 market would be any different, for at the end of 1984 the majority of the year's free agents changed clubs.

Carlton Fisk's timing couldn't have been better, or so he thought; it couldn't have been worse, as it turned out. The 1985 season had been a career year for him. He hit more home runs (37) and had more runs batted in (107) than any other catcher. Only six other players in all of baseball that year had both 30 or more home runs and 100 or more RBIs, and they were all under contract for the next season.

After filing for free agency, Fisk was named the catcher on the *Sporting News* American League All-Star Team and on the American League Silver Slugger Team. He had also appeared in the 1985 All-Star Game. Fisk thought about all the teams that needed catching help and decided to canvass the universe. He contacted every team in baseball, and then waited. And waited. And waited some more.

*   *   *

Willie Wilson was one of the lucky ones. What a difference a year had made in his life. Spring training in 1985 had been considerably more enjoyable than spring training of the prior year. Having put his drug problems behind him, Wilson was ready to help lead the Royals back into the playoffs. Best of all, his contract expired at the end of the 1985 season, and the Royals were anxious to keep him out of the open market. So on opening day, Wilson agreed to a four-year extension, making him one of the highest-paid players in the game. (Little did he, or anyone else, know that this would be the last contract covering more than three years that any player would receive for a long, long time.) And after that, things got even better for him. He led the Royals through the playoffs and then to a World Championship over the St. Louis Cardinals. In the World Series, he hit .367 and had more hits than any other player on either side. Perhaps best of all, he struck out only four times. He had a relaxing off-season.

Fisk's off-season was not.

Maybe Gussie Busch and Ewing Kauffman, the owner of the Kansas City Royals, were enjoying the World Series, but the other owners certainly were not. Ueberroth had called a meeting of all the owners on October 25, 1985, in St. Louis during the World Series. Like a stern schoolteacher reviewing term papers, he wanted to know if everyone had read their assignment (i.e., MacPhail's memorandum). MacPhail admitted later that Ueberroth "jumped" on those who had not and made sure additional copies were distributed. Then he asked MacPhail to summarize his recommendations. When MacPhail finished, the hush in the room was broken by Ueberroth's warnings.

"Look in the mirror and get out and spend big if you want," the commissioner chided, "but don't go out there whining that someone made you do it." (Ueberroth had read George Brett's comments.) Taking on the fervor of a Southern Baptist preacher, Ueberroth then conducted an "informal" poll regarding the owners' interest in the upcoming free agent market. One by one, the converts stood up and uniformly announced that they had no interest in free agents. As important, they announced to each other which of their own players they hoped to re-sign.

MacPhail's memo had hit home. "Don't sign players to long-term guaranteed contracts" and do not "give in to the unreasonable demands of experienced and marginal players. . . ." he urged. Of course, he was referring to potential free agents. Left unsaid was his final advice, which Ueberroth had made apparent: Do not sign a player who is still wanted by his former team.

A couple of owners missed the St. Louis meeting and were chastised. Ueberroth fired a letter off to them; and while he mentioned that he, of course, could not "order" the owners what to do, he reminded them that "each club is responsible for its own actions and the effect of its actions on baseball as a whole."

He didn't trust the generals to get the message down to the troops in the trenches. A couple of weeks later the commissioner spoke at the major league general managers' meeting in Tarpon Springs, Florida. "Don't be dumb . . . we have a five-year agreement with labor. It is not smart to sign long-term contracts . . . such contracts force other clubs to make similar signings." To make sure no one missed his message, he informed the general managers that he would want to know the economics of any club that signed a free agent.

Meanwhile Fisk waited, and waited, and waited. Oh, he got a few "We'll think about it" responses and a few other "We're all set at catching" comments. And then one nibble. George Steinbrenner couldn't resist. Maybe just one signing would be okay. He had attended the revival meeting, had stood up, and had taken the pledge with the others. But Carlton Fisk sure could help his team. On November 21, 1985, the Yankees offered Fisk a three-year contract at $750,000 per, a relatively small raise over his prior-year salary of $575,501. Steinbrenner immediately had pangs of guilt. But it wasn't as if he really felt close to Jerry Reinsdorf or his partner, Eddie Einhorn. After all, Reinsdorf had stood up at the All-Star Game party and said, "How do you know when Steinbrenner's lying? Answer: When you see his lips move."

The Yankees owner often referred to the White Sox owners as Mr. Reinhorn, and once said, "Those guys are the Abbott and Costello of baseball. You never know what to expect from them. They're a couple of pumpkins who should get their thinking straight. . . . Those guys are a pair of Katzenjammer Kids. They're characters."

With an offer from the Yankees, Fisk called Einhorn to see how much he and Reinsdorf were willing to pay to keep him in Chicago. Even though theoretically Fisk could sign with anyone else at any time, Einhorn did not seem to be in a hurry. "We are not prepared to make you an offer at this time, but let's talk after you see what's out there."

Steinbrenner then had second thoughts. He was so embarrassed about having made an offer to Fisk that he hadn't even told his own staff. Seeing the error of his ways, he picked up the phone and told Reinsdorf what he had done. The Yankees "offer" to Fisk was quickly withdrawn. Fisk was now under the gun. If he did not re-sign with the White Sox before January 8, he would be prevented from re-signing with them until May 1. With no interest and only one offer that was subsequently withdrawn, Fisk re-signed with the White Sox for the 1986 season, at a small raise.

Although there were no balloons, the owners' meeting in February of 1986 took on a festive air. The results were in, and it was a unanimous victory. Not one player had switched teams in the off-season (except those cut loose by their former clubs), salary increases of the free agents who'd re-signed with their clubs averaged a minuscule 5 percent, and the lengths of the contracts were vastly different than in prior years—of the twenty-nine free agents, nineteen had signed one-year contracts, six had signed two-year contracts, and four had signed three-year contracts.

Willie Wilson and Carlton Fisk had learned what every good comedian knows: Timing is everything.

If there were any doubts about the extent of the owners' boycott, they disappeared the next year. The 1986 free agent crop was the best group in history. It was not by coincidence. Unlike the Kansas City Royals in their negotiations with Wilson the prior spring, the clubs were in no hurry to re-sign players who were eligible for free agency. As they correctly anticipated, the players each club wanted back received no interest from other clubs on the open market, and all but eight re-signed before the January 8 deadline.

*　　*　　*

Tim Raines never did understand what was happening. He got up every morning at his elegant house in Sanford, Florida, had some juice and coffee while his son Little Rock ate breakfast, then went out for a three-mile run around the developed community. "Boring, but this whole thing is boring," he said one day in mid-March.

Raines was part of baseball's celebrated "Collusion Eight." Like Doyle Alexander, Rich Gedman, Bob Horner, Andre Dawson, Lance Parrish, Bob Boone, and Ron Guidry, Raines had not caved in to the January 8 deadline for re-signing with his old team, the Montreal Expos. "To my surprise," he said, "no one's called. Or, should I say, to my disappointment. I'm not surprised by anything anymore. I just can't believe that this is happening. I keep asking: What am I doing here?"

What Raines was doing was simply waiting for someone to come forward and try to sign him. After all, he had batted .334 in 1986, which led the National League. He had also led the league in on-base percentage. He had stolen 70 bases. Yet, here it was the middle of March and he didn't have a job.

"This isn't strictly a financial issue," Raines said in the den of his house. "The Expos' offer wasn't that bad, in fact it was reasonable [$4.8 million for three years], if there really is collusion. But after the year I had, is a hundred-thousand-dollar-a-year raise fair? If they give a five percent raise after someone wins the batting title, what do they do when the guy has a bad year? I don't think that raise is fair in my case, this particular year. It's not like I'm a flash in the pan [Raines's career average was .304, and in each of his six seasons, including the abbreviated year of the strike, he'd had between 70 and 90 stolen bases]. But, money aside, one of the reasons for free agency was to allow players to go where they want to go. I had some good years in Montreal. The Expos were good to me in most cases, including when I had my drug problem. But when you play in Montreal, you're what they call, 'Oh, an athlete who isn't a hockey player.' I'm not an egomaniac, but I'd like some recognition. In Montreal, I'll never get it. No endorsements. I've stolen a hundred bases, I've had a few accomplishments, I've always tried to be an up-front, pleasant person. But I've never had any endorsements.

"*Sports Illustrated* did a piece on Rickey Henderson and me, with the idea that we're two of the greatest leadoff hitters of all time. I sat around in the Astrodome waiting for Rickey so we could have our pictures taken together. We took them upstairs, on the floor of the Dome, and when the magazine comes out, who's on the cover? Rickey, in his Yankee uniform. I'm tucked inside, in the back.

"That's the way it is when you play in Montreal. How big a star could Andre [Dawson] be if he were in a media center? There just isn't a baseball atmosphere, and unless you're a Gary Carter, you're a nobody. So that's why I want to leave."

But after January 8, while there were teams like the Padres and Dodgers that lusted for the National League's premier leadoff force, the offers weren't there. The Padres made a token offer of two years for a total package of $2.3 million, but it was off the table before Raines could deliberate. "I was told back in the fall by Expo officials that if I didn't take what they were offering, I wouldn't get anything," said Raines. "I knew there was something going on, but that was more than a threat. I think it's illegal, but that's for Tom Reich, my agent, to determine. They told me I'd sit there until May."

So, all through March, while he read each day's spring training stories in the *Orlando Sentinel* and *USA Today* and watched his old friends on television, Raines was what he called "locked out— barred for not doing what The Man told me to do." Instead, after he ran, showered, ate breakfast, and read the papers, he went to a local club. Three or four days, he did weights. Five days a week, he worked out in a women's aerobics class.

So there was 5-foot-8, 180-pound Rock Raines, the original giggler, stretching and bouncing up and down with two dozen Florida women. "At first I felt pretty stupid and really self-conscious," he said. "But, after a while, I got used to it and they got used to me. Anyway, it's good training."

When his alma mater, Seminole High School in Sanford, let out at two-thirty, Raines went there. First, he'd take batting and infield practice, shag flies, and throw some BP with the baseball team. Players took turns hitting him ground balls at shortstop ("They don't remember me, but I played this position here once") and fly balls in left. He practiced throws from left field to second, third, and home, twenty-five to each. When he was finished with that, he went to the adjoining field, where he worked on sprinter's starts and low hurdles with the women's track team—"The boys were too good," he laughed. In actuality, the women's coach had worked with Raines when he was a football, baseball, and track star at the school. Then he'd drive home, shower, change, and prepare to coach then seven-year-old Little Rock's Little League games. "That," Raines said, "is the best part of this collusion BS."

While Raines sat in Florida, his former teammate on the Montreal Expos, Andre Dawson, plotted with his agent, Dick Moss, to devise a unique strategy to get a job.

Moss, Marvin Miller's right-hand man before he left the union to become an agent, outsmarted the system and the Chicago Cubs. He leaked it to the Chicago media that he would be pulling into Mesa, Arizona, visiting GM Dallas Green at Hohokam Park, handing him a blank contract, and telling the Cubs to fill in whatever they felt was fair to give Dawson. This caught Green off guard, and when Moss showed up, he first claimed to be unavailable. Then he directed a series of four- and twelve-letter word harangues at Moss. But Green also knew he had no choice but to sign Dawson. After all, Dawson was a superstar and one of the most respected *people* in the sport—so respected by Raines that he'd named his younger son Andre after him. Green wrote in $500,000, plus $200,000 in incentives.

Andre Dawson turned out to be a steal. In 1987, he was named the National League's Most Valuable Player.

Lance Parrish was the only other member of the "Collusion Eight" to sign with a new team, the Philadelphia Phillies, but that wasn't without its trying moments. Tigers general manager Bill Lajoie had been forced to tell Parrish that the team was limited to offering a two-year deal at less than had originally been discussed. Tom Reich, Parrish's agent, thought it was important for someone to at least break the logjam and move, and Phillies owner Bill Giles, thinking he had a good chance to win the National League East, wanted Parrish. So Giles and Reich worked out a deal at $1 million a year in late February. The $1 million was considerably less than what Parrish's real market value would have been, but it was $300,000 higher than what clubs were told was supposed to be the maximum bid.

A couple of years later, under cross-examination during the second collusion hearing, Giles spoke of the mixed emotions he had felt on signing Parrish. For the first time, an owner admitted publicly that there was an unwritten agreement among the owners to not sign another team's players unless the former club had no interest in re-signing him.

Giles wanted to sign Parrish before the January 8 deadline, but he waited because "despite the rules, teams shouldn't go after each other's players. It's a little bit like stealing, while trading for that player, even if he doesn't want to leave his club, is not stealing, it's just part of the game." So Giles waited until after January 8. Even though Detroit was prevented from re-signing Parrish until May 1, Giles knew he had broken from the pack by expressing interest in signing Parrish. The calls started. First, American League President Bobby Brown told him, "I don't want to lose one of my star players to the National League." Both Selig and Reinsdorf followed suit. "Don't do anything stupid," they advised. Giles was in a bind. The other owners—including Detroit's Tom Monaghan—had only a month before unanimously approved a motion that had allowed Giles to acquire an increased stake in the Phillies.

Giles also admitted that his reluctance to make Parrish an offer was based on another consideration: Ruly Carpenter's words had come back to haunt him. He was scared that if he signed Parrish, "it would open the door for Turner and Steinbrenner to get back into the free agent market." He told Reich, as he reluctantly made the All-Star catcher an offer, "I'm catching tremendous heat from all over everywhere." He did not have to worry about Turner or Steinbrenner, however. They had seen the folly of their ways.

As Parrish donned his catching gear for a new season in a new league, a former rival from the Boston Red Sox sat and wondered. Shea Stadium was a strange place for Rich Gedman to spend the opening day of the 1987 season. But one of his best friends, Bobby

Ojeda, was pitching for the New York Mets, and Gedman had nothing better to do.

Six months had gone by, but the memories of the sixth game of the 1986 World Series were still fresh. There had been two outs in the bottom of the 10th inning, with the Red Sox ahead by a run. There were two strikes on the Mets batter—Boston was only one pitch away from a world championship—when a wild pitch led in the tying run, followed by the famous grounder that went through first baseman Bill Buckner's legs as Ray Knight jubilantly bounded across home plate. The Red Sox had a shot in the seventh game thanks to Gedman's homer in the second inning. But their 3–0 lead didn't hold up and the game and the World Series ended with the Mets winning 8–5. That was the last game Gedman had played on the field. And yet there he was back in the same stadium when the gates opened for a new season.

The game off the field had been even more emotionally draining.

Gedman had had a solid career up to this point, and he was coming off one of his best years in 1986, during which he was named to the American League All-Star Team. Now his contract was up. Born and raised outside of Boston, he had the opportunity to again play for his hometown team. But even though he and the Sox had had a successful year in 1986, he knew that negotiations would be tough after the experience of the 1985 free agents, and he was right.

"The market has changed," Lou Gorman, the Red Sox general manager, stated at the first negotiating session. The Red Sox had no interest in reaching an agreement with Gedman on a multiyear contract based on what other players had received prior to 1985. They also correctly assumed that no other club had any interest in signing Gedman, since the Red Sox had publicly made it known that they wanted him back. At six o'clock on January 8, 1987, Gedman tried to buy some time. "I'm just a pawn in this game. Maybe there's price-fixing and maybe there isn't. But that's up to someone else to determine," Gedman commented to Gorman.

Gedman's solution to his own problem was a practical compromise. If he and the club could agree on a one-year contract, would they allow him to become a free agent again at the conclusion of the 1987 season? Under the Basic Agreement, a player must wait five additional years to become a free agent again, unless the club agrees to let him test the waters sooner. Since Gorman was convinced that the market had changed and was also emphatically denying any conspiracy, what did the club have to lose by agreeing to a one-year contract? After all, before the advent of free agency, all players were under one-year contracts.

The Red Sox would have no part of it.

The next morning Gedman found himself out in the cold without a job or even the opportunity to re-sign with the Red Sox until May 1. Maybe now, he rationalized, other clubs will be willing to talk to me, since they know the Red Sox can't re-sign me until a month into the season.

The Red Sox had other plans. They still considered Gedman to be their property and immediately sent telexes to all clubs, the commissioner's office, the PRC, and the headquarters of the American and National leagues. The memo detailed the club's last offer to Gedman, and made it clear that they intended to pursue Gedman and to make "every effort to sign" him as of May 1. They also stated that the club could not agree to Gedman's request to become a free agent again because "it was against the rules of baseball."

They were wrong. Clubs can, and many have, waived their repeater rights, and it is not contrary to "the rules of baseball" or the Basic Agreement. Boston's key point had been made to the other clubs, however: "Hands off Gedman—he's our property."

Meanwhile, at Shea, Ojeda was having trouble getting out of the first inning. It's a strange game, Gedman thought. Ojeda had been traded to the Mets by the Red Sox and was in uniform; Gedman, who the Mets or anyone else could have signed without having to give up a major league player in return, was not. After the January 8 deadline passed, Gedman would have thought he'd be a long way from New York on opening day. He thought he was going to be in Oakland.

After some prodding, the Oakland Athletics had showed an interest in signing Gedman. Gedman just wanted to play baseball in 1987 and not have to sit out. He accepted the Athletics' offer of a one-year contract, which was lower than the Red Sox offer. The key to getting the deal done was the agreement by Roy Eisen-hardt, the A's president, to allow Gedman to become a free agent again the following year. But Eisenhardt was concerned about signing Gedman. "I sure wish some team would break the logjam out there. It sure would be a lot easier for us if some other team signed a free agent first," he said over breakfast.

Two weeks later, Gedman was ready to sign. But Oakland changed its tune. Barry Rona and the PRC had gotten to Eisen-hardt. "Political considerations" was the A's response. Rona "felt strongly" that it was not in the "best interest of clubs" to waive the provision, Eisenhardt admitted. Sandy Alderson, the A's general manager, explained that Oakland was a "little fish" and decided that the waiver of repeater rights for Gedman "was not significant enough to go against the recommendation of the PRC."

Gedman shuffled out of Shea Stadium unnoticed. Six months before he had been mobbed for his autograph. Ojeda thanked him for coming down and wished him well. Gedman turned up the collar of his coat against the raw April wind. Slowly he walked to the cabstand. Well, in three more weeks it will be May 1, he thought to himself as he caught the shuttle back to Boston.

On May 1 Gedman signed a two-year contract with the Red Sox and had a month's pay docked. "You felt like you came back like a beaten dog," he said afterward. Indeed, he did get a beating. Five minutes before he signed his new contract, he was asked by Red Sox chief executive Haywood Sullivan to come into a private room, along with Tom Yawkey's widow. And then Gedman was tongue-lashed. He was called greedy; a dupe for the union; a disappointment to all the little people in Boston who had sup-ported him over the years. "I know what you're thinking. You are thinking there is collusion going on. Of course we talk. We talk all the time, and you talk to people all the time too," Sullivan shouted. As Gedman got up to leave, Sullivan's parting shot was: "I don't give damn who you tell about this."

By the time May 1 came around, the careers of the Collusion Eight had dramatically changed. Only Parrish and Dawson had signed contracts with new clubs, and at less than market value. Bob

Horner was frozen out and moved on to Japan. And Raines, Boone, Gedman, Guidry, and Alexander re-signed with their original teams and started anew, theoretically having been put in their place. Raines rejoined the Expos late, at Shea Stadium, where he promptly hit a grand slam homer to win the game; he finished the season with a .330 average and an astounding 123 runs scored in 139 games.

But four years later, when he was finally traded across town from his best friend, Andre Dawson, to the White Sox, there were still strains of bitterness. "No collusion payment is going to come close to making up what we had stolen from us," said Raines. "Sure, I finally got traded, and the White Sox gave me a good contract. Sure, Jack Morris, Jack Clark, and guys like that got second-look free agency. But Tim Raines in 1991 is four years older, and guys who run tend to lose some relative value in their thirties. Do you think Morris and Clark are worth close to what they were four and five years ago? Some guys will never recoup their pride, or their losses." Rich Gedman, relegated to being a backup journeyman in the National League, was one of them. So was another key player from the Red Sox–Mets World Series.

Ray Knight was the 1986 World Series MVP. He was the *Sports Illustrated* cover boy of the Series, and, beyond that, he was one of the fiery veterans who formed the personality of the world champions. When Eric Davis popped him with a stand-up slide during the 1986 season, Knight flattened him with one punch. He was a two-time All-Star who after a number of foot and shoulder operations wasn't at the peak of his career, but was still a hard-nosed .298 hitter (with 76 RBIs) who'd just led the Mets to the world championship, scoring the winning run in Game Six and belting the game-winning seventh-inning homer in the seventh-game. He was also turning only thirty-four years old that December.

Because of his growing popularity in New York, Knight wanted to remain with the Mets. But in the five weeks after the World Series, the Mets were slow in responding to him. Frank Cashen told Knight's agent, George Kalifatis, that he would go no higher than $800,000, hardly a meaningful raise from the $760,000 Knight had made in 1986. Finally, as the December 7 deadline approached, Cashen agreed to go two years at $1.6 million. "No way—not for the Series MVP," said Kalifatis.

"If I knew then what I know now, I'd have taken it," said Knight four years later. "But how was I to know the owners had gotten together the way they had? They got to the deadline and told me to take it or leave it. I felt betrayed. Emotion plays a big part in everything, and it played a part in my negotiations. When the Mets told me there was no way they'd go to salary arbitration, I couldn't believe it."

The Mets put forth their take-it-or-leave-us offer on December 7; Knight and Kalifatis refused. "The next morning I woke up and realized that my career in New York was over," said Knight. "It was a very strange experience and feeling."

Knight started making calls. The one man who genuinely seemed interested was Orioles GM Hank Peters. "Negotiations kept getting put off, but Hank kept promising that he'd make a legitimate offer," said Knight. "Finally, we got his offer. It was for around four hundred fifty thousand dollars. One year. I couldn't believe it."

"I called [manager] John McNamara in Boston, and he told me he really wanted me to play some first, some third, and DH. At that point, I figured it was better than taking nearly a fifty percent pay cut. Johnny Mac told me that he'd get back to me and that we'd hear from Lou Gorman. At that point, we were supposed to give a yes or no to Hank Peters or the Baltimore offer was off the table. We had to let them know by Monday afternoon, but McNamara promised me they'd have an offer by Monday morning. Kalifatis reached Gorman that morning. 'Haywood Sullivan will be out of town until Wednesday,' was Gorman's reply. The message was clear: no Boston offer while Baltimore was still on the table. Only, we didn't understand that the whole process had been rigged so only one team at a time could make offers.

"We were able to get an extension from the Orioles, and McNamara and Gorman promised they'd make us a proposal on Thursday. But when the time came, they put it off again. The whole thing was rigged, and I had no choice but to go to Baltimore for what they had decided would be my value, and that value was supposed to be a lesson to any player who didn't sign with his old team for what they wanted to give him. If I'd have been able to go to salary arbitration, I would have made around one-point-two million, easy. But that's not the way the thing was rigged."

Ray Knight, the Collusion Eight, and the other free agents from 1986 soon became the standard-bearers for the next major grievance that the union lodged against the owners for continued price-fixing. Peter Ueberroth, of course, dismissed the grievance as lacking any merit.

The commissioner was pleased with the course of events. "Be honest with each other; exchange information," he urged the owners. As in the old E. F. Hutton ad, when he spoke people listened. In June, the PRC announced that the 1987 salaries of the 1986 free agents—the greatest group of players ever available on the open market—were on the average 16 percent *lower* than the previous year. In addition, more than 75 percent of the new contracts were for only one year. For the owners, it was too good to last. The arbitration decisions came down in favor of the players.

The clubs had defended their actions as a sweeping "culture change" in baseball, based on legitimate business reasons. The economics of the game made obsolete the easygoing, family-style methods of the past, they argued. The opening of the books in 1985 had brought them to their senses, as well as to "the hiring of a new type of bottom-line executive." Finally, "the continuing bitter litigation between the parties" and the "actions of certain players' agents" created the "atmosphere of distrust and fear of entrapment." The arbitrators didn't buy it. First, Tom Roberts found for the players regarding the 1985 grievance. A year later, Nicolau rendered his decision.

"The differentiating factor was not the player's agent, the player's prominence . . . or the possibility of a long-term contract, but whether the former club wanted the player," Nicolau announced in supporting Roberts's finding that the owners were guilty of collusion. If the former club wanted the player, "there was no competitive bidding such as there had been in the past." It was left to the parties to negotiate a settlement. The price tag was $280 million.

*   *   *

And how did the principal actors view those years? MacPhail, predictably, believed that the clubs were motivated by what was best for the game itself. They had all come to the same conclusion after seeing the deteriorating finances of the industry when Ueberroth opened the books. They were convinced that the rapid escalation of players' salaries was threatening the game and that certain franchises, such as Cleveland and Pittsburgh, would have to move to survive. In MacPhail's view, fixed competition would destroy the game, cause several clubs to fold, and result in players losing jobs. This, he pointed out, would be in no one's best interest.

"Hogwash," Miller replied. The collusion conspiracy, according to the founder of the Major League Baseball Players Association, was worse than the Black Sox Scandal of 1919. "It was an agreement not to field the best teams possible—which is tantamount to fixing not just games, but entire pennant races, including all postseason series." Miller held such contempt for the owners' strategy that he compared it to the conspiracy to keep blacks out of baseball before the Dodgers signed Jackie Robinson.

Donald Fehr put the union on alert. "This is a case of deliberate, intentional decision to violate the Basic Agreement and destroy free agency, as the owners have been trying to do ever since the Messersmith decision."

Naturally, Barry Rona saw it differently. "The owners' conduct," he remarked, "in no substantive way differed from that of players' agents." During the hearings, Rona boasted that he was seriously thinking about becoming an agent, and that he could "put a lot of them out of business." Little did he know that within two years he would be fired by the owners, then denied certification to become an agent by the Players Association.

Meanwhile, the fans were oblivious to it all. Record attendances continued. Andy MacPhail, in the tradition of his father, Lee and grandfather Larry, built a World Series champion as the Minnesota Twins defeated Busch's Cardinals in 1987. Peter O'Malley's Dodgers won the World Series the next year thanks to the heroics of Kirk Gibson, a recently signed free agent. (Gibson, a free agent in 1985, had found no takers and returned to Detroit. With the collusion awards, he was allowed to become a free agent again. The Dodgers quickly signed him. All he did for them was win the MVP of the National League in 1988 and hit one of the most dramatic home runs in World Series history.)

Despite the arbitrators' decisions, most owners stood fast. "That signing really finished O'Malley off," one irate owner stated. "Here he is, preaching fiscal restraints, and then he goes out and signs Gibson. It shows he only cares about the Dodgers, and not the rest of us. The O'Malley influence, or what was left of it, is out the window."

As usual, Peter Ueberroth had the last word. "I don't think there was collusion involved, because I don't think the owners could collude if they were forced to do so by threats on their lives." Ueberroth compared the owners to sheep; as soon as one or two clubs decided to follow a course of action, he stated, the others simply followed.

Ask ten different people their views of Peter Ueberroth and you will get ten different answers, with one common observation: He always stays ahead of the curve. When George Nicolau announced his ruling against the owners in August of 1988, Ueberroth quickly announced that he would not seek reelection for a second five-year term, and that furthermore, even though his term was not up until January 1, 1990, he would leave earlier, once a transition was in place.

Ueberroth definitely knew what was around the bend. He had come in and done his job. According to his statistics, the clubs had operated at a loss of $277 million in the five years before he took office, but had a $435 million pretax profit during the last four years of his term. For four consecutive years, major league baseball established new highs in season attendance. And average salaries had risen from $344,000 to $429,640.

He was also leaving baseball with one more present. After forty-one years, NBC would no longer be "the baseball network." The last holdover from the earlier age had been outbid by CBS. Ueberroth was delivering to the owners the largest television package in the history of the game. But he also knew that the golden goose would be cooked, fought over, and eaten before the contract was up. Peter Ueberroth quickly made his exit. He was not going to be blamed by the owners for that carcass also. If they were going to shower free agents with millions from the new television contract, he didn't want to be around when the television screen went blank—far sooner than even he could have imagined.

CHAPTER SIX

FOOL'S GOLD

CBS HEADQUARTERS, DECEMBER 1989

"And that's the way it is, March 9, 1981." With those famous words, Walter Cronkite turned the anchor desk of CBS News over to Dan Rather.

CBS had always been known as "the news network." And the news department was directly responsible for its number one rating among the networks. For over one hundred weeks, CBS had held the lead position against NBC and ABC. As the summer of 1981 began to fade away, the executives at Black Rock (CBS headquarters in Manhattan) were not concerned with the baseball strike that was gripping the American sports public. That was NBC's loss, not ours, they chuckled. News brought the high ratings, and high ratings produced higher advertising revenues. The streak continued under Rather. It had reached two hundred weeks when the first crack appeared.

By 1984, "CBS Morning News" was a distant third in the ratings behind NBC's "Today Show" and ABC's "Good Morning America." There was concern, but no panic, at Black Rock. After all, the morning news shows are not major revenue sources for the networks. But CBS's strategy to fix its morning show sent tremors throughout the network that are still being felt today. To improve its ratings, CBS hired Phyllis George, a former Miss America with little television and no news background, to anchor "CBS Morning News." The message was clear: No longer would personalities for news-related shows be hired based on their news-reporting skills. They would be hired as entertainers first and reporters second.

Coupled with George's hiring, CBS began to make staff reductions in its news departments throughout the world in order to reduce expenses. Suddenly, CBS abandoned its heritage and lost its viewers. By early 1985, it had fallen out of first place in the annual ratings, and its stock took a pounding.

Ted Turner came calling. Thwarted by Peter Ueberroth in his attempt to saturate local television markets with free Atlanta Braves games, Turner had successfully developed a national cable news network, CNN, but he was still playing in the minor leagues. A major franchise, he realized, could be had. Turner put together a plan to buy CBS. Black Rock quickly responded by putting into place expensive defensive barriers to prevent the brash Southerner's assault, but it was costly. Network executives cried "greenmail" as they absorbed a $1 billion hit to keep Turner at bay. It had taken over one hundred years, but one Atlantan, at least, had learned some "carpetbagger" tricks of his own. Wobbling under the heavy debt load it needed to finance the repurchase of its stock, CBS made deeper cuts to keep the network afloat.

Sitting in his spacious Manhattan office, a private investor watched the Turner attack with keen interest. As Turner retreated south with his bags full of cash, Larry Tisch, a CBS stockholder, continued to add to his holdings. By 1986 he controlled nearly 25 percent of the company. Fearing another Turner holdup, CBS's board of directors, led by chairman Tom Wyman, decided that a friendly sale would be more suitable than a hostile takeover. After all, ABC had recently been sold to Capital Cities, and NBC to General Electric. But where could Wyman find a white knight to ride to the rescue and prevent the Tisch takeover from happening? His friend at Coca-Cola answered his phone call. Coke would be a player, continued Fay Vincent, chairman of its entertainment division.

Francis T. ("Fay") Vincent, Jr., had built a successful career by taking phone calls from friends he had met while a student at Williams College and Yale Law School. The first had come from Herbert Allen, who had been two years behind Vincent at Williams. In 1978, Allen's holding company, Allen and Co., was the majority stockholder of Columbia Pictures Industries, which was reeling under the disclosure that its studio chief, David Begelman, was guilty of embezzlement. Columbia's board of directors was about to fire its president, and Allen was looking for a strong successor who was above reproach. The Securities and Exchange Commission seemed like a good place to look, Allen decided.

Vincent certainly didn't fit the image of a Hollywood mogul. Even though he was only forty at the time, he was already heavy-set, with a broad, round face punctuated by a thick set of eye-glasses. His plain, off-the-rack suits seemed appropriate for someone who was the associate director of the Corporate Finance Division at the Securities and Exchange Commission. Physically unimposing, Vincent walked with difficulty and relied on a cane for support. Pranksters had locked him in his room when he was a freshman at Williams. Attempting to climb into the adjacent room, Vincent had fallen four floors as he slipped from the icy ledge of the window. He broke his back and was partially para-lyzed. It was Vincent's strength and determination to overcome his hardship that had always impressed Allen. Allen also needed someone who knew the securities laws to clean up the mess at Columbia. Vincent took the job, and over the next ten years made himself wealthy and Allen wealthier. In 1982 Coca-Cola bought out Columbia for $750 million, doubling Columbia's market value at the time, and Vincent was put in charge of Coke's entertain-ment division.

In 1986, Vincent presided over Coca-Cola's $450 million acqui-sition of Embassy Communications and its $200 million purchase of Merv Griffin Enterprises. With these acquisitions Coca-Cola became the largest television programmer in the world, with more hours on television than any of its rivals. Now, the opportunity to buy a major network to televise Coke's acquisitions was too good for Vincent to pass up.

Tom Wyman had known Fay Vincent for years and felt comfort-able negotiating with him. Turner was merely a pest, Tisch a 500-pound gorilla. Wyman realized that CBS was either going to be sold or taken over by Tisch. Resigned to the first option, the chair-man of CBS offered the company to Coca-Cola. The price was agreed on, but Vincent and his bean counters, Coke's investment bankers—Allen and Co., of course—needed ten days to study the books.

Tisch moved quickly. Opposed to the buyout, he needed help. In came the founder of CBS, William Paley, to throw his weight behind Tisch. The board sided with Tisch and Paley. Wyman was fired, Tisch was named CEO, and the acquisition was called off. Little did either Tisch or Vincent realize at the time that they would become partners in the future, a partnership Tisch would live to regret.

CBS's problems got worse. The losses mounted and the ratings plummeted. Then the unthinkable occurred: The network went dead. On September 11, 1987, Dan Rather—the handpicked heir to Walter Cronkite and the legendary Edward R. Murrow—walked out of the studio at the commencement of the six-thirty evening newscast. For six minutes, Rather protested the decision by the network to telecast the conclusion of a U.S. Open tennis semi-finals match instead of breaking for the evening news. The CBS news division, on which CBS's reputation had been built, suddenly realized that it was less important to the network than were two teenage girls playing tennis.

The fallout was inevitable. As the ratings and revenues fell further, Tisch and the other top executives fought hard to keep the affiliate stations around the country in the family, as many were considering switching to rivals ABC or NBC. It was time for drastic action, and Tisch knew it. He began to disassemble CBS by selling off such assets as its lucrative record division, and slowly, its war chest was replenished. Tisch was now ready to completely break with the past. Sports programming, not news, would be the foundation of CBS's future.

"My goal, and the goal of everybody at Black Rock, is to get back to the number one position. It's going to be a hard fight, but we're ready for an all-out assault at number one. This is one of the new building blocks in the resurgence of CBS," Tisch announced. CBS was going to corner the market on sports programming, regardless of the cost.

Tisch looked to his top lieutenant, CBS Sports president Neal Pilson, to lead the charge. Pilson was the epitome of a company man,

and had gained Tisch's confidence during the palace revolt in
1986. Very Madison Avenue, a button-down-shirt-and-rep-tie
kind of an executive, Pilson played fraternity hockey in college,
and that sport's strategies fit him well. Charge hard, fore-check
constantly, and be prepared to take a hit. And always keep your
eye on the goal. Pilson planned to score early and often for Tisch.

ABC, the self-proclaimed "network of the Olympics," felt that
it had overspent on the 1988 Winter Games and suddenly pulled
out of the bidding for the 1992 Games in Albertville, just as the
process was beginning. Competing against only one rival, Pilson
outbid NBC by $68 million for the 1992 rights.

Arthur Watson, NBC Sports president, walked away from the
table and blasted CBS's strategy. "Mr. Pilson talks a lot. He talks
of restraint, of keeping rights fees at reasonable levels, of not
overbidding. But then he goes out and overbids for the Olympics.
What he says and what he does are two different things. Pilson
can't go around saying he'll keep sports rights fees down. Sooner
or later you're going to pay the piper and have major losses."

"Arthur Watson can run his business, I'll run mine," Pilson
scoffed in response. As it turned out, fate would not be kind to
either.

Sooner and not later, Watson's piper came to collect from Pilson. But Watson never got the satisfaction of crowing over his
rival's disastrous losses. Arthur Watson was replaced as head of
NBC Sports in April 1989 because GE was convinced that he had
made the same mistake he accused Pilson of: overpaying by $100
million for the 1988 Seoul Olympics. GE felt he had also failed to
keep baseball on NBC, when his nemesis Pilson had again outbid
him. And ten months later, Watson suddenly dropped dead.

For four decades, NBC had been *the* baseball network. Since the
advent of division play, it had shared the All-Star Game and postseason play with ABC, but its exclusive Saturday "Game of the
Week," shown throughout the season, cemented its claim as the
official broadcast partner of major league baseball. The weekend
games were considered a trophy purchase by NBC over the years,
even though for several reasons they never attracted much of a
following.

The length of the baseball season means that games in the spring do not have the excitement of games that affect pennant races five months later. Also, the winter sports are all at their playoff peak when baseball hits the air in April and May. The summer months attract even less of an audience. Most fans have better things to do—like attending a live game—than staying indoors and watching baseball on Saturday afternoons. By the time fall rolls around and baseball interest should be at its peak, three factors work against weekly national games. First, unless the local team is involved in a pennant race, interest is limited. Second, college and professional football games start, with weekly hypes leading to once-a-week showdowns on Saturdays and Sundays. Finally, cable outlets carrying local teams cater to their markets at the expense of the national network game.

But NBC continued to broadcast the weekly games throughout the season at a loss because of its relationship with Major League Baseball. In return, NBC was always given a share of the crown jewels: the All-Star Game and postseason play.

Baseball's All-Star Game in July is the only all-star contest of the four team sports that achieves a high television rating. It comes in the middle of the season, is played during prime time, and pits two leagues that otherwise only confront each other on an individual team basis in the World Series. The postseason games are important to the networks for another reason.

Unlike the Super Bowl, which is a made-for-TV event on one day, baseball's postseason play can extend for almost three weeks, with the World Series games potentially overlapping two full weekends. By coincidence, the fall rating season for the networks occurs in October. Also, the networks roll out their new shows in October, and a captive market in prime time gives them ample opportunities to showcase the new sitcoms and detective shows. The World Series is an attractive buy, and the networks know it. Audiences grow for each game as the national audience gets to know the two teams better. A seven-game series, like the 1991 contest between the Atlanta Braves and Minnesota Twins, is a programmer's dream. With all the extra-inning games and close contests decided by one run, the Braves-Twins seventh game resembled a bout between two punch-drunk, staggering heavyweights fighting to see who would still be standing when the final bell rang. This is what the networks hope and pray for. A short series between two small-market teams lacking drama is what they fear. Besides losing lucrative advertising time to sell, a short series denies the network the opportunity to hype its prime-time entertainment shows for the new season.

As the television contracts with Major League Baseball were expiring in December of 1988, NBC was confident that it would receive at least a piece of the game, as it always had in the past. Watson and NBC were in for a shock.

Since 1985, Peter Ueberroth had been predicting to the owners that the new television contract would be less remunerative than the prior one. His dealings with the superstations had also convinced him that cable would play the major role and would "be used to change the dynamics of how baseball is viewed." It was obvious that the "Game of the Week" was a loss leader for the networks and that a national cable package allowing alternate games in various markets would be more successful. Besides NBC's Saturday afternoon games, ABC had bought the exclusive rights to twenty Monday or Thursday night games and nonexclusive rights to Sunday afternoon games. But ABC got more people to watch reruns than it did prime-time baseball, and as a result, it broadcasted only eight games in 1988.

Ueberroth and his broadcast lieutenant, Bryan Burns, were convinced that baseball's daily menu of games across the country was far more attractive to cable companies than to the networks. The proliferation of cable networks had dramatically increased the need for programming. Additional programming—particularly programming of interest to the local market—leads to new subscribers. Since cable networks are valued on a multiple of their subscriber base, signing up subscribers is every cable operator's goal—not only for the additional operating income, but also for the add-on value to the franchise. And only baseball had a sports product that is available six months a year.

As a negotiating ploy, Ueberroth waited until the excitement surrounding the 1988 playoffs hit a peak to announce that Major League Baseball might take the games in-house and create a baseball-only cable channel. But baseball would still retain a network partner for the crown jewels, the commissioner added. To get the pot open, Burns reminded the networks that Ueberroth had the power to negotiate a new TV package without ownership approval, and confided that he might consider selling the package outright to one bidder.

The opportunity to exclusively own the crown jewels was too enticing for CBS to pass up. Pilson saw Ueberroth's pitch as a hanging curveball over the middle of the plate. Swinging for the fences, he was sure that he'd connected for a home run. Watson was convinced that Pilson had struck out.

Announcing the biggest one-network sports deal ever, CBS agreed to pay Major League Baseball $1.1 billion over four years for the exclusive right to broadcast the All-Star Game, the playoffs, the World Series, and twelve regular-season games each year through 1993. CBS's bid was 37 percent more than ABC and NBC had paid under their combined prior contracts.

After having predicted a smaller TV package, Ueberroth waited a month to give the owners another going-away present. In January of 1989, he awarded baseball's first cable contract to ESPN, a subsidiary of ABC, for $100 million annually, commencing in 1990. Even though ABC's Monday night ratings had declined by 25 percent since 1984, advertisers' cost for regular-season commercial time on the games had risen by 35 percent over the same period. Concerned about its ability to charge higher fees for a product attracting smaller audiences, Capital Cities focused instead on acquiring the weekly games for its cable affiliate.

ESPN was chosen over the other bidders, including Ted Turner's TNT, because of the size of its subscription base—over 50 million. Ueberroth and Burns wanted to make sure the maximum amount of homes possible could see their product. To protect the local television outlets, it was agreed that blackouts of ESPN telecommunications would occur in the markets of the teams involved if they were being televised locally. Ueberroth had delivered a financial windfall. Starting in 1991, each club would receive approximately $14 million from the national television contracts.

For most clubs, the infusion of TV money couldn't have come at a better time. Under the prior agreements with NBC and ABC, each club received approximately $7 million each year; now that figure was $14 million. And under Ueberroth's leadership, merchandising revenue to each club had increased from $35,000 to $2.5 million annually. So, the outgoing commissioner had increased each club's revenues by $10 million a year. And the first annual dividend increase of $10 million was exactly the amount needed by each club to pay its share of the collusion settlement claim. Not a bad trade-off, not bad at all, the owners nodded to each other.

Ueberroth was reminded of his prior dire predictions regarding the new television package. "I was wrong," he said. "The marketplace and the game have changed since then." And no one was more responsible for those changes than Peter V. Ueberroth.

Ueberroth never quite fit in with the baseball crowd. The pace of the game played on the field often mirrors the games played in the hallways and back rooms. More gossip, innuendos, and rumors are heard daily among owners, general managers, agents, and reporters than at any Washington hot spot. There is a "smallness" to baseball that Ueberroth found boring and childish. Sitting with the commissioner at a game, one had the feeling that his main preoccupation was the number of seats in the house, and not the merits of whether both leagues should adopt or abolish the designated hitter rule.

Ueberroth said upon leaving, "When I came here I wanted to accomplish three things—financial stability, control of the substance abuse problem, and the creation of more goodwill for the game. But this is a strange business. The owners run their primary businesses entirely differently from their sports businesses. In baseball they compete and have to be friends and make trades, and then they try to outsnooker the other guy."

When Ueberroth arrived, some clubs were losing as much as $10 million annually. He justifies the collusion years by arguing that when he opened the books in 1985 twenty-one clubs were losing significant amounts of money, and that by the end of 1988 all twenty-six clubs were operating in the black. But the cost to baseball was expensive. His years in office left the union with a heightened sense of anger and distrust toward the owners. And the owners blamed him for their $280 million collusion payment.

Ueberroth brushed off the drug problem by stating in his address to the owners at the winter meetings in 1988 that "we've overcome it, thanks to the players, their union, and all of you who decided you didn't want drugs to ruin the reputation of your game." No players were present to hear his remarks. But even if they had been, many obviously would not have admitted what they knew: Drug usage was still a part of the game.

And what about the fans' feelings for the game? True, for four consecutive years, starting in 1985, baseball was enjoying record attendance. But except for the World Series, fewer television viewers tuned in to baseball in 1988 than in 1985. While the NBA was dramatically expanding its game internationally, promoting its superstars to an adoring public, and selling its sport as the game of the 1990s, baseball's image was going in the opposite direction. Fans had become fed up with the constant labor disputes, escalating salaries, and off-field antics of stars such as Darryl Strawberry, Dwight Gooden, Wade Boggs, and Roger Clemens.

Ueberroth remained an outsider to the end. As he left office, he chastised the owners for their resumption of spending to sign free agents, even though two collusion decisions had come down against them for following his advice. He now admitted for the first time that the warnings he had given to the owners to spend more wisely had led to their collusive behavior.

The owners had been outsmarted, overmatched, and manipulated by the agents, he scoffed. In his opinion, players deserved the money because of the owners' stupidity. They would spend themselves into bankruptcy again, he warned. He had had enough.

It was not the political arena that got his attention; it was the go-go world of mergers and acquisitions whose siren Ueberroth heard. Junk bond king Michael Milken had wined and dined him at the Predator's Ball in Los Angeles. He had even found time to negotiate the sale of E. F. Hutton to Shearson Lehman Brothers while acting as baseball's commissioner. Playing the role of an agent, he had received a $1 million fee on the transaction. Overseeing grown men fighting for control over spoiled, rich adolescents, some of whom were high on dope, no longer interested

Peter Ueberroth. Trying to save Eastern Airlines from bankruptcy and rebuilding the inner city of Los Angeles were far more intellectually challenging to the man referred to as the "can-do commissioner."

Bud Selig sighed. Five years had passed by too swiftly. But it was time to look again. Fortunately, Selig had anticipated that Ueberroth's reign would be for one term only. He had correctly surmised that Ueberroth would either quit or upset enough owners to be fired.

Naturally, Ueberroth took the lead in naming his successor. When Chub Feeney resigned as president of the National League in 1986, Bart Giamatti, Selig's original choice for commissioner, had accepted the job. As a member of Coca-Cola's board of directors, Ueberroth had gotten to know Giamatti, another board member before he became National League president. Three years later, in September of 1988, Ueberroth took his recommendation to a joint meeting of the owners, who quickly approved Giamatti as his successor. The owners were relieved.

"He'll have a different kind of relationship with the owners," said Expos owner Charles Bronfman. "He's more collegial than Peter, so I expect there will be more committee meetings and informal get-togethers." And Chicago's Jerry Reinsdorf bluntly stated in supporting Giamatti's appointment, "We just got tired of Peter doing everything by himself."

Giamatti, the former English professor from Yale, knew that he needed to have a strong business-oriented individual at his side to expand on the marketing plans initiated by baseball under Ueberroth. Another Coca-Cola director came to mind. Fay Vincent had recently been shifted by the giant soft drink outfit out of its entertainment division to its international operations. Vincent found selling Sprite to Indonesians about as exciting as directing an SEC audit, so he gladly accepted Giamatti's phone call and offer to become the first deputy commissioner of baseball.

Bart Giamatti and Fay Vincent thought they were going to have a lot of fun running baseball. But Ueberroth knew better, and that's why he, like Walter O'Malley before him, left the gray skies of New York for the sunshine of Southern California.

Pete Rose's gambling problems, George Steinbrenner's banishment, and a massive earthquake followed in Ueberroth's wake—and those were the *noneconomic* problems. As Ueberroth had learned, baseball was far from all fun and games. Giamatti died of a heart attack five months to the day after he succeeded Ueberroth and one week after permanently suspending Rose, baseball's all-time hit leader.

Baseball in the 1990s started with the problems that had been left over from the turbulent 1980s. The owners locked the players out of spring training in an attempt to force an ill-conceived wage scale system down their throats. Vincent fired Barry Rona on the eve of the negotiations and then tried to exert his commissioneritis and resolve the differences. This infuriated his employers even more. When the 1990 season finally got under way, the clubs received their bills for the $280 million collusion payment. The 1990 World Series, between Cincinnati and Oakland, two small-market teams, ended in a four-game sweep by the Reds, leaving CBS and ESPN with hundreds of millions in losses on their new television deals. As the commissioner, owners, agents, and network executives headed for Miami to open up the 1991 winter meetings, it was obvious to most that Ueberroth's era in baseball had come to a close, that Giamatti's had never gotten started, and a few also knew that Vincent's was probably nearing the end too.

PART II

PRESENT CONFLICT

CHAPTER SEVEN

THE RABBI'S PARABLE

MIAMI BEACH, EARLY DECEMBER 1991

The rabbi was quickly losing his audience. He was only half-way through the invocation before the annual banquet of baseball clubs, and already most of the major league owners had made plans to slip out the back door. Actually, the majority of them had never even shown up.

Once a year, in early December, all the executives in baseball hold a convention. The 1991 meetings were held at the Fontaine-bleau Hotel in Miami Beach. The major league officials dreaded the week, which used to be a great time to make trades. In the old days (read: before free agency), general managers, like Bill Veeck's Roland Hemond, would camp out in the lobbies hawking their wares. Once, just before the trading deadline, Hemond set up a card table in the middle of the lobby, put up an American flag, and hung a sign that said "Open for Business." Several big name players changed hands just before midnight curfew.

Now the December trading deadline has been replaced by a deadline for teams to offer salary arbitration to any of their former players who have become free agents. If the clubs refuse, they can't sign the player until May of the following year. As a result, media and owner attention is focused on the free agents and their representatives during the first week of December. Most general managers would rather be back in their home offices than here, getting upstaged by agents, who now control the player movements that take place during the winter conventions.

The minor league people usually have a great time at the winter meetings. Small-town operators who languish in obscurity all year cherish the opportunity to vacation in a big city and rub elbows with the likes of Ted Turner and George Bush, Jr. By eavesdropping on a simple conversation between two baseball men, it's easy to figure out who they're affiliated with. One group is preoccupied with the cost of popcorn and peanuts, the other with salaries and no-trade clauses. Except for the fact that they congregate at the same hotel, giving the outside world the appearance of a unified convention, major and minor league officials actually only meet together twice as a group. Traditionally, on Monday the commissioner gives his "State of the Game" address, and on Tuesday night the National Association of minor league clubs hosts the annual banquet.

In 1990 the meetings were held in separate locations, because the operating agreement between Major League Baseball and the minor leagues had expired. As usual, the fight was over power and control. "It's simple," said Miles Wolff, then owner of the Durham Bulls. "The commissioner wants to control the minor leagues." Joe Buzas, another minor league owner, was more blunt: "We're under a gag rule, but I don't give a damn. Vincent wants to be another Kenesaw Mountain Landis. But this is our business, our blood, sweat, and tears. My first twenty-one years as a minor league owner were hell. Now that we've built it up, they want to take over and get rid of us." At the time, Vincent made no secret of his plans to exert his commissioneritis to invoke the now-famous "best interest of baseball" rule so that his approval would be needed for all minor league franchise moves, ownership sales, and expansion of new teams.

Eddie Einhorn had really gotten the minors riled up several years before when he announced to the press that the minor league system was inefficient and costly. "We spend over three million dollars to develop one prospect who may not even make it to the bigs." Einhorn's solution was to disband the minor leagues and have all the major league clubs contribute to one development program from which players would be drafted.

Einhorn, who is in his early fifties, headed the partnership, along with his Northwestern Law School classmate Jerry Reins-dorf, that purchased the Chicago White Sox in 1981. Commuting between Chicago, New York, and Europe, Einhorn is always on the run. On his way to Miami for the meetings, he was stopped by a security guard at Chicago's O'Hare International when a huge serpent-shaped knife was discovered in his carry-on bag. Einhorn shrugged in embarrassment, saying that it was a present for his son from a recent trip to Nepal that he thought he had unpacked when he returned from the Goodwill Games in Cuba, where he had given Fidel Castro Bo Jackson's jersey. Or maybe it was after his trip to the World Figure Skating Championships in Europe; he couldn't remember.

Einhorn is not a baseball traditionalist. He is a man of the mo-ment who more than any other executive in the game today un-derstands that baseball is a part of the entertainment business, and that the international markets are clamoring for new sports pro-gramming. He is also the person most responsible for developing the tremendous popularity of college basketball on television. In 1968, he promoted the famous University of Houston–UCLA game that showcased the matchup between Elvin Hayes and Lew Alcin-dor (a.k.a. Kareem Abdul-Jabbar). Soon thereafter he sold his suc-cessful independent basketball network to CBS and became the executive producer of "CBS Sports Spectacular."

When George Steinbrenner was elected vice president of the U.S. Olympic Committee in 1988, he recommended that Einhorn be hired to act as its television consultant, which led to his orches-tration of the 200-hour television package that CBS rolled out in 1990. Since then several other sporting associations, such as the U.S. Figure Skating Association, the International Skating Union, the World Volleyball Association, and the U.S. Gymnastics Fed-eration, have retained Einhorn as their television consultant. Ein-horn lives out of a suitcase, jumps from one time zone to another, a ball of energy on the prowl for the next deal. First and foremost, he is a promoter. All one needs to know about him is summed up in the White Sox press guide: His favorite pastime is watching professional wrestling.

"The Japanese do it right." It's their baseball player develop-ment system and not their sumo wrestling tournaments that Einhorn is referring to. "Each club controls sixty players who are affiliated with the parent club from high school, through college, and then on an industrial team which plays in the same city as the major league club." As with their style of running businesses, the Japanese emphasize a unified-group approach to coaching and training throughout their entire organization. American baseball instead employs a hierarchical system where typically a player moves up the ladder from the instructional league to rookie ball, to an A league, then to an AA league, next to an AAA affiliate, and eventually to the majors. Along the way, he comes into contact with different owners, managers, coaches, and cities, often being presented with vastly different coaching techniques, working conditions, and playing facilities. Einhorn believes that the Japanese are far more efficient.

"As an example, the Tokyo Giants know that all their minor league players are within an hour's drive of Tokyo. On any given day, they can bring the hottest phenom into town and suit him up.

"Yes," a frustrated Einhorn continued, "we could learn a lot from the Japanese about the game of baseball."

Einhorn is not a popular figure with the minor league owners. They are quick to remind anyone who'll listen that as the producer of "CBS Sports Spectacular" he was responsible for bringing to television such critically acclaimed sporting events as "The Challenge of the Sexes" and that ultimate competitive confrontation—men racing each other up a hill with refrigerators strapped to their backs. These and similar "Sports Spectacular" events soon became known as "trash sports." Einhorn is quick to defend these shows by pointing out that sports, after all, is not about life and death and shouldn't always be taken so seriously. (Tell that to the guy who broke his back when the Kenmore slipped.) With over two hundred hours of programming per year to produce, Einhorn did occasionally persuade the network to air less gripping events. In 1980 he won an Emmy Award for "The Gossamer Albatross, Flight of Imagination," a documentary on wildlife that aired on CBS.

In 1990 Einhorn was the senior American League representative on the negotiation committee with the minor leagues, and he backed down on his proposals to change the minors. The present system was too entrenched. "Anyway, we're in a recession and you can't just put people out of business," he said, his voice becoming louder, rising in frustration.

Soon after the 1990 winter meetings, the minor leaguers, over-matched in negotiations, accepted the demands of the major league owners. Besides the requirement that each minor league club contribute a percentage of its ticket revenues to the major leagues, the minors had to assume more of the travel expenses. The major league clubs would only continue to cover the costs of salaries and meal money for the minor league players and um-pires, as well as of the equipment used. The minor league owners warned that the money now going to the major league owners would come out of their maintenance budgets. As one minor league general manager said, "It is the difference between putting in new showers. It is the difference between putting in a new drainage system. Every dime that they extract from me is coming out of maintenance for this stadium, because that's where we put our profits." Left unsaid was the implied threat that the million-dollar bonus babies in whom the major league clubs were invest-ing might suffer serious injuries on shoddy fields caused by the lack of available funds to fix them up.

Naturally, the major leaguers saw it differently. In 1991, the minor leagues drew 26.6 million fans, their highest figure in forty years. Over the last five years, minor league franchises, like the Durham Bulls and South Bend White Sox, that were purchased for thousands have started to sell for millions, while the major league farm directors complain to their bosses that the facilities are still substandard.

Unlike in prior years, it was not a happy group of minor league operators who arrived in Miami. The rabbi couldn't resist the temptation to be the great healer. With a nod toward Fay Vincent, who was sitting up on the stage with the heads of the various minor leagues, the rabbi rambled on. "The problems of baseball can be solved if we work together. I am reminded of a story I read about a young girl who got lost several years ago in the great Pacific north woods. A search party went out, with no success.

And then someone had an idea: Let's all hold hands and walk through the woods together and we will be able to find her." The rabbi's words echoed through the hall in a feverish pitch.

"How do you all hold hands when you are walking through a woods full of trees?" Einhorn, one of the few owners in attendance, blurted out as he stood at attention next to the White Sox table.

"At long last," the rabbi continued, "the searchers came upon the girl lying in the woods." Einhorn remarked that he knew the girl didn't have a chance if it had taken the search party as long to find her as it was now taking the rabbi to tell the story. He was right. "The girl was dead," the rabbi exclaimed oddly, and then disappeared backstage, leaving a stunned audience trying to understand how his story related to all the bickering in baseball.

The rabbi was a tough act to follow, but the next morning the lobby was full of candidates. TV cameras didn't know in which direction to turn.

In one corner, Jeff Smulyan, the owner of the Seattle Mariners, was pleading his case to allow his players to pack their bags and move to St. Petersburg.

Then there was Wayne Huizenga, owner of the Florida Marlins, one of the National League's new expansion teams, and he was irate. He had just paid $95 million for the *privilege* of spending $50 million more to field a team that is expected to lose one hundred games in 1994. He was not about to stand idly by and watch an established team move to Florida and dilute his potential cable market.

Miami and the other expansion team, Denver, were creating a nightmare for the schedule makers. National League President Bill White was trying to explain to a group of reporters why the Atlanta Braves are in the Western Division and the Chicago Cubs and St. Louis Cardinals are in the East. With the two new clubs joining the league in 1994, the other clubs were considering a realignment. The Tribune Company people, owners of the Cubs, held their own impromptu press conference and announced that they had no interest in realignment.

Before he succeeded Bart Giamatti as the president of the National League, White had been an announcer for the New York Yankees. All of a sudden, his tenure in the Bronx Zoo—the affectionate name given to Steinbrenner's Yankees during the years that Reggie Jackson and Billy Martin shared the spotlight—seemed tame by comparison. "One of the major problems with the game today is that the guys on Park Avenue never played it," White said in frustration. As the highest-ranking black official in baseball, White also could no longer contain his anger over the racism that he announced was still present in baseball. White decided to quit. Bobby Brown, president of the American League, had already announced that he wanted out too, but the AL owners persuaded him to stick around for one more year.

Across the hall, in the press room, former California Angel Wally Joyner broke down in tears as he announced that he had just signed a contract for $4.2 million to play for the Kansas City Royals in 1992. His tears were not from laughing all the way to the bank, but because he was being "forced" to leave the Angels because team owner Gene Autry's wife, Jackie, considered him a burr under her husband's saddle.

Waiting in line to get his breakfast at the hotel cafeteria, Whitey Herzog, the new president of the California Angels, shook his head and wondered why he had given up fishing to come back to this. His final offer to Joyner had been more than Kansas City's. "I feel like a marriage counselor," he exclaimed. He then turned his ire on agent Dennis Gilbert, standing behind him in line. Herzog had been a buddy of Gilbert's ever since Gilbert had played in the minors under him. Gilbert is now the hottest agent in the business, representing such stars as Jose Canseco, Bret Saberhagen, Danny Tartabull, and Bobby Bonilla—the cause of Herzog's anger. Herzog told Gilbert to take a hike and never call him again on a player. Herzog was convinced that Gilbert and Bonilla had used him and the Angels in bidding up his contract with the New York Mets. Bonilla had just signed a contract with New York for $29 million, making him the highest-paid player in the history of the game.

A solitary figure roamed the hallway looking for a job. Any job. After years of experience and success in leading the Los Angeles Dodgers to a couple of World Championships, he hoped that his actions would speak louder than his words. Unfortunately for him, they didn't; baseball had branded him an outcast for his statements to Ted Koppel on ABC's "Nightline" that "blacks lacked the necessities" to be successful in front office positions. No one had any interest in hiring Al Campanis.

Around the corner, Marvin Miller's old sidekick, Dick Moss, was trying to land a job for catcher Gary Carter. He was driving a hard bargain, and the Montreal ownership, remembering prior battles with Moss over many players, was in no hurry to remove Carter from the "former" category. Meanwhile, Carter, wearing his ever-present gold necklace with the diamonds that spell out his self-conferred nickname, "Kid," was working the crowd with his best routine.

Suddenly, an entourage made its way through the crowded lobby. The bright lights of the television cameras illuminated the broad, round face of baseball's leader. Leaning on his cane, Fay Vincent, in his high-pitched voice, spoke briefly with a few reporters and then, surrounded by his aides, exited the hotel to an awaiting limousine.

An illness had prevented Vincent from attending the meetings in 1990. As he disappeared from sight, many in the Fontainebleau wondered why he had bothered to show up in Miami at all. The lobby was as dense as the rabbi's forest, but nobody was holding hands . . . only press releases given out by all the opposing camps.

CHAPTER EIGHT

THE FRAGILE ALLIANCE

When National League President Bill White told the media in Miami that the owners were considering a realignment that would move Atlanta and Cincinnati into the Eastern Division and Chicago and St. Louis into the West, one broadcaster, reporting back to his New York station, said, "Finally, logical divisions." Granted. But logic isn't necessarily good television programming, and the Cubs are not just a baseball team; they are TV programming for WGN in Chicago, which next to Atlanta's WTBS happens to be the nation's biggest superstation.

Needless to say, the Tribune Corporation, which bought the Cubs from the Wrigley estate, objected to the geographical change. Along with the realignment, it was proposed that an unbalanced National League schedule be implemented. That would see each team play either eighteen or twenty games within its own division, and either six, seven, or eight intradivision games. The Cubs would then be playing anywhere from twenty-seven to thirty West Coast games—which would mean more than twenty games with a starting time of 9:30 CDT (10:30 EDT). "This isn't just self-interest, it's bad business, period," said one Cubs official. "That's a lot to ask of the Cubs. The other owners want us to cut back on our rivalry with the Mets, and on top of that, start twelve to fifteen percent of our televised games after the kids go to bed! How many working people can stay up past eleven in the summer? That's crazy. Anyway, do you think the Tribune people don't realize that it would be hurting WGN and helping WTBS? They'd have only six or seven ten-thirty [EDT] starts all year if they were in the East."

* * *

"The problem with talking about baseball as a business is that baseball represents so many different types of businesses," explains Brewers owner Bud Selig. For instance, the Braves and the Cubs are viewed by their owners as cheap programming for their flagship stations, WTBS and WGN. The Yankees, Red Sox, Blue Jays, and Phillies aren't necessary TV programming, but local television revenues are a very big part of their year-in, year-out operational budgets. In back-to-back winters, the Red Sox signed nine players to contracts worth more than $2 million annually, yet they did not raise upper-box, grandstand, or bleacher ticket costs for four years.

The Cleveland Indians are owned by the Jacobs family as part of their real estate investment in the reconstruction of the downtown Cleveland area. The Kansas City Royals, in one of the game's two smallest markets, are owned by pharmaceutical magnate Ewing Kauffman, who after selling his Marion Labs in 1989 received $675 million in cash, with no heirs. The California Angels are owned by Gene Autry, with an aging dream of simply buying a World Series each year. The Cardinals and Blue Jays are owned by Anheuser-Busch and Labatt's, respectively, as part of the business of selling beer. The Oakland Athletics are owned by the Haas family—the Levi Strauss people—and were bought in 1980 simply to keep the club on the Easy Bay for the sake of the community. Eli Jacobs headed the group to purchase the Orioles after the death of Edward Bennett Williams. After limited partner, club president, and former Williams partner Larry Lucchino worked out a deal to get the State of Maryland to put up the bonds to finance a new stadium, Jacobs basically ran the franchise with the same game plan he used for any other property—keep costs down over a five-year period, make as much profit as possible, then make a killing reselling it. He bought the club for $60 million; he put it on the market in 1991 at $120 million without any additional personal investment, and then increased the asking price to $200 million in 1992 after the club moved into its new publicly financed stadium.

"Baseball represents several different businesses," says Oakland general manager Sandy Alderson. "But there are also different purposes in owning a team. To some, it's maintaining the

Marvin Miller, former head of the
Players Association. *United Press International*

Bowie Kuhn, commissioner of
baseball from 1969 to 1984.
National Baseball Library, Cooperstown, New York

Laurence Tisch *(left)*, head of CBS,
and Peter Ueberroth, former baseball
commissioner. *Kimberly Butler Photography*

A. Bartlett Giamatti died less than one year after succeeding Peter Ueberroth as commissioner. *Baseball America*

Lee MacPhail served as American League president and chairman of the Player Relations Committee.

National Baseball Library, Cooperstown, New York

P eter O'Malley, owner
of the Los Angeles Dodgers.
*National Baseball Library, Cooperstown ,
New York*

E ddie Einhorn *(left)*, part-owner of the Chicago White Sox, and Fay Vincent,
who on September 7, 1992, resigned as commissioner of baseball.
Chicago White Sox

B̲ill Giles, owner of the
Philadelphia Phillies.
© Rosemary Rahn

H̲igh-powered agent
Scott Boras. *Baseball America*

Dennis Gilbert, agent for Jose Canseco, Bobby Bonilla, Danny Tartabull, and other high-priced talent. *Beverly Hills Sports Council*

Donald Fehr, executive director of the Players Association. *Baseball America*

Tony LaRussa *(left)*, manager of the Oakland Athletics, and Jerry Reinsdorf, owner of the Chicago White Sox and Chicago Bulls. *Chicago White Sox*

George Nicolau became baseball's permanent arbitrator in 1986. *Kimberly Butler Photography*

Sparky Anderson *(left)*, manager of the Detroit Tigers, and Bud Selig, owner of the Milwaukee Brewers. *Larry Stoudt*

Richard Ravitch, head of the Player Relations Committee since 1991. *Major League Baseball*

V eterans Stadium, home of the Philadelphia Phillies. *Philadelphia Phillies*

T he highly celebrated Oriole Park at Camden Yards, Baltimore, Maryland. *Jeff Goldberg, ESTO Photographics © 1992*

team and community. To others, it's ego, and in those cases, winning at all costs. While most owners want to win, once in a while you get someone who simply is in the business to make money. People used to criticize George Argyros, but he was a very successful owner because he accomplished what he set out to do."

George Argyros, a Southern California real estate developer, bought the financially strapped Seattle Mariners in 1981 for $13 million when they were a fifth-year expansion team with an underfinanced ownership group headed by actor Danny Kaye. He refused to allow the payroll to rise, instead either allowing top players to go to free agency (like Floyd Bannister and Mike Moore) or trading them off (Mark Langston, for instance) for younger players.

The Mariners annually made Argyros richer, and in 1989 when he finally sold the club, he got $78 million from a group headed by Jeff Smulyan of Emmis Broadcasting and Michael Browning of Morgan Stanley. Not only did he make nearly a 600 percent profit, but while Argyros was an owner during the collusion period, and reported to be one of the concept's biggest supporters, he was not liable for the collusion damages. Smulyan's leveraged broadcasting empire was hit hard by the deflationary economic environment of the early 1990s, and when his lenders called his notes, he found himself in dire financial straits. Besides the massive debt burden he found himself under to outside lenders, he had to also come up with the $10 million collusion settlement, unlike the new owners in San Diego and Montreal, whose previous owners assumed the damages as part of the sale agreement. "George Argyros would never have been considered a 'good owner' in the sense that the public labels and judges owners," says Alderson. "But he laughed all the way to the bank. He got exactly what he wanted out of the game. Not many others can lay claim to that."

When Smulyan and his group bought the Mariners in 1989, it was their original intention to keep the team in the city and make baseball work in the Pacific Northwest. "After all, the market is far larger than Kansas City, Cincinnati, or Milwaukee," Smulyan says. "It is the eighteenth-biggest television market in baseball. It should be viable, based on numbers. The problem is that baseball isn't part of the culture [in Seattle]. People don't spend the winter anticipating the baseball season. It isn't in the local business mindset to buy boxes and keep the team in the city, the way they did in Pittsburgh." Microsoft, one of the world's largest and wealthiest computer-related industries, is based in Seattle, but until July 1991, it had a ballpark advertisement in Minneapolis's Metrodome, not in Seattle's Kingdome.

"Unlike a lot of cities threatened when a team has the option of leaving," adds Smulyan, "there is no relationship between the politicians and the ball club. If anything, the relationship over the years has been a nightmare." When King County formulated plans to build a new arena adjacent to the Kingdome that would be used by the National Basketball Association's SuperSonics, one of the agreements was that basketball fans could use the Kingdome parking lots, whether the Mariners were playing or not. The city finally introduced bus lines to the Kingdome from downtown; problem was, they stopped service at 7:00 P.M., which just happens to be game time. "No local politician had ever been to a Mariner game," said one club official. "So no one ever thought about going home from one."

Smulyan, who built much of his fortune in the radio and communications business, said in March 1990 that because of the size of the market, if he could "get out and convince people that the Mariners are committed to winning in Seattle, we can harness the market and get up near the middle of clubs' local radio-TV revenues." By June 1991, Smulyan realized that he couldn't make it. He was strapped, facing big interest payments with little income. The club had to continually reuse old baseballs in batting practice to save money. Even though the team was in borderline contention in the American League West pennant race, it could not afford to go out and get a right-handed slugger to put in the middle of the batting order behind Ken Griffey, Jr.

The Seattle manager, Jim Lefebvre, got so frustrated that he told reporters that Smulyan was financially so tapped that not only could the team not afford to make a deal to get it into the race, but Smulyan didn't want to win because it would make the Mariners' attempt to move the franchise even more difficult. Smulyan got wind of Lefebvre's comments and fired him after the 1991 season, even though the Mariners had posted their first winning season in history. Lefebvre was one of the lucky Mariners. The Cubs quickly hired him as their manager.

Tracy Ringolsby of the *Dallas Morning News* wrote that the Mariners were akin to the fictitious Cleveland club in the movie *Major League*—a team whose owners did not want them to win. Smulyan denied that was the case. "But," he added, "there may come a point where we are convinced that baseball and Seattle have no future."

By October, Smulyan had exhausted attempts to create television revenue, as no local station was willing to work out any deal except for the Mariners to go in-house, produce their games, and buy airtime. By November, Smulyan was saying that he did "not want to own the Mariners in Seattle." He put the club up for sale, which triggered a clause that if no one came in and met his appraised value ($100 million), he automatically could get out of his Kingdome lease and move to St. Petersburg, a market with a promising and growing television market. To baseball's chagrin, Nintendo's Super Mario came to the rescue.

"In Seattle in the off-season, the only baseball that is talked is whether or not the Mariners will move," says Jeff Smulyan. "And even that is muted. But in Boston, what holds up the talk shows? Likewise, in New York, if the Mets make a couple of moves, what are people talking about? On the one hand, in some baseball markets, (like Boston and New York) it is not incumbent on the club to make moves to sell tickets or television subscriptions. But on the other hand, those teams, because of their fan support, are expected to go out and spend all off-season."

If one is an owner in a city where baseball *is* the culture, it can be a high-stakes business. For example, take the Boston Red Sox. Baseball dominates local talk shows. Both the *Globe* and the *Herald* run one or two daily stories, year-round. "At least during the season, the team can win a couple of games and appease the media and the fans," says John Harrington. A former Boston College business professor who started in baseball as an American League auditor, Harrington moved to the Red Sox in the same capacity, left to enter the insurance business, and then returned as the spokesman and power behind the throne of Mrs. Jean Yawkey when he agreed to run the Yawkey Foundation, which is the primary general partner of the club. The Yawkey Foundation is responsible for managing the day-to-day affairs of the different interests owned by the late Tom Yawkey.

Tom Yawkey is often referred to as the last of the great sportsmen who owned sports franchises before the modern era. While he probably was not the last, he certainly was one of the most enduring. Between his apartment at the Ritz Carlton in Boston and his plantation in South Carolina, for forty-four years he oversaw his two favorite holdings—the Boston Red Sox and a 40,000-acre wildlife preserve.

Upon entering the foundation's office, one is immediately reminded of Yawkey's two loves: On one wall is the head of a deer, and on the opposite wall is an autographed picture of Ted Williams—obviously, two of Yawkey's greatest trophies. A reminder that he was the sole owner of Fenway Park as well as the team, a framed section of tin from the "Old Green Monster" hangs next to Williams. Even the magazines on the coffee table carry the themes: *Ducks Unlimited* and a World Series program.

John Harrington is the trusted overseer of the Yawkey Foundation. As such, he was advisor and confidant to Yawkey's widow until her death from a massive stroke in 1992. His official title is executive director and trustee of the Yawkey Foundation. "Trustee" is the perfect title for Harrington; the Boston Red Sox and Fenway Park—more than any other sports franchise and stadium—are viewed by the public as belonging to the region and not to one individual.

When her husband died, Jean Yawkey wanted to keep the Yawkey name involved with the club, although she personally did not want to take an active role in its ownership. Several suitors for the franchise, including the parent company of Rawlings Sporting Goods and a group headed by former Red Sox outfielder Dom DiMaggio, were turned down by the estate.

During his later years, Yawkey had become close to Haywood Sullivan, who was in charge of the Red Sox' minor league system. Jean saw the fondness that her husband had for Sullivan as the two men would sit in the owner's box and discuss prospects in the farm system. Owners are usually more excited when talking about prospective stars down on the farm than they are discussing players on their major league roster. This probably is based on the perception that these kids have not been "exposed" to anything but the desire to make it to the big leagues. Thus, with only one eye on Yastrzemski in left field, Yawkey always had both ears tuned to Sullivan as he would recite the exploits of kids in the minors named Evans, Lynn, Rice, and Fisk. As Yawkey's physical strength diminished in the early 1970s, it was Sullivan who was his constant emissary, both around Fenway Park and the American League.

It was not surprising that Jean Yawkey wanted to let Sullivan run the club after her husband died. However, Sullivan clearly did not have the financial ability to raise the money necessary to purchase the club from the estate. Turning to Edward G. ("Buddy") LeRoux, Jr., the former trainer of the club, Sullivan found his partner. LeRoux had been successful in raising money through limited partnerships to purchase real estate. He quickly put together a group of investors, who came forward with an offer. Mrs. Yawkey informed the group that she would recommend that the trustees of the estate accept the offer, on two conditions: first, that she herself be allowed to contribute as a limited partner to keep the Yawkey name involved with the club; and second, that Haywood Sullivan be given a general partnership interest with Buddy LeRoux. The LeRoux consortium jumped at the chance, particularly since its offer was below that of others.

At first, the other owners in the American League did not want a former trainer and a farm director in their brotherhood, particularly since the Boston Red Sox had been in one man's hands longer than any club in the history of baseball and was considered the flagship franchise of the American League since the demise of the New York Yankees. The estate was notified that the new group would be rejected for membership, but that the franchise shift would be approved if Jean Yawkey was prepared to step up to the level of general partner. Reluctantly, the widow decided to take on the additional role. For her general partnership interest, she threw in the real estate, i.e., Fenway Park. To this day, many have wondered why she was so generous as to "buy" her general partnership interest when she was elevating her husband's former employees to ownership status. "Imagine how I felt," Dwight Evans commented at the time. "One day Buddy's giving me a back rub, the next he's giving me my paycheck." LeRoux enjoyed his new status, often referring to himself as the "skunk at the lawn party" after attending an owners' meeting with Peter O'Malley, Gussie Busch, and other baseball old-timers.

Jean Yawkey made another mistake. The general partnership of the club was divided into three equal partnership interests. In hindsight, Yawkey's widow should have created five partnership interests, taken three interests for herself, and given one each to Sullivan and LeRoux. They certainly wouldn't have refused. Without her, they would have been back as paid employees. Over the past ten years there have been many differences between the general partners, which have resulted in several messy lawsuits. As a result, the publicity surrounding the battle for control of the Red Sox among the various owners has rivaled the coverage given to the team on the field. After a decade of bickering, attention finally shifted back to the team itself when Jean Yawkey bought out Buddy LeRoux's interest, after LeRoux really laid out a spray and hired none other than Marvin Miller, the owners' greatest adversary, to represent him in appraising the club's worth.

No one understands the media attention that the Red Sox operate under better than John Harrington, a native New Englander. And the intense interest in the club by the public is not limited to the summer months, Harrington points out. "If we don't do something in the winter, one week seems like an eternity, and fans and the media get all upset and think we're not trying to do anything. It puts a lot of pressure on us, and some of the criticism is occasionally undue and gets out of hand, but it all comes with the territory. People care, which is why the franchise is so great."

The off-season media scrutiny of the Red Sox is so intense that it isn't unusual for general manager Lou Gorman to call radio and television shows to answer criticism. For instance, before the 1991 winter meetings, *Boston Globe* columnist Dan Shaughnessy—a frequent Gorman critic—was in the studio of Red Sox flagship station WRKO host Dan Roan. "The Red Sox are flip-flopping," said

Shaughnessy. "All fall, Lou is promising all these trades for Chuck Finley, Randy Johnson, whomever. Now he's saying he may have to sign another free agent instead." Shaughnessy also criticized Gorman for such past moves as letting Mike Boddicker and Bruce Hurst leave as free agents, signing Matt Young, and trading Jeff Bagwell, who became National League Rookie of the Year.

The inside line at the studio rang. "This is Lou Gorman. I'd like an opportunity to refute some of Mr. Shaughnessy's statements," Gorman told the producer.

Onto the air went Lou. "I'd make that Bagwell-for-Larry Andersen trade a hundred more times," he said, and went on from there.

"But that winter scrutiny keeps us in the spotlight all winter, and as long as people are talking about us, they're talking about buying tickets," Gorman contends. Normally, the Red Sox have nearly 60 percent of their tickets sold by the first of January. In Seattle that would be a huge plus, but Boston is dependent less and less on the actual gate. In addition, revenues pour in from the sale of luxury boxes, from the 600 Club (the private club that customers can join by purchasing four seats in a glassed theatre behind home plate for five years at a total of $125,000, not including food or beverages at the dinner club), and from the team's cable outlet, New England Sports Network (NESN), of which the club is the largest shareholder. The luxury boxes, which sell for $60,000 a year, are sold to businesses and wealthy individuals, and there is a waiting list for them. But the 600 Club and NESN fluctuate. "When the Red Sox went out last winter and signed Roger Clemens [for five years and nearly $22 million], then made all the free agent signings [Jack Clark, Danny Darwin, and Young, an investment of nearly $27 million], it created an excitement that carried over to our subscribers," says NESN general manager John Claiborne, who once was the GM of the St. Louis Cardinals as well an assistant to the GM in Boston. "In the early 1990s, Massachusetts has been in a serious recession. Now, I understand sports is a diversion and that the Bruins [the other major attraction on NESN as well as the co-owner of the network] have been strong, but the fact that every winter the Red Sox have done something—

Jeff Reardon and Tony Pena two years ago, then last winter's signings—have excited the public and given them reason to believe that the Sox will be in the pennant race all season."

During the winter meetings, Claiborne acknowledged a front-page story in the *New York Times* claiming that the economic decline in Massachusetts was the worst of any state's in the country since such figures began to be compiled in 1948. "But if the Red Sox make one impact move, we might even gain subscriptions," said Claiborne. Not long after, the Red Sox signed former Cy Young Award winner and 1987 World Series MVP Frank Viola to a three-year, $13.9 million deal.

"The Red Sox can and have to do something like that every winter," says Smulyan. "They can also afford it. We don't have to, but then, we cannot afford to, either. The chasm between big and small becomes larger and larger. What you get is a situation that without some rebalancing between large- and small-market clubs, the small-market teams cannot afford to sign their own players because they'll all wait to get the big teams to bid against one another."

Which is exactly what happened in the case of Bobby Bonilla. The Pirates—who were bailed out in 1985 by Pittsburgh Associates, a group of nine investors (including Westinghouse, Alcoa, and Mellon Bank) that was assembled to keep the Pirates in Pittsburgh for the sake of the local economy—are a small-market team. From the winter of 1990–91 through the 1991 season, the Pirates tried to sign Bonilla. His agent, Dennis Gilbert of the Beverly Hills Sports Council, refused offers of up to four years, amounting to $16 million. He set a price: five years, $23 million. "All we could do was guess what would happen when we hit the market, and that was our best guess," said Bonilla.

When he did get to the market in November, he had three big markets in the bidding—the California Angels, the New York Mets, and the Philadelphia Phillies, armed with a new infusion of cash from local television. The Angels opened the bidding at five years, $27.5 million. At the same time, in came the Pirates for one last try at $23 million. Too late. "What chance did we have?" asked

Pirate chairman Doug Danforth. "No matter what we came in at, the Mets would have come in higher." Pirates manager Jim Leyland added his view: "It's no different than my going into a store to buy a gun. If I have ten dollars and another guy has twenty dollars and there's one gun, who gets the gun? The richer guy. That's the baseball business. Only in this business, the owners are supposedly in the *same* business. But they're greedy. They want to win, so the big-market guy can be greedier than the small-market guy. He can have whom he wants." Bonilla got $29 million for five years from the Mets, who also signed thirty-five-year-old Eddie Murray for two years for $7.5 million and traded for pitcher Bret Saberhagen, who figured to get more than $6 million to forego free agency in 1993.

"We're in a very competitive TV market," said Mets GM Al Harazin. "We have to compete, not only in terms of baseball, but against basketball, football, and hockey. In New York, the battle for the entertainment dollar is a tough one." The Yankees lead the way, with close to $50 million a year in radio and television rights fees; on the other hand, Seattle, Kansas City, St. Louis, and Milwaukee opened the 1992 season without a local television contract. So, once collusion ended and teams were free to spend to increase revenues, the division between small- and large-market clubs began to get greater. After the 1991 season, the first nine $3 million free agents (with the exception of first baseman Wally Joyner, who took a one-year contract from Kansas City) signed with teams in the ten biggest markets. At the owners' meeting in Miami, they were told that in 1992 there would be six teams with larger payrolls than the total gross revenues of six small-market franchises. "When you've got one end of the spectrum making more than $100 million in revenues, and at the other end teams are making $35 million, what sense does it make?" asks Twins general manager Andy MacPhail.

White Sox co-owner Eddie Einhorn was more specific in his description of the differences that exist between clubs. "When you buy a team you buy a market." And the baseball markets are divided into three groups:

1. Supermarkets: New York Yankees and Mets, Boston, Chicago Cubs and White Sox, Los Angeles Dodgers, California Angels, and Toronto Blue Jays—the three biggest cities, and the gold mines of Toronto, and Boston. Philadelphia isn't far behind. Every one of these franchises has a revenue possibility of $100 million annually.

2. Convenience Stores: Philadelphia, San Francisco, Atlanta, Oakland, Baltimore (and Washington), Texas, Houston, St. Louis, San Diego. Average revenues for the mid-markets are approximately $60 million.

3. Lemonade Stands: Seattle, Milwaukee, Kansas City, Cincinnati, Pittsburgh, Cleveland, Minnesota, Montreal. All could be in the $35–$45 million range in revenues.

Within each group, there are complexities. The Cubs are different from the White Sox because they are entertainment for the Tribune Corporation, which owns WGN and also shows the free White Sox games. The Dodgers, who were bought by the O'Malley family, have been a testament to the capacity to make money in sports. Every year at their postseason organizational meeting, general manager Fred Claire tells his baseball people, "If it comes down to money, then money is never an issue with the Dodgers."

The complexities are even more at play in the second group. Houston owner John McMullen operated in the seventh-biggest market in the country, but he was like Argyros in that he simply wanted to make money and sold the club for a huge profit. Since he owned the Houston Sports Authority—which includes the Astrodome, an amusement park, and motels—he has always wanted to tie them together into one package worth somewhere in the vicinity of $175 million. When he sold out in 1992, he received about $125 million for the club and the Astrodome lease.

Baltimore owner Eli Jacobs also wants to run the Orioles on a high-profit, low-cost margin, then sell for a huge gain. The Braves, on the other hand, are a toy for Jane Fonda's husband Ted Turner, and are, like the Cubs, cheap programming (for years, they have played games at 5:30 P.M. on Wednesday nights because of WTBS's Wednesday night movies). However, as cable multiplies and Turner's cable properties continue to grow, they become more significant players.

The Cardinals are but one arm of the Anheuser-Busch multinational corporation, expected to sell beer but to show a profitable ledger like every other division. The Texas Rangers were purchased in 1989 by a group headed by George W. Bush, who bought 53 percent of the club from Eddie Chiles for $46 million. But the group has a large debt service and has been tied to a $40 million revenue ceiling until the Rangers get into their new park in 1994.

Down in the small markets, the Jacobs family in Cleveland can sit on a rebuilding, $8 million payroll until they get into their new park in 1994, and then invest. They figure that a "new Indian era" can be marketed as a major part of the revival of downtown Cleveland, particularly the Flats area, which just happens to be in the process of being redeveloped by the Jacobs family.

Montreal is another story. The Expos are sold by Seagram's billionaire Charles Bronfman to a local group of French investors headed by the now club president, Claude Brochu. Bronfman, fed up with the escalation of player salaries, told Bud Selig that he'd rather give his money to Jewish charities than to spoiled baseball players. Brochu's group is highly leveraged, the market is not oriented to baseball, players do not want to play in Quebec because of the tax, language, and customs problems, and, worst of all, the growing Quebecois movement makes baseball an increasingly difficult proposition. At one point during the winter meetings, when told that the Red Sox were negotiating with Milwaukee on a deal for pitcher Chris Bosio—and that part of the deal was that Boston would take Dan Plesac and his $2.5 million contract—Expos general manager Dan Duquette said, "It must be nice to not have to worry about money. It's incredible how different the jobs are when you're the general manager of the Red Sox and the general manager of the Brewers, or Expos. Two different businesses, two different jobs."

Because the big-city clubs are unwilling to share the bulk of their local television revenue with the smaller teams, the pressure to win and stay solvent has put general managers from the smaller markets in the pressure cooker. The owners expect them to make astute trades, be knowledgeable on the complicated waiver rules, develop blue-chip prospects who can be rushed to the majors, and keep their payrolls in check. But the free agent bidding and arbitration process blows the lid off their plans. The game is out of their control too.

The majority of the general managers returned from Miami without making a trade. Most of the veterans were either free agents, made too much money, or had no-trade clauses in their contracts. And the general managers didn't dare trade for a young player until February 20, since the last arbitration case was scheduled for that day. The crapshoot season was about to begin.

CHAPTER NINE

HIRED GUNS

Ⓑ

THE ARBITRATION SEASON, FEBRUARY 1992

S everal baseball officials were standing on the sidewalk outside the Royal York Hotel in Toronto hours before the 1991 All-Star Game when a cab pulled up and out climbed Cincinnati general manager Bob Quinn. The Reds were the defending world champions, so their manager, Lou Piniella, was managing the National League team, and he had brought with him five players and a couple of his coaches. After the Reds had won it all, Quinn, a lifelong baseball man whose grandfather once owned the Red Sox, whose father ran both the Phillies and the Braves, and whose brother-in-law was the Orioles' general manager, Roland Hemond, had been named the Major League Executive of the Year by two different news outlets. Yet the reason his arrival was newsworthy was that it was widely known through the industry that the general manager of the defending world champions had had to pay his own way to get to Toronto.

The Reds were not playing well at the time and were far behind the first-place Dodgers. Their best pitcher, Jose Rijo, had hurt his ankle sliding into second base in June, and soon thereafter the pitching staff fell apart. Quinn was under considerable pressure to make trades to patch the pitching staff, which he had thus far been unable to do, and had even been criticized by Piniella for his inaction. But pay his own way from Cincinnati to Toronto for a traditional baseball gathering?

For Quinn, this was all part of life with Marge Schott. Almost all the front office personnel who had been in place in July 1985 when

119

she became the official owner—president and chief executive officer, for those who like titles—had left or been fired. She wanted to get rid of all her scouts, "because all they do is watch games," and soon thereafter, scouting director Larry Doughty and more than half Schott's scouts quit. She tried to replace the ticket department with volunteers. She complained that the public relations department was handing out too many pregame press notes—too much paper. One winter the club had a small morning press conference, at which coffee and doughnuts were provided. The next morning, she offered the leftover doughnuts to the office employees—at a quarter apiece, of course—then tried to get the bakery to take back their day-old, picked-over food.

Marge Schott has also made a fool of herself with her players on many occasions. The Reds' owner was famous for her affection for her dog, Schotzie. Before the first game of the 1990 World Series, several of her players had agreed to perform a musical rap in uniform, with the proceeds to be donated to a local charity. As they left the locker room, Schott suddenly handed the players new hats with earflaps that resembled dog ears. She informed them that unless they wore the hats she would not permit them to wear the team uniform for the performance. Barry Larkin and the others decided on their own what was in the best interests of baseball: The benefit was done in street clothes, sans earflaps.

Bob Quinn at one point worked more than six months for Schott without a contract. Another time, when he was holding Schott's line in contract negotiations with Eric Davis and his agent, Eric Goldschmidt, he found himself savaged in the papers by Goldschmidt, who then praised Schott, which resulted in Marge giving Goldschmidt what he wanted for his star client.

So, as Quinn handed the bellman a bill and headed toward the door to the Royal York Hotel, he smiled, shook hands, and, as he passed Royals general manager Herk Robinson, said, "Maybe we can get together and talk." In between Quinn's checking in and checking out—and paying his bill, of course—he met with Robinson and worked out a trade that sent Todd Benzinger to the Royals for veteran Carmelo Martinez. "In this business," Quinn said a week later in his Cincinnati office, "you do what you can, any way you can." At least Quinn had made a trade, even though it wasn't for a pitcher.

There are owners, and there are players. Between them, there are general managers on the one hand, and agents on the other. "This was once a reasonably simple, uncomplicated job of managing the baseball operation," says Harry Dalton, who after more than twenty-five years as a general manager of the Orioles, Angels, and Brewers was "reassigned" in October 1991 when Milwaukee owner Bud Selig restructured his front office. "The general managers, who often were developed by running minor league clubs, oversaw everything from players to uniforms to tickets to promotions to hot dog rolls, made trades, did contracts, oversaw the minor league and scouting departments, and made sure the grounds crew was doing its job," Dalton explains.

"It was a far, far different era before free agency," Dalton continues. "To begin with, the contracts were basically one-way affairs. What could a player do? There was no free agency. Arbitration didn't come into place until 1973, and in its infancy the dollars hardly had grave consequences. Today, the preparation for arbitration is virtually a year-round job. Contract negotiations take teams, with lawyers and specialists. There are grievances over virtually everything, and waiver and technical rules have become so complicated one needs specialists for them. Many in management would argue that players and their representatives—agents, as well as the Players Association—have reached the point of being out of control. But they'd probably argue that where once the owners and general managers set the rules, because the players had no real rights, now players simply are commodities whose rights enable them to operate in a free market, as unusual as that market might be. So if owners are willing to pay what the players and agents want, they pay it."

The January 1976 McNally-Messersmith decision affected everyone in baseball, but it was particularly hard on the old-line general managers. For years, Dodger GM Al Campanis—who'd risen as a career Dodger minor leaguer and player to operator of minor league clubs to the top post under owner Walter O'Malley—dictated to players what he felt like dictating, because he was the general manager of the *Dodgers* and what could anyone do about it? Buzzy Bavasi, once with the Dodgers, then with the Padres and Angels, had the same sort of lordly relationship. Across the continent, Red Sox general manager Dick O'Connell in 1974 told Carlton Fisk, "You're going to have to deal with me, because I do not talk to agents."

Fisk at the time was one of the first clients of Providence-based agent Jerry Kapstein, who would advise Fisk what he should hold out for, then wait to hear what happened when O'Connell and Fisk met. The media had not yet grasped agents, and when Fisk, after being Rookie of the Year in 1972 and starting two All-Star Games, asked for $60,000 in his third year, he was trashed by columnists in both the *Boston Globe* and the *Boston Herald* for his avarice. "What does a pipe fitter think when he hears that Carlton Fisk is demanding $60,000 after two major league seasons?" wrote the late *Boston Globe* columnist Ray Fitzgerald.

In May 1976, O'Connell was dealing with another world, that of free agency. Three of Kapstein's clients—Fisk, Fred Lynn, and Rick Burleson—had not signed 1976 contracts and could become free agents at the beginning of the season. "It was all new, and no one really understood where it was headed," recalls O'Connell. "But one thing was clear—the agent, in this case Kapstein, had become an important part of the power process. In the back rooms of our offices at Fenway, we had our traditional baseball people sneering at the whole thing. Haywood Sullivan, Ed Kenney, Frank Malzone and people like that, who came from the traditional baseball mainstream, promised that agents would go away, that they'd never last."

O'Connell had read the changing world that previous year and had hired what effectively were two assistant general managers, former Oakland executive John Claiborne for baseball matters, and a young John Harrington on the business side (O'Connell also had brought in longtime television executive Gene Kirby to oversee radio, TV, and marketing activities, as the Red Sox became one of the first teams to market beyond the live gate by putting nearly one hundred games on local television). Both Claiborne and Harrington were convinced that the open market was going to push salaries out of sight, and, as the season wore along, Claiborne argued that the best course of action was to tie players up with long-term deals. "There was a lot of division in the office," says O'Connell. The traditionalists thought the outsider Claiborne was selling out the store. The August Sunday when Kapstein came to Fenway to meet with O'Connell, Claiborne, and Harrington to finalize the deals on Fisk, Lynn, and Burleson, the Public Relations Department tried to have him kept out of the park. Kapstein stood at the gate, and when the guard called the PR office, he was hung up on.

All three players were signed to five-year contracts, and each deal was obsolete within two years. Three months after the signings, O'Connell and Claiborne went to the first free agent "draft," made Twins reliever Bill Campbell their first pick, and by nightfall had become the first team to sign a Messersmith-era free agent, making Campbell the first millionaire product of the new system, with a five-year deal for $1,075,000. One year later when the Red Sox were sold to a group headed by Sullivan, sure enough, O'Connell, Claiborne, and Kirby were all fired.

The times became tough for Buzzy Bavasi, who in trying to rebuild the Angels after the 1977 season traded second baseman Jerry Remy to Boston for pitcher Don Aase and some cash, which he planned to use to sign free agent outfielder Rick Miller. Problem was, when Bavasi was discussing Miller after he had signed him, he told writers, "This gives us a right-handed-hitting outfielder, something we needed." Buzzy had confused the left-handed-hitting Miller with right-handed-hitting Dwight Evans. Campanis was another old-time baseball executive who was stung by the new way of acquiring players when he was forced to plunge into the market in 1980, signing Don Stanhouse and Dave Goltz to five-year contracts that turned out to be disastrous.

Back before Messersmith, players dealt with the general managers, and the owners were in the background. But as players became market figures, owners had to make bottom-line decisions, right from the inception of the free agent system. It was clear who was making the decisions. When Reggie Jackson visited New York, George Steinbrenner took him to dinner, and in Texas, owner Brad Corbett dined with the players and in spring training had them play catch with his children. In the late seventies, the role of agents grew, for negotiating and business reasons, and agents learned the ways of the business. If one knows that the owner makes the decision and that the general manager is a go-between, why not try to get to the owner himself?

The way the system evolved was that players tended to put all their faith in their agents, because the players knew that they themselves were not experienced in that field. However, owners did not put the club's power in the hands of the general managers, because the owners controlled the bottom line, and owners were businessmen who made business decisions. As players began to deal directly with owners, who wanted to be known for bringing stars to their communities, general managers lost much of their power and veneer. So when powerful agents like Dick Moss or Tom Reich wanted to effectively close deals with the Yankees, they went directly to Steinbrenner, and each was very effective in persuading Steinbrenner to sign their clients for big bucks. Some, like Steve Kemp and Ed Whitson, were out of New York within three years, money in hand.

When the 1992 season began, the only general managers who had been in place for more than five years were Toronto's Pat Gillick, Boston's Lou Gorman, Oakland's Sandy Alderson, Minnesota's Andy MacPhail, Texas's Tom Grieve, and San Francisco's Al Rosen. In one stretch from 1990 to 1991, half the GMs in the game were changed. "With all the pressures of winning and making money, there are a lot of general managers who are caught squarely in the middle," says MacPhail. "In my situation, I'm very fortunate. I work for an owner [financier Carl Pohlad] who gives me a budget, parameters, and allows me to do what I feel is necessary. Other general managers, however, aren't always so fortunate."

When Pohlad bought the Twins from Calvin Griffith, who ran everything himself, he hired MacPhail, who brought in a new staff, including personnel and scouting directors, and quickly separated the business and marketing departments. "And we're a small market," says MacPhail, who oversees everything.

The Oakland setup is virtually the same. Alderson has separate scouting, development, and major league operating chiefs, all of whom report to him. When Walter Haas bought the floundering franchise from Charley Finley in 1980 as a community service, he pioneered the marketing for the nineties, hiring Andy Dolich and a huge creative promotional department that changed the ballpark to an entertainment complex with three different types of score-boards, Dolby stereo, and a virtual food mall; marketed such con-cepts as BillyBall and the "tradition" of the A's, which goes back to Lefty Grove and Connie Mack; and put together a community relations team that was years ahead of its time. But while Alderson and MacPhail are still general managers in the old sense, only with modern structures beneath them, they are what they are because their owners are hands-off operators. If someone wants to nego-tiate with the Athletics or Twins, he knows Alderson or MacPhail has the authority to make the decision.

But that simply isn't the case with most clubs, where the own-ers clearly are the decision-makers. In Milwaukee, Bud Selig changed his office when he moved Dalton aside. Where Harry had some control over everything from scouting to the bullpen coach, Selig's new setup brought Sal Bando in as the baseball operations chief and others to run the business and legal departments—with Selig obviously making the final decisions.

Most of the White Sox offices at the new Comiskey Park are taken up by marketing and business people. Far in the back, gen-eral manager Ron Schueler has his office, next to that of scouting director Larry Monroe. Reinsdorf hired Schueler to make baseball decisions—to advise ownership on who can play and who can't, on who deserves to get the money and who doesn't. Everyone knows that Reinsdorf makes the dollar decisions, so that when it came time during the winter to discuss with agent Dennis Gilbert free agent deals involving Bobby Bonilla and Danny Tartabull, Reinsdorf asked Schueler for his input and advice, then went where he wanted to go with the deals. As it turned out, Reins-dorf's complicated offer to Bonilla involved deferred compensa-tion and insurance deals. "It was really the best offer," said Gilbert. "But it's hard for a player to grasp."

Even though ownerships have diversified with multinationals like the Tribune Company, Labatt's, and Anheuser-Busch competing with community business groups such as the Pittsburgh consortium, the general manager's job has become more defined in each case. The Tribune knows what it wants from its Cubs; it wants a personnel director, be it Jim Frey or Larry Himes, who it feels can find, develop, trade for, and recognize talent. Over the years, the Toronto job had become so diversified that where Pat Gillick used to run the Blue Jays like an old-time GM, now he is more of a personnel director and, when it comes to complex contracts, works as part of a team with club president Paul Beaston and assistant GM Gordon Ash, an astute negotiator.

The Pirates ownership consortium hired former Anheuser-Busch wonderchild Mark Sauer as club president, and he knew what he wanted as GM: a young personnel man—who, since Sauer worked for the Cardinals after leaving the Sea World end of Anheuser-Busch, turned out to be Ted Simmons, former minor league director for St. Louis. Sauer then hired legal counsel and looked for outside negotiating help. Since Simmons's predecessor, Larry Doughty, had lost three players, including now Phillies outfielder Wes Chamberlain, because of waiver technicalities and snafus, Sauer also immediately searched for an office technocrat.

"There are strains and pulls in every direction," says Alderson. "If a player isn't in the lineup, an agent wants to know why. It's a very complex job. Trades are the easy part, although they aren't easy to make because of all that's involved in contracts these days."

Nowhere are the complexities more evident than in arbitration. On the owners' side, the club keeps detailed records and statistics on each player, pro and con. The Player Relations Committee's computer spews out books of relative materials. Then almost every team hires an outside arbitration firm to handle the case.

The most successful arbitration consulting firm is run by former Astros general manager Tal Smith. His Houston-based company, Tal Smith Enterprises, has eight to ten employees, including labor attorneys, statistical analysts, and financial consultants. "It is such an essential part of the business that we use an arbitration team," say Reich, whose brother Sam heads a team that spends three to four months preparing potential cases. "There is no such thing as too much preparation for a one-hour presentation," says agent Randy Hendricks. "Every case impacts the industry significantly," says Reich. Since salaries of players with comparable statistics are the key criteria for an arbitrator to consider in reaching his decision, each time a new salary plateau is reached a roar can be heard from the Players Association's office.

In February 1992, when Moss won his case for David Cone and hauled in a record $5.4 million award, Moss said, "I hope this record lasts one day." The next day, the Reich group argued the Ruben Sierra case, asking for $6 million. It won.

"The process has come a long way in twenty years," says Don Fehr, who can remember when agent Bob Woolf of Boston, better known as a football and basketball agent, tried arguing the case for Toronto pitcher Dave Lemanczyk by handing the arbitrator several stories about himself as a sports attorney and expert; Fehr and Lemanczyk called time out, dismissed Woolf, and tried to argue the case themselves. Things were so simple in those days that the Rangers took Jim Spencer to arbitration over $3,000, and the A's actually filed a figure on Mike Edwards that was higher than what he filed at. Today, however, Tom Reich, the Hendricks brothers, and other well-known agent firms may spend upward of six figures in preparation. While every case takes on a life of its own, there are a few general maxims about the process that both agents and general managers agree on:

1. Try to settle the case beforehand, particularly if the arbitrator found for the other side in his last decision.

One of the problems with the system is that an arbitrator can be fired by either side if that side doesn't like his decision. For instance, in 1987, University of Massachusetts law professor Glenn Wong—a noted college basketball player at the University of New Hampshire, a former employee of an agent, and coauthor of a two-volume book on sports and law entitled *Law and Business of the Sports Industries*—had to decide five cases. "I knew the way the business works," said Wong, "but, honestly, all five cases were, in my mind, clear-cut." In every case, including Boston Red Sox vs. Dennis ("Oil Can") Boyd, Wong ruled for management. The Players Association had him dismissed.

Many arbitrators like to hear cases, even if they only get $500 per hearing. They like to meet players, they get publicity, and, most important, they get a reprieve from what is otherwise a tedious occupation. They tend to balance their decisions out.

2. Don't ever try to figure out how an arbitrator makes a decision.

An arbitrator is not allowed to either comment on his decision or give a written opinion. It's left up to the parties to guess what influenced him. Maybe he's a fan of the player. Maybe his wife yelled at him that day. One year, the California Angels had two players go to arbitration, Gary Pettis and Dick Schofield. The Angels thought they had clearly won the Schofield hearing and lost the Pettis case. The rulings were 1–1, but in the opposite order.

In another case involving Cincinnati, Reds general manager Bob Quinn walked out of a hearing and congratulated Randy and Alan Hendricks on their case for Greg Swindell. To everyone's surprise, the Reds won.

3. Picking a number to submit is the hardest part.

Since the arbitrator must pick either the club's or the player's number, the important number often isn't either filing figure, but the midpoint. If, say, the player files at $1 million and the club at $600,000, it's up to the agent to prove that his client is worth more than $800,000. In single-figure arbitration, $800,001 wins $1 million against $600,000. Clubs thus try not to get too low, or players too high.

Tim Teufel's 1986 case demonstrates some of the inherent problems with the system. Teufel had three solid years starting at second base for the Twins, from 1983 through 1985. He was first eligible for arbitration in 1986, but just when he got close to signing with the Twins, he was traded to the Mets, right before the filing deadline. The Mets essentially refused to negotiate, claiming they didn't know whether or not he would be a starter. As the system dictates, Teufel filed based on what he'd done, not on what his role in New York might be.

Wally Backman, the Mets' incumbent second baseman, had had his case heard the previous day. Backman lost. Backman had filed for a salary that was higher than Teufel's asking figure. But the Mets' number for Backman was lower than Teufel's request.

As the Teufel hearing began, the arbitrator asked Teufel's representative whether, considering the Backman ruling, he didn't consider the entire exercise a waste of time. The arbitrator was prejudicial and naive to the process. First, he had made up his mind that Backman was the Mets' starter and Teufel the backup. Second, he did not understand that the case was based on Teufel's past, and not future, performance.

The Mets pointed out that the Twins had replaced Teufel with Steve Lombardozzi and that Teufel had been acquired to platoon against left-handers. Teufel had argued that his performance over a two-year period, as reflected in the official statistical ratings (the Elias ratings), warranted his salary request. Then Tal Smith made a presentation on the "shortcomings of the Exhibit A [Elias] ratings," because, as Smith pointed out, "they are restricted to a two-year period and neither reflect nor give weight to the entirety of a player's career. For example, an examination of the National League rankings for first basemen and outfielders discloses that potential Hall of Famer Pete Rose ranks thirty-sixth of thirty-eight." Smith argued that statistics are altered for disabled-list time, and argued that the volatility of short-term performance rankings blows salaries out of whack.

After a 1985 season with the Twins in which Teufel was a regular, played 138 games, and hit .260 with 10 homers and 50 RBIs, he filed at $360,000 and "lost." Teufel actually got a raise, even though the arbitrator found for the club. As many owners have said, "The player never loses; it's only a question of how much of a raise he gets." The following year, after a season in which he was platooned, appear in 93 games, and batted .247 with four homers and 32 RBIs, Teufel "won" at $590,000. One can only suspect that this was the classic makeup call.

In 1985, Smith represented the Red Sox in their case against Wade Boggs. At the time, Boggs had played three major league seasons. He filed at $1 million and the club at $675,000, and Smith's presentation included

- Club won-loss records for 1982–1984, which showed Boston tied for sixth in the American League over that time;
- Club attendance, showing Boston's decline over those three years, from ninth to thirteenth to fourteenth;
- A section, titled "The Basic Agreement," in which Smith argued that each year of major league service brought a player additional benefits;
- Charts on the origin of 1984 contracts and on mean and average salaries by service time and position;
- A section titled "Salary Summary for Boggs," showing that the club's offer of $675,000 exceeded the mean for all players by $338,000, exceeded the median salary by $440,000, exceeded by $247,000 the mean salary for third basemen, and exceeded by $357,000 the mean salary for all players with three years of service time.

In the summary, Smith pointed out that only two players with Boggs's service time made more than $675,000. "These two players, Cal Ripken and Dave Righetti, rank first and third, respectively, in Exhibit A [Elias] rankings among all players with three years' experience."

In Teufel's case, Smith had argued that the Elias rankings had shortcomings. In Boggs's case, Smith argued that they were significant.

Boggs won.

What Boggs won was, of course, not only $1 million for himself, but a new plateau for others as well. As arbitration awards affect everyone's clients, the representation business has changed dramatically. Where fifteen years ago Kapstein operated his own business out of his house, first in Providence and later in San Diego, now the big agents are big companies. The most difficult part of the job these days is recruitment, which often requires young, enthusiastic members of the company who are willing to beat the college campuses and minor leagues for future revenue-producing stars.

The Players Association has tried to monitor and register agents, but with little success. When Kapstein became club president of the Padres after marrying owner Joan Kroc's daughter in 1989, he was banned from being an agent. But while association general counsel Gene Orza has investigated charges of illegal recruiting inducements and players being given shares in the action for producing new clients, no formal charges have been filed against agents.

Now that players are multimillion-dollar concerns, their needs are as complex as those of any small business. In the late seventies and early eighties, players rushed to shelter as much of their income as possible, and by the middle and end of the decade, a number of players were bankrupted by failed schemes, shelters that were disallowed, and dry oil wells. Some players whose names were attached to airlines and shopping malls gone bad actually had to get legal divorces to try to save some of their children's possessions.

Agents fall into many groups. There are the traditional big boys, like the Hendricks brothers. But agents have gotten into the business for as many diversified reasons as owners. Gilbert and Alan Nero (Wade Boggs's agent), among others, are insurance salesmen, and often take lower fees because they make their money off the premiums from insurance policies. Eric Goldschmidt, agent for Darryl Strawberry, Eric Davis, and many others, built a client base out of Los Angeles based on his being a financial planner, and more and more former minor leaguers are recruiting young players through their contacts in the bushes

Gilbert's Beverly Hills Sports Council has one full-time associate just to take care of Jose Canseco. "Jose is a business unto himself," says Gilbert. "There are his routine needs, his investments, endorsements, shows, memorabilia . . ." Yes, and, once upon a time, even his 900 number. "He's show business, and has to be represented as a movie or rock star. Another player is a different story."

In June 1991, the San Diego Padres' first pick in the free agent amateur draft was a right-handed pitcher from Georgia Southern University named Joey Hamilton. He was represented by Scott Boras, the California-based agent and attorney who has long been active representing high school and college players. Boras and Padres general manager Joe McIlvaine, a baseball purist, had a long-running battle stemming from amateur signings, and as the Hamilton negotiations dragged on, it became a test of wills. Boras had always been willing to advise top picks to turn down what he deemed inappropriate offers and go to college, and his advice had worked for Alex Fernandez—who turned down the Brewers and two years later tripled his money from the White Sox. McIlvaine made some comments about Boras that were printed in *Baseball America*. Boras filed suit against McIlvaine; when McIlvaine apologized in a later issue of the newspaper, the suit was dropped.

Hamilton was due back at school the first week of September, and as soon as he attended one class, the Padres would lose their draft rights. McIlvaine refused to budge and was going to let Hamilton go, but Boras got to owner Tom Werner, who gave Hamilton the money and signed him.

Before the 1992 season, McIlvaine was unable to reach a settlement on pitcher Andy Benes's contract. Benes had been the first player taken in the 1988 June Free Agent Draft. Coming off an excellent 1991 season in which he won fifteen games for the Padres, Benes was still ineligible for salary arbitration. Boras went to Werner again, and got a $100,000 raise over McIlvaine's renewal number.

Werner had the power; Boras knew it, and sidestepped McIlvaine to get his clients signed. On one side were the players, Benes and Hamilton, and on the other the owner, Werner, who needed them. Boras and McIlvaine were in the middle, and Boras realized that McIlvaine could be finessed out of the equation by one phone call to Werner.

Boras then successfully completed his triple crown victory over McIlvaine. Just before spring training, the agent convinced an arbitrator to make Benito Santiago, San Diego's All-Star catcher, the highest-paid catcher in baseball history, at least for a year or two.

McIlvaine would not forget. He would get even, somehow, somewhere; it was just a matter of time. The other twenty-seven GMs could relate to his frustration, but first they would need help in their battle to regain control over the young players. As was the case when they got together to hold down salaries to free agents, the owners were only too willing to assist their general managers.

CHAPTER TEN

BO'S LEGACY

T he reputation of Scott Boras was still being built. In that same June 1991 draft, the Yankees made nineteen-year-old pitcher Brien Taylor of Beaufort, North Carolina, the first pick in the country. Taylor's mother Betty was ready. First she hired Boras and then she went to battle with the richest club in baseball for the bonus. Ms. Taylor insisted that her son should get what Todd Van Poppel had received the previous year, when Van Poppel received more than $1 million from the Oakland Athletics.

The Yankees insisted that Van Poppel was a special case because he wanted to go to the University of Texas, and they offered Taylor $600,000. Ms. Taylor held out. Brien hadn't qualified academically for an Atlantic Coast Conference or Division I school, and columnists in New York ridiculed the notion that he was holding out for Van Poppel money. One story pointed out that the Taylor family lived in a trailer. The Yankees then sent a local Major League Baseball Scouting Bureau representative to talk to Brien himself. The scout asked him, "Would you like to drive my Cadillac?" Taylor declined, and the scout tried to enter the trailer when Ms. Taylor opened the screen door to let her son in. Quickly closing the door, she advised the scout to learn some Southern manners before he made another attempt to solicit her and her son.

Again and again, Ms. Taylor proudly held out. The kid applied to and was accepted at North Carolina's Louisburg Junior College, which had produced major leaguers Greg Briley and Bill Haywood. Finally, hours before Taylor was to attend his first class, which would terminate the Yankees' rights to him, the team of Ruth, Gehrig, and Mantle gave in and Taylor got $1.55 million, the biggest bonus in baseball history.

Two months later, baseball owners began structuring a new draft procedure to insure that no high school or college kid would ever hold up an owner again. They put together a plan similar to the National Hockey League's by which a team would retain a high school player's rights for five years after he graduated from high school. Fay Vincent and his deputy, Steve Greenberg, insisted that the new rule was passed only to try to induce more baseball players to go to college. "It doesn't say much for our industry that we're trying to pay kids not to go to Stanford," said Greenberg. "It's a poor message for the industry to send out."

Greenberg, who played baseball at Yale and in the minor leagues, may believe that, but in reality the owners didn't want any high school kid holding them up for any million bucks again. "Let colleges pay to develop these kids until they're twenty-one," said one owner. It was money and power, and having more college-educated players was hardly foremost in anyone's mind.

And since Van Poppel the year before had received his lucrative bonus, some critics have attributed another motive to owners' action. "There's no question that most black kids saw this unfold and said, 'They won't let some nigger kid do this to them again,' " says Marlins scout John Young, a black man who runs inner-city programs throughout the country. "It was a message that, once again, this is a white man's game. Not that it necessarily is, but the perception is there, and it's a problem for baseball, especially with all the concurrent stories about the lack of blacks in front offices and dugouts." The Players Association filed a grievance complaining that the new rule could not be put into place without its agreement. Boras then announced that he would challenge the rule in court, implying that baseball's antitrust exemption would be put to the test once again.

As the "Taylor Rule" was being debated, much was being written about the fact that since the beginning of the 1991 season, there had been thirteen managerial changes, and the only black who had been hired was Hal McRae in Kansas City. East Coast columnists pointed out that there were no black third base coaches (which wasn't true, since Jerry Manuel coached third for the Expos) and that Don Baylor, who interviewed for several of the managerial jobs, had been bypassed and had called the process "a joke." (Finally, in 1992 the Rockies named Baylor as their first manager.) Meanwhile, higher up the management ladder, only a few blacks hold meaningful front office positions and none were interviewed during the rash of general manager firings between 1989 and 1992. And there are no minority owners.

In 1984 in Boston, coach Tommy Harper spoke out against certain members of the Red Sox getting passes and eating at a segregated Elks Club in Winter Haven, Florida (even though the all-white club had stopped issuing passes to white players five years before, some clubhouse attendants, equipment men, and scouts still ate at the establishment). Harper was reassigned to the minor leagues the next year and subsequently fired. He filed suit against the club, and was awarded nearly half a million dollars. That scandal received two years of headlines in the Boston papers, especially considering the fact that when the Red Sox had tried out Jackie Robinson in 1945, a voice from the stands had been heard to bellow, "Get the niggers off the field"—and the Red Sox had become the last of the original sixteen teams to have a black player, finally integrating twelve years after Jackie Robinson became a Dodger.

Darryl Strawberry wrote a book with black broadcaster-journalist Art Rust, Jr., in which he claimed he felt like an outsider because the Mets were a predominantly white organization after 1986. The book was met with considerable criticism in the New York media. "It seems to me that a lot of writers don't want a black guy writing a book and giving a different viewpoint than that of the white media in New York," said Rust. "That's also the way Darryl viewed it. This book was a black man's viewpoint, and people don't want to hear it."

In 1987, the fortieth anniversary of Robinson's breaking of the racial barrier in baseball, Peter Ueberroth tried to make it a priority to attract blacks into management. But the issue didn't generate much media coverage until Al Campanis shocked the nation with his outspoken comments on Ted Koppel's "Nightline."

The media attention resurfaced with the managerial question in November 1991, and the persistent perception that it is a game owned, run, managed, and reported on by whites continued.

Rather than grabbing a quick-fix solution, Vincent saw the problem as a developmental one. "The biggest reason minorities aren't getting hired in these openings isn't a matter of racism," he said at the time. "'It's that there is no base of minorities being developed in baseball. Where we have to direct our attention is to all levels of the game, and try to provide opportunities for minorities to start out as minor league coaches and managers, assistant farm directors, and so forth. That way we will develop a base so in the next few years, when there are openings, there will be a pool of solid minority candidates."

While problems in the front offices and dugouts received most of the media attention because they were easily documented, baseball faces another troubling problem: the talent supply. In 1991, *Sports Illustrated* did a marketing study showing that the only baseball player among the twenty-five most identifiable athletes in America was Bo Jackson, and he was also a football player. Baseball isn't getting the same great athletes that football and basketball are getting, and while some feel it is the perception of baseball as a white game, that isn't exactly accurate. Bobby Bonilla is a New York Puerto Rican, Danny Tartabull a Miami Cuban, and Barry Larkin a Cincinnati black, and they are three of the highest-paid players in the game.

The problem is the system. In high school, where are the crowds and the cheerleaders? They're at the football and basketball games. Baseball is the year's afterthought, and to a seventeen-year-old, American Legion or some form of sandlot ball is usually more important than the high school game. If one lives in New England, baseball is actually fourth on the totem pole, below ice hockey. Naturally, if a seventeen-year-old wants the glory, the crowds, the media, and the girls, he is going to play football or basketball, first and foremost. Vince Coleman, the speedy black center fielder for the New York Mets, was a kicker on the Florida A. & M. football team when he was drafted to play baseball. "I didn't even know which teams were in the American League or the National League. I sure knew, however, who was in the AFC [American Football Conference] and the NFC [National Football Conference.] Grow-

ing up in Jacksonville, Florida, I never watched or cared for baseball.''

Go to most high school baseball games in April; you're lucky if
there are one hundred spectators. Then, if a kid is extraordinary,
he gets all the recruiters' attention. A standout football or basketball prospect gets a stack of mail daily, phone calls, glitzy visits to
college campuses, and notoriety from all the recruiting handbooks
that have become so popular throughout the country. When one
of the top twenty high school basketball players makes his college
decision, it makes the front sports page in *USA Today*. Colleges
recruit baseball prospects, but to a far lesser degree.

The result is that the pool of American blacks playing professional baseball is actually smaller today on a percentage basis than
it was twenty years ago. *Baseball America* did a study that showed
that from 1971 to 1991, the percentage of American blacks in the
major leagues had remained about the same (obviously, the per-
centages of minorities had increased because of the expanding
Latin American talent base). But more significantly, the percent-
ages in the minor leagues had dropped dramatically. Also, *Baseball
America* showed that only 5 percent of all college baseball players
are blacks. ''Fans have gotten used to seeing the Michael Jordans
and Bo Jacksons and want to see great athletic skills,'' says White
Sox owner Eddie Einhorn. ''Baseball has to do something to encourage the kids to play. The traditional talent supply system now
works against us, and to keep the product improving and attractive, we have to do something about it.''

One thing that may have happened is the ''Bo Jackson Effect.'' The
Royals and White Sox may have been frustrated that Jackson
wouldn't devote his attention solely to baseball before he got hurt
and needed a hip-replacement operation. Bo never became a great
baseball player. ''He's a highlight film, a barnstormer who might
do something you've never seen any night you see him,'' said
former Kansas City coach Bob Schaeffer. ''But he never became a
great hitter or player.''

However, Jackson received so much attention and made so
many memorable commercials that he became larger than the
sport, and his greatest claim to baseball fame may one day be that

he began showing the way for other great athletes to decide on the baseball millions. But only a few gifted athletes, probably, will choose to pursue *two* professional sports after their college careers, as Jackson did. Deion Sanders was the first to follow Bo's example, and then fellow Falcon Pro Bowl safety Brian Jordan played baseball, but only in the summers, with the Cardinals organization.

"The difference is that in baseball you have to ride buses and build up to the big money," said Jordan at the time. "Big-time college football—even the University of Richmond, where I went—is better than any minor league life. If you go to UVA [University of Virginia] or Florida State, you live a big-league life, and when you get drafted, they pay you big money up front if you're good. I never think about getting hurt in football, but I do think about the baseball money and the fact that I have a good time playing baseball. If the Cardinals would sit down and make it attractive to me, I'd probably quit football and play baseball." A month after he made these remarks, the Cards paid Jordan $2,400,000 to quit football.

Bo's football injury, which has jeopardized his baseball career as well, has had a strong impact on players considering both options. Ironically, Bo appeared to be leaning toward quitting football for good the year he was injured. Sanders and Jordan have admitted that they will stick with baseball if the money is equal. But for baseball to really compete with football for the top young players, it must convince high school draftees that even though their chances of making it to the pros are only one in ten, baseball is prepared to pay for their college education and give them a substantial signing bonus. (The football alternative would require four years of playing in college before the player could be drafted and receive a larger football bonus.) Since a player can be a pro in one sport and remain an amateur in another, if baseball was more flexible in allowing its draftees to complete their studies in the spring and to return to school to play football in the fall, it would have a better chance of signing most of its prospects.

Toronto general manager Pat Gillick has always gone after the exceptional athletes. He once signed New York Islanders stars Clark Gillies and Bobby Bourne to contracts with the Houston

Astros. He's signed such multisports stars as Danny Ainge and Jay Schroeder, and lost out on Sanders and Jackson because of Canadian taxes. "Years ago, baseball could just sit back and get the best athletes," says Gillick. "Now we have to be creative. But it can be done. Baseball has a lot to offer in salary, longevity, stability . . . all we have to do is use our heads and swallow our pride to admit that we do have to compete with the other sports. Those other sports are competing with us for the entertainment dollar."

Will Jackson, Sanders, and Jordan attract other similar athletes? "No question, if baseball's interested," says Jordan. "What we're beginning to see is two-sport athletes going to schools that allow their football or basketball players to play both sports; it used to be that you couldn't do it."

If major league baseball encourages the colleges to allow kids to play baseball in the spring as well as permitting to play in the summer programs, Jordan and others are convinced that you'll see a lot of good athletes going to college on football or basketball scholarships insisting that they also be allowed to play baseball. The more baseball competes, the more it will attract the great athletes. Sure, Bo may be gone, but look how fast Deion became a household baseball name.

Carlton Fisk remembers his first introduction to Sanders. It was a meeting Sanders would not forget either. Appropriately, baseball's oldest everyday player met one of its youngest at home plate in the House that Ruth Built. The shock waves from their confrontation brought out into the open a simmering hostility that continues to boil among what used to be a united group of ballplayers. More and more, the veteran players who were taught the game in a different era resent the young players who are being paid millions while ignoring the fundamentals the veterans consider an integral part of "playing the game the right way." Sanders's failure to run to first on an easy out occurred at the wrong time against the wrong player.

CHAPTER ELEVEN

MUTINY IN THE RANKS

$\bigcirc\!\!\!\bigcirc$

SPRING TRAINING, MARCH 1992

Several years ago, Bart Giamatti, then president of the National League, addressed a group of businessmen at the Harvard Club in Boston on the similarities between managing a university and running a major league ball club. He had been enticed to leave New York on a hot summer day upon being informed that his beloved Red Sox were about to start a weekend series with the Yankees. As he waited for a cab to take him up Commonwealth Avenue to Fenway Park, Giamatti casually remarked that the big money that many of the players were getting would ultimately lead to the breakup of the Players Association.

"Baseball is a part of the entertainment business," said Giamatti. "Look what happened to the movie industry. First, the big studios had all the talent under contract. Then the stars refused to tie themselves up with one studio. Like baseball free agents, movie stars saw their worth skyrocket. In order to pay the marquee performers, the studios were forced to pay less to the supporting actors. As a result, the Screen Actors Guild came about to protect the spearcarriers, not the stars. The baseball players' union is facing the same problem. The stars have different needs than the players who are trying to hang on to a job. I see some real conflicts brewing," Giamatti said as the cabbie closed the door and sped away.

As it turned out, the Players Association would outlive Giamatti; but, as he predicted, its membership is deeply divided be-

141

tween aging veterans and young players. As with everything in baseball, money is at the root of the problem.

When the 1992 spring training season began, more veterans than ever before—over one hundred—made their way to Florida and Arizona without a contract for the upcoming season, looking for a job. They had cringed each time they had read about a new multimillion-dollar signing in the off-season. For, as they knew, every time a club's payroll was ratcheted up, the older players were squeezed. Some teams, like the Oakland A's, were so tapped out that they wouldn't even invite an unsigned veteran to their camp, regardless of his salary expectation or ability to contribute.

The first casualty of the spring was Pittsburgh's Bill Landrum. Having led the Pirates in saves for three consecutive years, he re-signed with the club as a free agent in February for $1,700,000. Less than a month later the Pirates, under new management, got out of his contract by releasing him. Teams have, of course, been releasing players for years during spring training. However, in Landrum's case, the Pirates didn't claim he lacked "sufficient skill or competitive ability"; they just had second thoughts about paying his salary. Landrum quickly filed a grievance against the Pirates, even though the Montreal Expos picked up his contract.

Ten miles down the road from the Pirates camp in Bradenton, Florida, Dwight Evans sat on a stool in front of his locker in the Orioles' makeshift locker room in Sarasota, an ice pack slowly melting over his leg. The early days of March had been unseasonably cold and wet in Florida, but a veteran attending his twenty-fifth spring training knew what he had to do to be ready for the season's opener. The year 1991 had been a transitional one for him, and even though the Orioles' season had been disappointing, Evans had been pleased with his own performance.

His goal had always been to finish his career where it started, wearing the same red, white, and blue uniform. But that had all ended when the Red Sox decided Evans was through and refused to exercise the option in his contract for the 1991 season. The Orioles took a chance on him, and got just what they had hoped for. He had been the team's top pinch hitter as well as its leading run producer both with men in scoring position and with the bases loaded. He had hit a solid .270 in 101 games, and most encouraging, his back had held up. Unlike his last year in Boston, Evans played sixty-seven games in right field and had continued to show the brilliance that had marked his nineteen-year career as an outfielder with the Red Sox.

Evans arrived in camp in February, a month earlier than required under the Basic Agreement. He was excited about the upcoming season. The transition had gone far better than he had anticipated, he thought. No longer did he feel uncomfortable wearing an Orioles uniform. The younger players had looked up to him in 1991 and he was optimistic about the team's prospects for the new season.

The Orioles had not been sure what to expect from Evans in 1991. Evans himself had candidly admitted that he could not guarantee that his back would be okay. But after his strong performance in 1991, the club aggressively pursued him in the off-season, even though he had become a free agent once again. All of baseball was raving about the Orioles' new stadium, with its homage to parks of another era, like Fenway, and the chance to be the opening day right fielder in Camden Yards influenced Evans's decision to re-sign with the Birds. Convinced of the sincerity of their interest, Evans agreed to a new contract calling for a base salary of $900,000—which, while considerably more than the minimum wage, was less than the majors' average salary. The club assured him that as long as his back stayed healthy he would go north with the Orioles from spring training. At the team's request, he even attended its board of directors dinner in early January to share his enthusiasm about the club's chances in 1992.

During the contract negotiations, Larry Lucchino, the Orioles' president, had told Evans that he fully understood that veteran players prepare differently than younger ones during spring training so that they do not wear themselves out during the early games but peak physically by the end of camp. Before the 1991 season, Frank Robinson, manager of the Orioles that year, had allowed his right fielder to work out on his own schedule during the early weeks of March, and it had paid off. So Evans planned to follow the same workout program as veterans and rookies arrived for the 1992 spring training season.

On his first day in camp, Evans pulled a calf muscle. Johnny Oates, the Orioles manager, told his veteran not to push it, and again assured him that as long as he was healthy he would be going north. Evans wasn't overly concerned about the pulled muscle—after all, what player doesn't go through spring training with aches and pains? Soon he was back in the lineup, and while known as a notoriously slow starter in the spring, he got a few hits in the early games.

On Saturday, March 14, Evans felt a slight tightening of his hamstring during an exhibition game. He continued to play and drilled a single up the middle in the fifth inning. He was scheduled to have an off day on Sunday, and Oates took Evans out of the game so he would be ready for the night game on Monday, March 16. The trainer wasn't concerned. Just a little ice and a day's rest, he advised.

As Evans applied the ice pack, he wondered whether this team would be good—and lucky—enough to win it all so he could finally capture the World Series ring that had eluded him in 1975 and 1986. The opportunities for individual success were also a motivation. Opening day would mark his twentieth year in the major leagues. He was more proud of that pending accomplishment than of the other—15 home runs would give him 400 for his career. But he also knew that of all the eligible players who had hit over 400 home runs, only one (Dave Kingman) had not been elected to the Hall of Fame, and that Kingman had not been the premier defensive outfielder of his generation, as Dwight Evans had.

The other players filed off the field and into the locker room. Dressing quickly, most were anxious to escape the baseball environment as quickly as possible. Some had tee times; others had dates waiting at the beach. Evans's penetrating eyes focused on one young player, as he recalled their conversation in another locker room the day the team had been mathematically eliminated from the 1991 pennant race. "Man, you guys really had it tough," the young ballplayer had said to the veteran. "The playoff and World Series money was a big deal to you guys. Fortunately, we don't have to make the playoffs to make the big money. Hell, the licensing share now is more than you ever made from the World Series."

Evans remembered how he had taken the player aside and chosen his words deliberately: "I can believe you would think those things, but what I can't believe is that you would have the balls to say them publicly. Don't ever say that again to me or to any other veteran." The player had walked away with a confused look on his face, having had no clue as to what Evans had meant, or why the ring that Evans coveted cannot be bought.

Gazing down the row of young athletes, Evans spotted another player, who was turning up the volume on his tape player while throwing his unopened mail in his shoulder bag. He had been a well-publicized rookie on the Red Sox in 1987. Arriving at his first major league camp in Winter Haven, he had worn a T-shirt that read, "IF YOU HAVE ANY QUESTIONS, ASK MY AGENT."

Evans had had his career year in 1987, hitting 34 home runs, driving in 123 runs, and batting over .300 for the year. Late in the season, he found himself in the bottom of the eighth inning of a close game behind in the count against a young pitcher who had just been called up from the minors. Stepping out of the batter's box, Evans noticed that the on-deck hitter was not studying the pitcher (to perhaps find some small nuance in his delivery against the veteran slugger that could give him an edge when it was his turn at bat), but instead had his back to the plate as he stood by the first base railing signing autographs. That rookie was now his teammate, once again, on the Orioles. He had also pulled his hamstring muscle, and had played fewer innings during the spring than Evans.

"Yes," Evans thought to himself, "they are different."

Evans was looking forward to relaxing on his off day on Sunday. Instead, he was called to the park, where he was notified that the club was releasing him. The Ides of March had come, and Evans had gotten the knife. The excuse given was that the Orioles could not count on Evans because of the injuries he had suffered during the spring. But Evans knew the real reason for his release: By releasing him on March 15, the club was only liable for thirty days' termination pay. The club had decided to go with younger players, including the two who Evans had seen the day before, rushing out of the clubhouse. The Orioles were also scared that Evans might severely pull his hamstring, which would have forced them to put him on the disabled list and prevented them from releasing him.

Evans knew that he was being forced out because a business decision had been made. Thus another veteran who could help a team win a pennant—whether by providing leadership and stressing fundamentals or by having the ability to produce coming off the bench—had been given his pink slip. A younger, cheaper player would be kept instead.

So after he'd played professional baseball for twenty-four years, Evans's career had come to an end. On the field, it had ended with a single up the middle (he had been given just twelve at bats during spring training). Off the field, it had just abruptly ended. No testimonial, no gold watch, no accolades in the papers, and no public or private acknowledgment from the Boston Red Sox. For twenty-two years he had put on their uniform. He had been the consummate professional, even when personal tragedies had tugged at his family through the long seasons. He ended his career with eight Gold Gloves, an all-time Red Sox record. In every imaginable Red Sox career batting statistic, he is in the top four with Ted Williams, Carl Yastrzemski, and Jim Rice.

But the Red Sox had no public comment after Evans was released. After all, he wasn't their property anymore. He had chosen to become a free agent. After all, he could have retired after the 1991 season. It was his choice to put on another uniform, they had told the press.

And, as he'd played only one season in Baltimore, the Orioles certainly did not consider Evans part of their family. So, across the country, the only way a baseball fan would have found out that Dwight Evans was not playing would be if he or she had caught a small transaction buried in the back of the local paper's sports section: "The Baltimore Orioles placed Dwight Evans on waivers for the purpose of giving him his unconditional release." No other club called; he must be physically unable to play, they assumed. "It's too bad about Dewey," said Lou Gorman, the Red Sox general manager. "But I guess he just can't play anymore." Nobody bothered to ask Evans what he thought.

Of course, it happens to every veteran. And too often an aging player, like a heavyweight boxer, tries to go one more round than he should. Evans had thought about retiring after the 1991 season. But he knew that he could still hit. His only uncertainty was his back. He had no such fears on March 15, 1992. He knew he could still contribute, both on and off the field. But young players were approaching their arbitration years, others couldn't be sent back to the minors, and Eli Jacobs, the Orioles' owner, had his club on the market for sale. The veteran—and his salary—had to go.

Evans paid for his own flight home to reunite himself with his family. The Orioles, and baseball, would soon begin the 1992 season with one less veteran who'd played before 1976 and bridged the two eras. There were now only twenty left.

Deion Sanders—brash, flashy, publicity-seeking—is the prototypical modern ballplayer. He sees the money everywhere—arbitration awards, free agent salaries, card shows, home shopping networks, licensing shares, endorsement tie-ins—and he wants a part of it all. After just one year in the majors, Sanders had a .183 lifetime average with nine home runs. But he had already drawn more national coverage, magazine articles, and "prime time" radio and television interviews than Dwight Evans had received in the prior twenty seasons combined.

As Evans left Sarasota, the White Sox were just starting a spring training game in the same town, with their young ace, Jack McDowell, on the mound. Beginning his fourth year with the Sox, for the first time in his career he had been eligible for salary arbitration. The prior spring he had refused to sign the White Sox's offer, so the club had renewed him at its figure. McDowell had fired Dennis Gilbert as his agent and had his brother and father handle his arbitration case. Neither had ever negotiated a baseball contract before. McDowell "lost" his hearing, but his salary increased almost tenfold, from $175,000 to $1,600,000. He was bitter; he had asked for $2,300,000.

McDowell, like Deion Sanders, Jose Canseco, Barry Bonds, Ken Griffey, Jr., and most of all the other great young talents today, feel the same way about the state of the game. "We didn't create the system, but we're entitled to everything we can get. I can't worry about the older players. They're trying to take my job away. Meanwhile, the owners screw all the young players while they can. Look what they did to me. They sent me back to the minors in 1989, when I could pitch better than most veterans on their staff. They stole a year of arbitration from me to save money. I don't feel any loyalty or need to 'pay my dues' to the White Sox." Jack McDowell, a professional guitarist in a rock band when not pitching for the Chicago White Sox, expects to be paid as an entertainer. Most of his young contemporaries feel the same way.

The young players today are certainly no more materialistic or egocentric than former stars like Babe Ruth and Ty Cobb—or for that matter, Reggie Jackson and Pete Rose; there just seems to be a different arrogance, or swagger, about them that is not as likable as it was in prior stars. Children of strikes, lockouts, and other labor-management confrontations, most of the players coming into the game today fool no one when they repeat the trite phrase, "I'd play the game for nothing."

Like the club owners, who fight among themselves based on where they fall within one of three market classifications, the players are also divided into three camps. The first group consists of young players and prospects, like Deion Sanders, who have not been in the majors for three years, are totally under the control of their clubs, and have no leverage in salary negotiations because they are not eligible for salary arbitration. The second group is made up of players who are either salary-arbitration eligible (like Jack McDowell) or close to or at their free agency year (like Barry Bonds) and are considered "impact players."

The third group consists of the rest—like associates in a big law firm who will never make partner and will not be "offered" new contracts, or like aging senior partners being shoved out the door. Dwight Evans fell in the third category.

The Chicago White Sox, like most clubs, have players on their roster who fit all these categories. One of them, Carlton Fisk, was, in his words, "not a happy camper." As McDowell threw strikes to Ron Karkovice, the White Sox backup catcher, Fisk pumped iron in the team's weight room. "I know," he said, his voice full of sarcasm, "they'll say, 'I told you so. See, age has finally caught up with him and he can't play anymore. That's why we didn't pick up the option on his contract.' But nobody mentioned that Mike

Gallego, who is thirty-two and signed with the Yankees as a free agent, is out with the same injury."

What had started out as a minor bruise in his heel had turned out to be an inflamed tendon and bone spur under his foot. Fisk called the representatives at Nike, the shoe company that has hired him as a spokesman to wear its shoes, to get their opinion. They told him that the injury he had suffered is very prevalent among runners and that with time it would heal. But time is not something a forty-four-year-old catcher has a lot of, and even though the doctor had said there was no correlation between the injury and age, Fisk knew that the White Sox would say there was.

"This game grinds on you," one of baseball's all-time greats continued. "It's not the playing of the game, the joy in winning, the frustration in defeat, or the thrill of being part of a collective effort to achieve something very special that can only be appreciated by those who have gone through it. It's all the other things that wear you down. The front office just doesn't understand that my job is more than just calling balls and strikes or trying to hit the ball over the fence."

Like his ex-teammate, Dwight Evans, Fisk is angered by the attitudes toward the game shown by many young players. His daily responsibility is to be "an attitude adjustment counselor," either through dealing with it head-on or through leading by example. "There is a comfort zone that a lot of the players slip into. You know, they're making such big money, and as long as they don't embarrass themselves they're content. They come into the game with such egos that they don't ask questions. They just think they know it all, as they wait impatiently for the big contracts."

"That's why I quit when I did," Greg Luzinski, known as the Bull for his intimidating physique, was saying from his 150-acre spread in the tall pines outside of Cherry Hill, New Jersey. Luzinski had been a great power hitter for the Phillies during their championship years of the late 1970s. He ended his career with the White Sox in 1984, although he was only thirty-three and had an offer to play again for over $500,000.

"I thought it was bad then. Well, it's gotten a lot worse in the last ten years. Koos (pitcher Jerry Koosman) and I decided we'd had enough. Nobody seemed to enjoy sitting around the clubhouse, having a few beers, and talking baseball. Instead, it was shower and get out fast. Of course, Pudge Fisk would stick around. But he'd always be in the weight room working out." Luzinski's son, Ryan, the Dodgers' number one pick in the June 1992 draft, listened intently to his father's story, and just nodded in agreement. That's one of the reasons he was so highly rated by the scouts. No attitude problem with the Baby Bull.

One young player was fortunate enough to get an "attitude adjustment" lesson very early in his career. In his twenty-fourth major league game, Deion Sanders, a member of the New York Yankees at the time, came to the plate against the White Sox on May 22, 1990 with a runner on third base and one out. Popping up to the shortstop, Sanders casually trotted a few feet down the first base line, then abruptly turned to the home dugout before the ball was caught. It was a hot night, and Fisk, who had been drafted by the Red Sox before Sanders was born, got a lot hotter. "I'm looking at this kid, and thinking to myself, 'Can you believe this?' "

Two innings later, Sanders came to the plate again. "Run the 'bleep' ball out, you piece of 'bleep,' " Fisk barked at him.

"What?" an astonished Sanders replied.

"I said," Fisk repeated, "run the 'bleep' ball out, you piece of 'bleep.' "

"The days of slavery are over," Sanders yelled back.

Quickly, both dugouts and bullpens spilled out as fifty players and four umpires converged at home plate. But no blows were thrown, and the game ended without further incident.

"There's a right way to play this game, and there's a wrong way," Fisk told the New York and Chicago media as they surrounded his locker after the game. "Sanders wants to turn it into a racial issue. He's black, I'm white, and he brings up that slavery stuff, which had nothing to do with it. I'm a member of the opposing team—the *opposing* team—and *I'm* offended by his dogging it. The issue isn't race, the issue is professional pride."

Deion Sanders has no clue as to who Thurman Munson was. But Carlton Fisk had groveled in the same dirt around the very same home plate on more than one occasion with his greatest adversary many years before. Fisk was thinking as much about the former Yankee captain who died in an airplane crash as he was about the newest two-sport phenom to hit baseball.

"The game deserves better," Fisk continued. "Some of these kids playing now just don't appreciate what they have, what this game is. I mean, some players in baseball have earned the right to be animated. Reggie Jackson, Rickey Henderson, Dennis Eckersley are good examples. Eckersley upset Dewey Evans during the playoffs when he struck him out, then made that little gesture, like boom-boom with a pistol, 'I got you.' Well, that sort of thing gets on your nerves, but Eckersley has earned the right to show his emotions. Sanders? He hasn't exactly earned his stripes, has he? Did he even hit his weight last season? Come on. If you're going to do something, do it the right way, or don't do it at all. In certain ways, everything seems so backwards now. Players now are getting paid for potential more than performance, and all that does is create a very large comfort zone—too large."

While "Prime Time" Sanders hasn't completely changed his act, many players have noticed a change in his personality over the last two years. He no longer wears all the heavy gold jewelry he was famous for and he clearly has toned down his act in the baseball locker room, even though his macho image is still very intact in football. He has confided to several friends that he is beginning to understand that the culture of baseball calls for a different approach. If he truly understands it, baseball has Carlton Fisk to thank for the lesson.

Fisk's foot continued to throb as he forced the barbells up for one more repetition. "That's why the White Sox handled my situation in the way they did in the off-season. Too many young players in the 'comfort zone' are receiving contracts they don't deserve. The owners then turn to those who have been around for a while and tell us that they are sorry but they can't pay us what we're worth because they have to keep their payrolls in line."

Fisk had had an outstanding year in 1991, hitting 18 home runs and piling up 74 RBIs while having the second-highest percentage among catchers throwing out runners attempting to steal. He assumed that the club would pick up the option on his contract, which would have paid him the same salary (approximately $2 million) in 1992 that he earned in 1991. Instead, the club said no thanks, allowed him to become a free agent again, and opened the negotiations at a base salary of $500,000, which would have made him one of the lowest-paid starting catchers in the game. "It's a business decision," club owner Jerry Reinsdorf said. The White Sox then turned around and signed Fisk's backup, Ron Karkovice, for the same $500,000. Coming into the 1992 season, Karkovice had played four years in the major leagues. Fisk, of course, would be starting his twenty-first year.

Fisk finally settled for a base contract of $1 million, more than a 50 percent cut from what he made in 1991. No other club offered him a contract when he filed for free agency. Larry Himes, the new general manager of the Cubs said, "Why should I make an offer to Pudge when I know he wants to finish his career with the White Sox? He'll only use our offer as leverage with the Sox." Himes had been Fisk's GM on the White Sox before he was fired in 1990. The young Cub pitching staff could certainly have used Fisk's experience and leadership. But Himes was probably right. "You know, even for the money and the satisfaction of proving the White Sox wrong, I just couldn't see myself going crosstown to play for the Cubs. You give so much of yourself to a team, and to the league; the loyalty factor plays heavy on you." "Loyalty" is not a word heard very often around baseball these days.

Certainly the White Sox, who reportedly earned $17 million in 1991, could have easily exercised the option on Fisk's contract for his prior-year salary and avoided the negative press reaction and public outcry, which was solidly behind Fisk during the off-season. But Jerry Reinsdorf had heard worse and wasn't concerned. He explained the club's decision in a calm, dispassionate way.

"When I first bought the ball club, I wanted to reward our young star, Harold Baines, for the outstanding season he had had for us, even though he was not eligible for salary arbitration. Suddenly, several players who could go to arbitration used Baines's salary to justify their request. As one player said at the time, 'If I'm only half the player Baines is, then I deserve to earn half of what he makes.' That's when I learned my first expensive lesson about the game: You can't make decisions about paying a player in a vacuum. Every salary affects every other salary you have to negotiate. The players got what they wanted. Let them now fight over how the pie is going to be split among them."

Just before Fisk signed his one-year contract with the White Sox for $1 million, the club signed its other free agent player, Dan Pasqua, to a three-year contract for $6 million. Pasqua's offensive statistics were almost identical to Fisk's in 1991. They both played in 134 games, both had 18 home runs, and Pasqua had 66 RBIs to Fisk's 74. Pasqua alternated between the outfield and first base, and is not a threat to win a Gold Glove at either position. However, since he'd just completed his six years in the major leagues, the White Sox were concerned that another club might sign him to a contract, despite the fact that he had never been an everyday player in his major league stints with the Yankees and the White Sox.

Pasqua's signing just infuriated Fisk more. "The White Sox say they want me back, but not for the option price they asked for. They knew no one would make me an offer, so they lowballed their proposal to me. Then they go and sign Danny to a contract worth four times what they offered me. I smell collusion all over again."

The clubs blame the schism that exists between the players and their teams on the riches that have flowed the players' way through arbitration awards and free agency. "They don't care about a team anymore," one owner said in disgust. "They only want to make as much money as possible and then get out. In the old days, you saw more players start and end their careers with one team. Players didn't jump around as much back then, and the fans had real hometown heroes to root for."

It's true that in the days before free agency, there was a closer bond between teammates on a club, and a greater respect for the owner. Typically, the players came up through the system together and, with no control over their own destinies, developed a strong allegiance to their teammates. Players on opposing teams, conversely, were viewed with disdain. But once the players acquired leverage through collective bargaining to become free agents and move to other clubs, their attitudes changed. Between 1976 and 1990 the players' allegiance to the union became far stronger than their loyalty to their individual clubs. Marvin Miller and his successor, Don Fehr, have had great success in educating the players that they are the show and that only by sticking together can they prevent the owners from reinstating the reserve clause, capping salaries, reducing the players' pension benefits, and seizing control over all licensing revenues—in other words, wiping out the union's hard-earned gains from the prior twenty-five years.

The owners' public pronouncements that free agency has caused a greater turnover of players on teams, and therefore a lack of fan identification with one team, are unfounded. A recent study reveals that there were actually more annual changes to club rosters when clubs controlled player movement through trades than there have been subsequent to 1976, when both clubs *and* players started to have a say.

Another owner complaint is that the competition for star players has driven "marquee players" away from their original teams and that the days of a premier player playing his entire career for one team are over. No longer, the argument goes, will a player be synonymous with a city, like Al Kaline with Detroit, Stan Musial with St. Louis, and Ernie Banks with Chicago. But since the turn of the century, only fifty players who played for at least fifteen years in the majors played their entire careers with the same team. Eighteen of the fifty played at least part of their careers after 1976 and had the opportunity as free agents to move elsewhere, but chose not to. And seven—George Brett with Kansas City; Jim Gantner, Paul Molitor, and Robin Yount with Milwaukee; Alan Trammell and Lou Whitaker with Detroit; and Dave Stieb with Toronto—were still playing for their original teams at the conclusion of the 1992 season.

What will change in the future, however is that fewer players will play for as many as fifteen years. And certainly we will never see the likes of Ted Lyons again. Lyons played for the Chicago White Sox for twenty-one years between 1923 and 1946. During a remarkable stretch between 1924 and 1942 (except for 1931, when he was injured), Lyons started at least twenty games a season as a pitcher, and between 1926 and 1935 he was used as a pinch hitter or outfielder in several games when he wasn't pitching. In 1930, he led the league in games started with twenty-nine and innings pitched with 297, and won twenty-two games for the seventh-place White Sox, who lost ninety-two games. And to top it off, he hit .311 in fifty-seven games. Jerry Reinsdorf would have traded him before his 1930 free agent year.

Of course, the Red Sox did trade Babe Ruth the year before he would have been a free agent if the system had existed back then. In 1919 he had led the league in runs (103), home runs (29), RBIs (114), and on-base percentage (.456). He also won nine games for the Sox that year. If the Babe was playing today, he still probably would have ended up in New York after his sixth season. The difference, of course, is that he would have received the spoils of his labor from the Yanks, and *No, No, Nanette* would never have opened.

The yardstick players measure themselves by today is no longer the statistical benchmark of former players. Very few, if any, young players could tell you how many home runs Hank Aaron hit or how many consecutive games Joe DiMaggio got hits in; indeed, more than a few players don't even know who Hank Aaron or Joe DiMaggio are. The measuring stick today is salaries. So Rickey Henderson pouted when the A's refused to renegotiate his contract before the 1991 season because several players he deemed inferior to himself had received higher contracts from other clubs.

Since players now define themselves relative to where they are pegged on the salary scale, many, like Henderson, cannot accept the leapfrogging that takes place as one player's salary surpasses another's.

The A's were one of the first organizations to hire a sports psychologist to work with players in order to get a handle on the frustrated emotions that often affect play. Oakland's Harvey Dorfman, like his counterparts on other clubs, tries hard to solve the problem. Dorfman admits that he doesn't have the cure. "Nobody forced Rickey to sign his contract. And Sandy [A's general manager Alderson] even warned him that somebody else might make more than him before the contract expired. But within two years Rickey went from being the second three-million-dollar player to being about the fortieth. And while he was slipping on the salary totem pole he won the MVP of the American League. He feels that the A's should acknowledge the rapid change and restructure his contract," Dorfman said, a year later, as he watched a still discontented Henderson take batting practice before a 1992 spring training game.

"How can a player like Henderson who is making three million dollars feel that he's underpaid?" Carlton Fisk asks. "If a player is concerned about what the next guy is going to sign for, why doesn't he just sign for one year? But players don't want a one-year contract, they want the security of a multiyear deal. Well, you can't have it both ways. If you sign for the security, don't complain if someone else jumps ahead of you. Just smile and thank him, because your turn will come up again if you are good enough," the veteran, who has been through it all, sagely advised. A few, like Kirby Puckett and Cal Ripken, Jr., have taken Fisk's advice, but most others follow Henderson's lead.

Henderson's attempt to rationalize his public demands to renegotiate his contract, not based on what the A's were paying his teammates but on what other owners were paying their players, is probably the most glaring example of the fundamental problem that faces baseball today. Henderson, like most baseball players, refuses to believe that each club acts independently of other clubs, solely in its own best interest.

"Why put up with the charade?" one prominent player asked. "It's us versus them. The players are on one side and the owners are on the other. So if one club sets the salary scale they all should follow it. If they have a problem with the big cities overspending, then they [the small-city owners] should demand a greater share of their local TV revenues."

"Sure we'd like for Steinbrenner to give us a share of his local TV money, but it's not going to happen," Sandy Alderson, the A's GM, responded.

Henderson basically mailed in his performance that year, leading several of his teammates to openly state that Henderson's lack of effort had had a direct impact on the team's poor performance in 1991. As one of the A's said during 1992 spring training, "Sandy

Alderson should have just eaten his contract last year and released him. I can guarantee you we would have been better off and had a better record."

It was an uncharacteristically hot May night in Boston when Dave Stewart, the ace of the Oakland staff for five years, did what comes naturally for him: He beat the Red Sox for the eleventh straight time, including wins in both the 1988 and 1990 American League playoffs. Stewart, one of fourteen A's who could be free agents after the 1992 season, was intent on showing the club that he was not washed up at age thirty-four.

Like so many other veterans, his frustrations were directed as much toward his younger teammates as they were toward the front office. "Man, I'm not ready for this," he said. "For twelve years I've come to the park, done my work, given a hundred percent, produced on the field, and tried to lend a hand off the field to the community. But the young players come up either forgetting or never learning the fundamentals, expect the big contract right away, and are only interested in their own stats. And then the front office takes it out on those of us who have produced over the years." Suddenly, an unexpected smile appeared on Stewart's face. "Leave it to old Goose to put it all in perspective, though. He keeps telling me to remember that no matter how bad it seems, it's better than anything else we'll ever do for the rest of our lives."

Richard Michael Gossage (a.k.a. "Goose") was ending his career as Stewart's teammate on the A's after twenty years of stops in Chicago, Pittsburgh, San Diego, San Francisco, Texas, and Japan. Oh yes, and in New York with George Steinbrenner. Like Billy Martin and Reggie, Goose will always be remembered first and foremost as a Yankee. He signed with the Yankees as one of the first free agents in 1977. Five times he was on the mound for the final out as the Yankees clinched pennants.

Goose has lived through the changes that have rocked baseball over the last twenty years. "When I hang it up, I'm just going to walk away and never be involved with baseball at any level." The ends of Goose's trademark mutton chop mustache curled as he calmly talked of his impending retirement. "I have no interest in being around the young ballplayers or the front office people. The game's been good to me, and I'll always appreciate what it's provided my family. But why be involved with people you just don't agree with or like?" A mountain of a man with a barrel chest, Gossage for years had stalked the mound, throwing 95 m.p.h. fastballs at reluctant hitters. But his words—and the tone of their delivery— revealed a different person. The Goose, a proud veteran, looked forward to once again just being Rich Gossage, a gentle family man and honorary mayor of Breckenridge, Colorado.

As veterans such as Gossage, Stewart, Evans, and Fisk leave the majors, it is apparent that no longer do the teams with the best talent necessarily win. Those that do are the teams that can keep the three diverse groups of players focused on the same goals, even if the goals are purely selfish. Before free agency, when all players played under one-year contracts, September was often referred to as "Salary Drive Month." Today, successful managers get their players to start the engine in April. That is why the role of the modern-day manager, like Tony LaRussa of the A's and Jim Leyland of the Pirates, is so important. How he handles a pitching staff and the skills he displays on game day are still important in defining a top manager. But as important—or perhaps more so—is the ability of a manager to blend the various personalities of the players together to keep the lid on the pot.

"The players today are definitely better prepared physically," LaRussa says. "With the money they make, they can afford to work out all year. But the distractions—money, media, card show promoters, to name a few—take their attention away from the mental aspect of the game." LaRussa's best friend, Jim Leyland, concurs. "Look, I don't blame the players one bit for the money they're making. But I remind my players every spring that if they expect to get the big contract, they better pull together as a team, give a hundred and ten percent, and live and breathe baseball during the season."

As hundreds of former major league veterans are forced out of the game, clubs are left more and more with greedy young players who don't know any better and fabulously wealthy stars who have entered the "comfort zone."

As the owners continued to fight among themselves, they all agreed that they needed to somehow unite to force the players to accept lower salaries. But while their battles with each other and the union raged, the ultimate challenge to their old way of doing business was gaining momentum.

CHAPTER TWELVE

A NEW FOE
TAKES SHAPE

Marvin Miller, founder of the Players Association, knows it will work. Mike Traeger, former NBC vice president, is behind it. Agent Dick Moss and former major league owner David LeFevre thought it up. As commissioner, Bart Giamatti once said, "Frankly, it's an act that strikes me as something I would do if I were a responsible labor leader." Sal Artiaga, who recently resigned as president of the minor leagues, said that there was vast support throughout the minors for it. And Eddie Einhorn, the consummate promoter, not only is convinced that it will happen, but that it will be successful. What they all agree on is that a new baseball league will soon emerge to challenge major league baseball.

At first glance, David LeFevre seems to be an unlikely candidate to challenge baseball's establishment. A prominent New York attorney, LeFevre grew up in Cleveland, Ohio, the grandson of Cyrus Eaton, one of the great industrialists of the 1920s. LeFevre has been actively involved with major league baseball for many years. Originally a minority owner with hard-liner John McMullen of the Houston Astros, he sold his interest in the Astros and became an investor in the Cleveland Indians. In early 1984, he made a $41 million offer to buy the Indians from the estate of F. J. O'Neill. He withdrew the offer in December of 1984 when he felt that the estate was dragging its feet in selling the club. LeFevre turned his attention to the Orient, where he has since spent most of his time, working with Japanese clients. He recently persuaded several Japanese banks to bail out Phil Esposito, the former hockey star who had acquired the Tampa Bay expansion franchise in the National Hockey League. LeFevre now sits on the board of governors of the NHL.

As the relationships between the players and the major league owners hit a low point during the collusion years of the late 1980s, LeFevre started to explore the possibility of starting a new baseball league.

Dick Moss was convinced that several of his unemployed ballplaying clients could still cut it, even though they had been frozen out of the market. Hearing that LeFevre was interested in starting a new league, Moss approached him and mentioned that he was thinking about doing the same thing. The two of them went out and found a third partner, Doug Nelson, who as a consultant with McKinsey & Co. had worked on several projects for major league baseball in the past.

In November 1989 LeFevre revealed his plans. "We plan to open The Baseball League in 1991 with eight cities. ABC has made a proposal to us to broadcast our games. Their proposal is close to eighty percent of what we are looking for. We already have six owners lined up, including Donald Trump," LeFevre confided. "Edward J. DeBartolo, Sr. and Portland timber tycoon Bruce Engle want to join too."

DeBartolo, the man who changed the way Americans shop by bringing malls to the suburbs, would love to get back at major league baseball. On his deathbed in 1982, Bill Veeck had agreed to sell the Chicago White Sox to him. However, Bowie Kuhn and the ownership committee (in other words, Peter O'Malley) deemed DeBartolo nonacceptable because he owned several racetracks. DeBartolo knew that this was not the only reason he was rejected. After all, both George Steinbrenner and Dan Galbreath, former owner of the Pittsburgh Pirates, owned tracks as well. DeBartolo was convinced that Kuhn and O'Malley didn't want him in their brotherhood because he was Italian. Unsubstantiated rumors floated around baseball that he was involved with the mob. When DeBartolo's offer was turned down by baseball, Veeck threatened to move the team from Chicago. Then Jerry Reinsdorf and Eddie Einhorn came forward and bought the club.

Besides Trump, DeBartolo, and Engle, LeFevre mentioned that

he also had two other prominent owners lined up. They had been recommended to him by a highly unusual source, attorney Stephen Greenberg. Greenberg was a partner in a prestigious Los Angeles firm and was a prominent agent representing many major league players. He had known LeFevre from their days growing up in Cleveland, where Steve's father, Hall of Famer Hank Greenberg, was a part owner of the Indians. Soon after recommending the investors to LeFevre to help form a new league to challenge the majors, Greenberg was named deputy commissioner of major league baseball by Fay Vincent.

LeFevre and Moss carefully monitored the negotiations that were taking place between the players and the owners in the spring of 1990. The major league clubs publicly denounced the present system of compensating players as being too costly, and proposed a wage scale system with a salary cap formula. The players, of course, rejected the proposals out of hand and said that the problem with baseball was that the big-city clubs do not adequately share revenue from their local cable contracts with the smaller cities, and therefore expect the players to solve their economic problem for them by agreeing to lower salaries.

Moss and LeFevre nodded to one another that these were the exact kinds of problems that their new league was going to avoid. Their league would operate under a cooperative format in which television revenues would be shared equally among all the clubs, similar to the system used by the National Football League. The profits would be shared with the players, making the format similar to the revenue-sharing plan that exists in the National Basketball Association. As far as stocking the clubs with players, Moss and LeFevre realized that they would have to pay for a few superstars and then fill in the rest with marginal players. LeFevre shrugged off any concerns regarding the inferior product that might be put out on the field by saying, "The average public doesn't appreciate skilled baseball anymore, anyway."

With the 1990 spring training canceled by the owners' lockout, LeFevre said his league was ready to go, unless one of two things occurred. First, if the major leagues agreed to immediately expand to eight cities, his league would be doomed. Since baseball had not expanded since 1977, and had shown no inclination to rapidly expand anytime in the near future, the threat of expansion was minimal. "We will also be in trouble if the owners cave in and give such huge salaries over the next three years that there would be no incentive for players to jump to a new league." That, of course, is exactly what happened. But two other factors worked against LeFevre: the spotted owl and the recession. The owl became an endangered species in the Northwest lumber areas, and Engle's company's stock plummeted. Engle was no longer interested in a baseball franchise for the Northwest. Then the recession started, and no one was hit harder than real estate developers, who had amassed huge wealth during the 1980s. Two of the more prominent victims were Donald Trump and Eddie DeBartolo.

Eddie Einhorn owned the rights to the Chicago entry in the now-defunct United States Football League, which sued the National Football League in 1985 for antitrust violations. Although the suit was successful, the damages awarded—three dollars—were hard to split among the various promoters. One gets the feeling that if Einhorn had not teamed with Jerry Reinsdorf to buy the Chicago White Sox, he would have emerged as the commissioner of a new baseball league. "LeFevre and Moss were right, but their timing was lousy," he exclaimed. According to Einhorn, not only could a new league successfully challenge the majors, but if the present system of baseball does not change soon, within three or four years a new league could be even stronger than major league baseball. Einhorn is convinced that Moss and LeFevre made a tactical error by publicizing their new league as an alternative to major league baseball just before the owners' negotiations with the players over a new contract in 1990.

Commissioner Giamatti was smart enough to use this to the establishment's advantage. Before a Senate task force hearing on expansion, he argued that one of the reasons for the delay in major league baseball's decision to choose expansion franchises was the fact that the players' union was sponsoring a new league and that it was hard to figure out what cities would be available for major league expansion. He added, "I welcome the competition. Competition is what the game is all about." Giamatti had masterfully turned the attention away from baseball's delay in expanding by putting part of the blame on the publicity surrounding the new league. Because of Dick Moss's involvement, he suggested to the press that the new league was nothing more than a grandstand play by the union to force a settlement on various collective-bargaining issues. Eddie DeBartolo, Jr., the owner of one of the most solid franchises in the National Football League, the San Francisco 49ers, convinced his father that he should keep his focus on the collapsing real estate market and not rock the baseball establishment.

According to Einhorn, the time to announce the creation of a new league is not during labor negotiations between management and labor of the established league, but during a period of time when things are fairly calm. The perfect time to set up a new league will probably be within the next two years. First of all, the collective-bargaining agreement and new television agreements will be in place by 1995. Secondly, now that Miami and Denver have been awarded expansion franchises, it is highly unlikely that any new franchises will be added to major league baseball until the twenty-first century. The cities that were passed over are re-signed to the fact that they are not going to have major league baseball for a long time. Also, because of the astronomical salaries paid to the top players in baseball, all clubs have dramatically cut down on signing middle-level players who are still in the prime of their careers.

Historically, new leagues have come into existence in order to achieve one of two goals: either to have their stronger franchises merge with the existing league or to sue on antitrust grounds and receive a substantial settlement. Baseball enjoys immunity from the antitrust laws not accorded to other professional sports leagues. The U.S. Supreme Court first addressed the question in 1922 when the only remaining team in the old Federal League sued the National and American leagues to be allowed to join the major leagues. The complaint stated that the defendants had destroyed the Federal League by buying up some of its terms and inducing others to leave. The Supreme Court refused to hear the case because it concluded that baseball activities did not involve interstate commerce and thus did not fall within the reaches of the antitrust laws. In the court's view, baseball lacked the essential character of a business because it involved a personal activity and not the manufacture of a product.

Over the next thirty years, the Supreme Court significantly expanded its definition of interstate commerce. Likewise, changes within the baseball industry greatly increased the magnitude of its multistate involvement. By the 1940s the court was ruling in non-sports-related cases that "commerce," for the purposes of antitrust, had been extended to include personal services.

Most everyone began to agree that the old Supreme Court case would no longer protect baseball from antitrust attacks. Several lower courts began to question the value of the decision, and in 1949 an appeals court announced that it was prepared to find that the earlier case no longer controlled the baseball industry. A player by the name of Danny Gardella, who had been under contract to the New York Giants, jumped to the Mexican League. When he tried to return, the major league owners barred him from playing for a period of five years, based on a new "blacklist rule" they quickly adopted after Gardella and seventeen other players were lured south of the border.

When Gardella sued on antitrust grounds, saying that he was denied the ability to make a living, the district court dismissed the complaint, relying on the old "Federal Baseball" case. On appeal, however, the appellate court found that "Federal Baseball" should not apply. The famous jurist Judge Learned Hand stated what every fan already knew: Baseball was no longer a provincial sport, but an expanding business relying more and more on radio and television broadcasts to extend its appeal to a national audience. The case never made it to the Supreme Court, because Gardella settled his suit and signed with the St. Louis Cardinals, where the remainder of his big league career consisted of one at bat.

Since the basis of the "Federal Baseball" case appeared to be losing its support, lower courts challenged the baseball exemption through the 1940s and 1950s. Controversy over baseball's exemption once again made its way up to the Supreme Court in 1953. While the Supreme Court once more held up the original ruling of the 1920s, in its majority opinion it stated for the first time that the issue belongs with Congress and not with the courts. In essence, the court washed its hands of the issue, saying that Congress had passed the antitrust laws and that if it wanted to include baseball under them it should now pass a new law to specifically include the sport. After the 1953 case the Supreme Court position seemed clear, and predictably, lower courts found little reason to question it. Whatever encouragement the Gardella case had given courts to challenge the "Federal Baseball" decision had been effectively squashed.

It now became apparent that if any changes to baseball's exemption were to occur they would have to come from Congress. This became an obvious invitation to those upset with the exemption to take their case to Congress. However, once more the antitrust exemption was challenged before the Supreme Court. Even though in 1969 Curt Flood was denied the right to become baseball's first free agent, the Supreme Court stated for the first time that professional baseball is indeed a business and that it is involved in interstate commerce. The court even apologized for having granted the antitrust immunity to baseball while having denied similar status to other sports.

In essence, because the exemption had been upheld in the past, the Supreme Court reluctantly upheld it again. Adhering to the legal principle of *stare decisis*, the Supreme Court refused to overturn a prior Supreme Court's decision, particularly since it had sent a message to Congress advising it to rectify the wrong by passing a new law.

It now seems obvious that any challenge to the antitrust exemption for baseball will have to originate in Congress and not through a court challenge. But despite sabre rattling by various congressmen, major league executives are not concerned that Congress will pass a bill eliminating their antitrust exemption.

"Do you really think Congress wants to generate negative press coverage by taking up the taxpayers' time to push a bill through Congress in order to protect the interests of six-hundred-fifty spoiled millionaires or another wealthy Japanese who wants to buy into an American institution?" one owner scoffed. Probably not, but if enough cities form a new league because of their inability to persuade baseball to expand, members of Congress might respond to their constituents' anger over being denied a major league team in their community.

Losing the antitrust exemption would have a profound impact on major league baseball for several reasons. First, any action that the owners took would have to be supported by something more than the rules of baseball as spelled out by the owners in their Major League Agreement. As an example, rejecting foreign ownership would not be permissible unless the owners could prove damage to the industry by allowing it. Also, the whole minor league system would be subject to attack, including the drafting of high school and college players and the rules that tie a player to one organization for six years.

Ironically, even though the Players Association is the strongest union in sports, if baseball should lose its antitrust exemption a substantial threat to the majors would be for the union to decertify itself, similar to what has occurred in the National Football League. With no union to bargain with, the major league owners would lose control over the players during the first six years, as all players at the conclusion of their present contracts would become free agents.

Clubs could not be transferred or sold on the individual whims of the owners and the television territory issues would be challenged. Ted Turner's ultimate fantasy could happen: Every cable system in the country would probably have to offer Atlanta Braves games for free, without any compensation due the local teams for Channel 17's intrusion into their markets. Doing away with the antitrust exemption would definitely be costly to baseball.

While professional football, basketball, and hockey have been challenged by rival leagues over the last twenty-five years—which have led to mergers in all three cases—ironically, baseball, which is more vulnerable, has not been challenged since the 1950s, when Peter O'Malley and Horace Stoneman took their teams west. A rival major league, the Continental League, announced plans to establish teams in cities that had either been abandoned by major league baseball or had never had a franchise in the first place. This led to the first major wave of expansion in the early 1960s.

What is intriguing about a new baseball league is its potential to be a commercial success. "There is no question that a new league could run far more efficiently than ours," Einhorn has lamented. As an example, Einhorn points out that the White Sox spend approximately $7.5 million a year in their development program. If you're lucky, maybe two prospects make it to the Major Leagues each season. A centrally run development program owned by all the franchises in the new league would cost dramatically less to operate. "And while a new league was waiting for their young prospects to develop, they would have their pick of the litter from our top minor league players."

In football and basketball, the minor league system consists of the colleges. Any new league competing with the established players would have to get into a bidding war with the NFL or NBA over players coming out of college. In baseball, no high school players, and very few college players, go directly from school to the major leagues. Since most players in the minor leagues (unless they have some major league service) are neither members of the Players Association nor under contract to their parent clubs, a new league could have a feast at the expense of major league baseball.

Major league baseball has hundreds of millions of dollars invested in its farm teams through signing bonuses already paid to the players and "research and development expenses" invested in each player based on his years in the minors. A new league could simply offer the top minor league players guaranteed major league salaries to jump ship once their minor league contract expired. Since most minor league players have no idea when or if they will make it to the majors, the offers would be enticing. To round out its organizations, a new league could go after a couple of "marquee name" major league free agents and backfill with many veterans who are being forced out of major league baseball through the austerity cuts that all clubs are implementing.

The present player development system in major league baseball is so inefficient, clubs will admit, that their minor affiliates only have one or two "prospects" and the rest of the players are "suspects" being paid solely to provide enough bodies so the prospects can play a game. As Einhorn admits, "We're trapped. We can't disband the minor league system and start over."

*   *   *

Until Miami and Denver were awarded expansion franchises, baseball had not added any new teams since 1977. Over 40 percent of the top twenty-five U.S. markets do not have a major professional baseball team. The existing player development system is archaic and inefficient. Furthermore, the disastrous negotiations with players over the years has mandated through arbitration awards that each club act individually in its own best interests on labor issues, instead of teams resolving problems collectively. A new league would benefit from all the prior mistakes made by major league baseball by operating as a cost-effective partnership between the clubs themselves and the clubs and players. The conflicts that major league baseball faces today would not exist.

Einhorn knows where the money will come from to bankroll the new league and allow it to survive until its young players develop—television, of course. "Our present contract with CBS is a bad deal. It's bad for the network and it's bad for baseball.

Einhorn, along with Bill Giles, John McMullen, and George Steinbrenner, were members of the owners' television committee that Ueberroth was supposed to report back to during his negotiations for the present contracts. When Ueberroth informed the committee that he was leaning toward awarding the network contract exclusively to CBS, Einhorn told him that it was better to keep it on two networks and to keep two partners in play. "Instead we end up with one guy who's lost money on it and we've pissed off the others. Our former partners [NBC and ABC] have now gotten along without it, and we've lost our leverage in the next negotiations," Einhorn complained recently. The committee members asked Ueberroth if he could have gotten the same deal by keeping two partners instead of one. Ueberroth never got back to them with an answer, as he had already decided to award the entire package to CBS.

Einhorn also feels that the cable deal with ESPN was a mistake. While ESPN clearly offered the best financial package, Einhorn feels that baseball should have cut its cable deal with a rival company, such as SportsChannel. "Do you strengthen the number one player in the business or do you go with the guy breaking in and strengthen him? We should have taken less money, because all we did was go out and spend it. When the deal runs out and the dollars go down, how do we adjust backward under the present system?"

Since SportsChannel is half owned by NBC and has been negotiating to merge with TCI, the nation's largest cable operator, Einhorn sees all the makings for a television combination that will support a new league. TCI already owns 50 percent of Turner Network News and Prime and would be a formidable player with NBC to get revenge at the expense of major league baseball, CBS, and ESPN. "It's all there, waiting to happen," Einhorn is convinced.

But dealing with the challenge of a new league would have to wait. Besides the immediate problems, tough negotiations with CBS and ESPN were about to start. Tougher negotiations with the players would soon follow. Still, an emerging league, coupled with challenges to baseball's antitrust exemption, would be the biggest battle of all.

The business of baseball was hotter than the pennant races as the owners prepared for their June quarterly meetings in New York. Suddenly, another major confrontation was about to become public. The commissioner was under attack.

CHAPTER THIRTEEN

THE COMMISSIONER'S LAST STAND

350 PARK AVENUE, NEW YORK CITY, MAY 1992

The friendly confines of his office on the seventeenth floor overlooking Park Avenue provided only a momentary reprieve for the commissioner of major league baseball. The problems besetting his sport had not been contained within the four walls of the Fontainebleau Hotel six months earlier, Vincent sadly realized. The messages were piled high on his desk. Bud Selig, Jerry Reinsdorf, Jeff Smulyan, and the others could wait. First, he wanted to make sure the *Boston Globe* and ESPN got his side of the stories straight. The Cola Wars between Coke and Pepsi that Vincent had lived through seemed downright civilized compared to this.

Soon after accepting Bart Giamatti's offer in 1989 to become baseball's deputy commissioner, Fay Vincent was asked if he'd be stimulated in his new job. At Coca-Cola he had run a billion-dollar division. In his new position with baseball, he would be expected to work for half his prior salary, in the shadow of a gregarious, outgoing commissioner. "People define roles; roles don't define people," he responded. Vincent was wrong. Two events dramatically elevated Vincent from anonymity to the position of spokesman for all of baseball. Giamatti's sudden death four months into his term as commissioner and the San Francisco earthquake during the World Series two months later forever defined Vincent's role as commissioner.

Vincent had been hired by Giamatti to run major league baseball's day-to-day operations, handle broadcasting negotiations, increase marketing opportunities, and develop a global presence for baseball. It was a role that he felt comfortable performing. But in less than a year, he was thrust onto center stage, and soon became intoxicated with the aura that surrounds the office of the commissioner, especially the easy access to the national press. More and more he became preoccupied with how the media treated him, and he was known to surprise reporters who barely knew him with unsolicited phone calls to defend his actions.

Taken ill before the 1990 winter meetings in Chicago, Vincent had his office deliver to the owners a written copy of his speech in which he outlined to his bosses what he thought his job was. First, he viewed himself as a strategist, in charge of developing the framework for baseball's future. Second, the commissioner oversees the day-to-day operations of the central office of baseball. Third, the commissioner must act as a communicator to the twenty-eight clubs, "to keep them working together in areas where coordination is important." Finally, and most important in his view, the commissioner is "a spokesman for the game's integrity—it should go without saying that I take this responsibility [as judge and protector of the best interests of baseball] very seriously." Summarizing his job, Vincent stated, "It is incumbent upon the commissioner to guide our national pastime through turbulent as well as smooth waters."

Judge Landis, Bowie Kuhn, and Bart Giamatti would have applauded in agreement; Peter Ueberroth knows better. While agreeing with Vincent's definition of the commissioner's role, he would probably also admit privately what the others would not: that Vincent had left out one key responsibility. The commissioner's main job, whether he realizes it or not, is to make money for the owners. Protecting the integrity of the game has become a secondary consideration. The seas were indeed choppy and many owners were beginning to publicly question Vincent's navigational abilities as the waves grew higher. His ship was definitely taking on water, and even his decisive action against George Steinbrenner was not sitting well with the other owners.

*   *   *

Steinbrenner had thought that Vincent would be more lenient in his punishment of the Yankee boss for his involvement with Howard Spira, a known gambler. After all, Vincent and Steinbrenner had attended the same school, Williams College; sat at football games together; and occasionally met in New York, before or after Yankees games. It was Steinbrenner, shortly after Giamatti's death, who had vigorously pushed for Vincent's appointment. The Yankees would again score a victory against their most hated rivals, the Dodgers: O'Malley had appointed his commissioner, and Steinbrenner would now have his. He was wrong.

Steinbrenner had paid Spira $40,000, supposedly to provide incriminating evidence on Dave Winfield, then a Yankee player, who Steinbrenner had signed to a ten-year contract in 1981. A portion of Winfield's contract plus annual contributions from the Yankees were to be funneled into a charitable foundation to be run by Winfield. When Steinbrenner soured with Winfield's on-field performance, he began to have questions about the foundation's books and tax-reporting procedures. The Boss stopped making payments to the foundation. The player sued the club. And then Spira came into the picture. He testified that Steinbrenner gave him the money to "get" Winfield. Steinbrenner claims he was extorted into giving Spira the money based on threats made against himself and his family. The commissioner called for an investigation.

After months of negotiations with Steinbrenner, Vincent held a press conference to announce that they had struck a deal. Even though he was the majority owner of the New York Yankees, Steinbrenner agreed to go on the permanently ineligible list in August of 1990. As part of the agreement, Steinbrenner was banned from taking part in the team's day-to-day operations. And if he wanted to see the Yankees play, he would have to buy a ticket like any other fan.

Almost immediately, Steinbrenner had second thoughts about the arrangement. Daniel McCarthy, one of his partners and his business attorney, sued the commissioner on the grounds that Vincent had damaged the partnership by banning Steinbrenner. Several sportswriters laughingly disagreed, saying that Vincent had actually added value to the franchise by removing the Boss.

The Yankees partnership, controlled by Steinbrenner, chose

limited partner Robert Nederlander, a Broadway producer, to run the club during Steinbrenner's absence. A year later he resigned and Steinbrenner appointed McCarthy to act as the club's managing general partner until the Boss could convince Vincent to lift the "permanent" ban. Vincent demanded a meeting with McCarthy to discuss his role in running the club. A defiant McCarthy told Vincent, "We don't work for you; you work for us." Vincent, remembering that McCarthy had sued him the year before, rejected McCarthy's candidacy: "It's not in the best interests of baseball for McCarthy to be the permanent general partner of the Yankees." Steinbrenner, hearing the news while attending the Winter Olympics in France, returned angrily to New York to confront the commissioner. He then named his son-in-law as the surrogate president of the club.

To Steinbrenner's surprise, he found a group of unlikely allies when he publicly denounced Vincent for his handling of the investigation: the other owners. While acknowledging the commissioner's right to discipline and suspend the Yankee boss for his involvement with a known gambler, many owners were appalled at Vincent's heavy-handedness during the investigation. What really incensed the other owners was the fact that Vincent did not provide Steinbrenner with the basic constitutional rights that anyone, in or outside of baseball, is entitled to. Vincent, in essence, told Steinbrenner that the only right he had during the investigation was "the right against self-incrimination." Steinbrenner was not even given the right to keep confidential private conversations and correspondence between himself and his attorney.

As the owners continued to castigate the commissioner privately for his treatment of Steinbrenner, Vincent looked for a way out of his dilemma. The public—and particularly the average New York fan—was behind him. After all, for almost fifteen years Steinbrenner had been portrayed by the national media as the bully, the big city loudmouth who would go to any means and any cost to get his way. He was an inviting target for Vincent to hit, particularly since there had been an involvement with a gambler. The "Best Interests of the Game" power was created for issues like this. Nonetheless, Vincent now found his own job in jeopardy, even though Steinbrenner had signed the agreement. And why had Steinbrenner agreed to give up control over the Yankees? Because of his involvement with the U.S. Olympic Committee (USOC).

According to a high official in the USOC, Steinbrenner was afraid that if he did not relinquish control of the Yankees, Vincent would have suspended him for being involved with a gambler. "How could we have allowed him to continue his involvement with the Olympic delegation if he had been suspended from baseball because of a gambling tie-in?" the official rhetorically asked. Instead, Steinbrenner had agreed to resign from running the club without admitting any wrongdoing.

Vincent knew that the public fallout would be bad if he reinstated the Boss, but there were bigger battles on the horizon that he was more worried about. So he called Steinbrenner and informed him of his decision. Since he had originally planned to suspend Steinbrenner for two years before they agreed on the permanent ban, and since two years had gone by, Vincent told the Yankees owner he could return to the Bronx on March 1, 1993.

Steinbrenner immediately requested a meeting with the commissioner to discuss the March 1 date. While flying from Tampa to New York, he was suddenly informed that Vincent had changed his mind again. The commissioner told the press that he had been tipped off by some unnamed Yankees employees that Steinbrenner had secretly run the club from Tampa during his exile. If this was the case, the ban would not be lifted. However, after interviewing several Yankees officials, Vincent announced that maybe Steinbrenner wasn't responsible for the team losing ninety-one games in 1991 after all.

Vincent's public waffling on *l'affaire* Steinbrenner only further convinced most of the other owners that he lacked the leadership traits needed to hold the game together.

The commissioner had also embarrassed the owners in the spring of 1990 during their lockout of the players over collective-bargaining issues. As both sides were close to reaching an agreement, Vincent held a press conference to present his own settlement proposal, in which he suggested that the players give up their right to strike in return for the owners agreeing to end

their lockout. The substantive issues would be left for further negotiations once the lockout ended.

Don Fehr and the other union leaders found Vincent's scheme
ludicrous, claiming that if they accepted it they would be giving
up the only leverage they had (the right to strike) to reach a new
agreement. Vincent further weakened the Player Relations Committee's bargaining position by inserting himself into the process
and pretending to be a neutral party. The union took Vincent's
proposal as a thinly veiled attempt by the owners to derail the
settlement negotiations. They were incensed and almost called off
negotiations. Vincent was told by the owners to keep out of labor
matters. But Vincent couldn't resist. After all, wasn't he the commissioner of baseball, and wasn't it his job to do whatever was in
"the best interests of the game"?

Having upset both the players and owners, Vincent then took a
jab at one of baseball's sugar daddies. At the winter meetings in
Miami, the commissioner made light of ESPN's financial losses on
its baseball contract by saying, "Where would ESPN be without
baseball? There are only so many tractor pulls and billiard matches
you can televise." He later admitted that the comment was inappropriate, but the arrogance of the statement was not lost on either ESPN or CBS. For two years baseball's television partners
have been trying, with no success, to have Vincent at least admit
that baseball should try to work with them to alleviate their financial losses.

A couple of months later, Vincent made another public statement that he came to regret. Through the efforts of the local com-
munity in Seattle, including many key politicians, a prominent
group of local businessmen put together an offer to buy the Seattle
Mariners from Jeff Smulyan in order to keep the team in Seattle.
The financial muscle of the group would immediately make the
Mariners one of the most stable franchises in baseball. The ownership group consisted of the pillars of the business community in
Seattle, including executives from Microsoft Corporation, McCaw
Cellular Communications, Boeing, and Puget Power. However,
the majority owner would be the Japanese family that created the
Nintendo video games, whose American plant employed 1,400
people in Seattle. Before the Ownership Committee had even

studied the proposal, Vincent held a press conference and said baseball's ownership "has addressed" the issue of foreign investors and has "developed a strong policy against approving investors from outside the United States and Canada." He further stated that the approval of the Japanese offer was "unlikely."

The local press had a field day with Vincent's statements regarding local ownership, since none of the prior Mariners owners had lived anywhere near Seattle, while the president of Nintendo's American subsidiary and his family had resided in the Washington community for fifteen years and intended to stay there. The fallout from Vincent's comments was immediate. The congressional contingent from the Pacific Northwest, including Speaker of the House Tom Foley, announced that if baseball turned down the offer to keep the team in Seattle and allowed the club to move to Florida, there would be a bill submitted before Congress to remove baseball's antitrust exemption, as well as a costly lawsuit against the sport.

Before the owners had even responded to the ownership-transfer proposal, Vincent's comments had put them back on their heels. Vincent's own deputy, Greenberg, quickly stated that baseball's owners had never developed a public policy against foreign investment and that Vincent was out of order in his comments because he does not have the authority to speak for the Ownership Committee. But the damage had been done.

After the national press blasted baseball for its handling of the Mariners' ownership problems, Vincent suddenly decided that Super Mario, the hero of the Nintendo games, and his friends would be just dandy running a baseball team and that the commissioner would help lead the fight to keep the franchise in Seattle. But Vincent's attempt at exerting leadership only convinced many owners that once again he had meddled in business affairs outside of his jurisdiction.

Vincent's ego then suffered a serious bruise when the owners agreed to pay Richard Ravitch, a prominent New York businessman, a higher salary than the commissioner. The owners had hired Ravitch to do one thing: reduce labor costs as the head of the Player Relations Committee. The owners' hiring of Ravitch, and at a higher salary than Vincent's, sent a message to the commissioner. Stay out of labor-related matters, which we consider more important than and independent of your chores as commissioner.

Vincent was furious when he heard that Ravitch was to be paid more than he, particularly since Ravitch had been hired to replace Barry Rona, whom Vincent had fired. But the owners got their message across. They still remembered Vincent's failed attempt in 1990 to insert himself in the battle between the clubs and the players during the owners' lockout during spring training. The Ravitch hiring sent a clear message to the commissioner. Sooner and not later, Vincent, like his predecessors, would be gone from baseball.

As he made plans for the long Memorial Day weekend, Vincent looked at his phone messages. Which owner should he call back first? Should he randomly pick one from a small market or one of the heavyweights? Of course, it didn't really matter; in either case, someone was calling to complain. The commissioner decided he might as well see what Bud Selig had on his mind. Selig told the commissioner that he would meet him in his office to discuss a proposal he wanted to run by him. Vincent was in for a shock.

Soon after arriving at Vincent's office, Selig and Fred Kuhlmann of the Cardinals, another member of the Player Relations Committee, made their pitch. The PRC wanted to send a message to the players' union: Don't expect the commissioner, as had always been the case in the past, to be a participant in the upcoming labor negotiations. Kuhlmann and Selig then asked Vincent to agree to give up his "best interests of the game" power to intercede in labor negotiations.

If it hadn't been for Peter Ueberroth, the meeting would never have needed to take place. One of Ueberroth's conditions for taking the job of commissioner was that the owners agree to add a new major league rule to prevent them from unilaterally reducing the commissioner's powers during his term in office without his approval.

Vincent refused the owners request, and by doing so sealed his fate. His days as commissioner were now numbered. He quickly got on the phone to his public relations director, Richard Levin, and told him to get ready to go on the offensive.

CHAPTER FOURTEEN

STORM CLOUDS ON THE HORIZON

THE WALDORF-ASTORIA, JUNE 1992

April is a false start. The baseball season really begins after Memorial Day each year. Kids get out of school, the weather starts to warm up, CBS decides that maybe it's time to broadcast a game on free television, and clubs begin to find out if their pitching staff can hold up throughout the summer.

The 1992 season was no different. At least the outcome of the games played on the field bore a resemblance to prior seasons: June arrived with the Toronto Blue Jays, Minnesota Twins, St. Louis Cardinals, and San Francisco Giants ahead in their divisions. Over half the clubs in baseball were within a four-game winning streak of first place, and as usual, the Cleveland Indians were not one of them.

But the owners could have cared less. The clashes off the field were heating up too. It seemed that all the problems that had been confronting the sport suddenly ignited at the same time. And Commissioner Vincent was the lightning rod attracting the most attention.

As usual, an invitation to appear on a national television program—in this case "Larry King Live!" in Washington—got a quick and favorable response from Vincent. As the commissioner was leaving his office to catch the shuttle, Jerry Reinsdorf, between a couple of Bulls playoff games, called from Chicago. He told the

179

commissioner that he and Fred Kuhlmann, who besides being on the Player Relations Committee was chairman of the Ownership Committee, wanted to meet Vincent in Washington to fill him in on their committee's decision about the Mariners sale. The three met in Washington on Tuesday, June 2.

Vincent was not in a particularly good mood. His appearance on "Larry King Live!" had not turned out as he had expected. Instead of being able to use the show as an opportunity to expound on the wonderful game of baseball, he instead was blasted by irate Astros fans, who called him up because he had criticized them two weeks before in Houston for not supporting the team's efforts to find a new buyer.

Reinsdorf and Kuhlmann disclosed to Vincent that they and the other members of the Ownership Committee were going to recommend that the purchase of the Seattle Mariners by the Japanese be approved by all the clubs, provided that the new owners agree not to exert any control over the day-to-day operations of the ball club. As the ownership meetings were to take place the following week in New York, Reinsdorf and Kuhlmann wanted to make sure that the commissioner understood their decision so he wouldn't embarrass them again and release some statement contrary to their recommendation.

Sitting in his hotel suite, Vincent knew that the two club executives standing before him had more on their minds than just a briefing on the negotiations surrounding the Mariners sale. He was right. Having failed with Selig at his side, Kuhlmann was hoping that Reinsdorf's presence would sway the commissioner to agree not to step in during the upcoming labor negotiations. Again, Vincent refused. The two owners then instructed Vincent to meet them in Chicago two days later for a full meeting of the PRC.

At the Chicago meeting Vincent was informed that the impetus to remove him from labor negotiations had come from a cross-section of more than ten owners from both leagues. Reinsdorf urged him to reconsider his decision. "Look, if you're not involved, no one can blame you. You can tell the press that you don't have any power to influence either side during labor negotiations," Reinsdorf explained. But Vincent refused to reconsider his position and returned to New York to face the most trying week of his administration since the San Francisco earthquake two years before. The private feud between the owners and their appointed leader was about to be played out on a very public stage. But first the commissioner had to deal with another ugly public relations matter. The week would begin with a controversy involving drugs and the New York Yankees.

On Monday, June 8, Vincent called a press conference to announce that he was going to punish Steve Howe, a relief pitcher with the Yankees, who had pleaded guilty to a charge of attempting to possess cocaine. Vincent immediately told the assembled sportswriters that he was suspending Howe from baseball indefinitely. It was not the first time Howe had been caught in a drug sting; this was Howe's seventh suspension for drug abuse, going back to Bowie Kuhn's administration. Despite being disabled, suspended, restricted, and released on several occasions, Howe had outlasted three commissioners. Besides New York, his road show had included stops in Los Angeles, Minnesota, Texas, Tabasco (Mexico), and points in between. The odds were pretty good that he would be back, once again throwing his fastball in the majors, long after Vincent had departed. The Players Association, naturally, filed a grievance with arbitrator Nicolau to have Howe reinstated.

The independent arbitrator reminded the union that he was already hearing arguments on their grievance that the recently adopted changes to the draft of rookies should be ruled illegal, since it had not been negotiated with the players through collective bargaining. Scott Boras and other agents were testifying in Los Angeles against the draft changes when Howe's suspension was made public. Several other grievances were on the docket as well. But since Howe's hearing involved the playing status of an active major league player, his case took precedence over the others. Nicolau told the commissioner that he had to be more specific regarding the "indefinite" status of the suspension. So Vincent changed the "indefinite" to "permanent." Steve Howe would become the first player in major league history to be banned from the sport for a drug violation. The Players Association and Dick Moss, representing Howe, immediately filed another grievance to reinstate the pitcher.

No sooner had Vincent announced the Howe banishment than the phone rang in the commissioner's office. An embarrassed owner was calling to see if Vincent would give him a loan. Tom Monaghan and his ball club, the Detroit Tigers, were about to default on their biweekly payroll payments. The commissioner quickly authorized $5 million to be advanced to the Tigers from baseball's central fund, which collects royalties from the superstation teams and from the various corporations that have licensing agreements with major league baseball. Monaghan, the founder of Domino's Pizza, was in trouble: Pepsi-Cola's subsidiary, Pizza Hut, was making serious inroads into Domino's market share and the company was now being controlled by its banks.

Monaghan, according to one American League owner, "had sucked everything out of the Tigers for his personal gain." Along with six other clubs, the Tigers were up for sale. Vincent, however, downplayed the crisis, saying that lots of clubs borrow from the central fund all the time. "There was nothing unusual about the advance. I feel the story was blown out of proportion," he said. Naturally, the owners, trying to convince the players that the clubs really were losing money this time, were not thrilled by Vincent's comment.

On the eighteenth floor at 350 Park Avenue—one floor up from Vincent—Player Relations Committee director Dick Ravitch had been on the job for six months, but the walls of his office remained bare, giving the unmistakable impression that he could move out (or down one flight of stairs) in an hour's notice, if necessary. Ravitch was unknown to the local and national baseball media that converged on New York for the owners' meetings. But he would soon emerge as a key player in the internal battle that was about to rock baseball.

Ravitch looked at his calendar. He had less than six months to decide whether he would recommend to the owners that they reopen the collective-bargaining agreement with the players, which would quite possibly lead to a lockout of the 1993 season. If a lockout took place, Ravitch knew, it would be the big one. The hawks had warned him that if the players refused to accept a salary cap and wage scale formula to control spiraling salaries, the industry would have to be shut down. But before he even began to plot his strategy to confront Don Fehr and the union, Ravitch had two more important problems to deal with.

First, he knew that his biggest hurdle was to get a consensus of his twenty-eight owners and then hold them together during the negotiations. He was upbeat about his chances. "I bring a different perspective to this job," he said. "Having been successful in business, I understand that the twenty-eight club owners have different economic self-interests. I also understand that negotiations between the players and the owners have historically taken place in a fishbowl." The owners shouldn't be so concerned about pleasing the press, Ravitch scoffed. A sign hung on the door to his office as a constant reminder: "Today's newspaper is tomorrow's fish wrapper."

He would need help to resolve his second problem: finding a way to keep the commissioner out of the negotiations. "One voice has to speak for management," Ravitch concluded, echoing every PRC director's lament since the owners created their committee in 1967. Selig, Reinsdorf, and most of the other owners also agreed.

The club moguls arrived at the Waldorf-Astoria expecting a heated debate over the issue of the Japanese purchase of the Seattle Mariners. Instead, the foreign buyers agreed to the restrictions placed on the club's purchase—specifically, limiting their involvement in the day-to-day operations of the club—and the owners voted to approve the sale in less than an hour. Later that afternoon Selig called the PRC board of directors together to once again ask the commission to reconsider his position on removing himself from any negotiations with the players.

Seven of the nine PRC members, including the presidents of the American and National leagues, supported the move, with only the Mets' Fred Wilpon and the Houston Astros' John McMullen opposing it. Wilpon, the commissioner's strongest ally among the owners, was opposed to any dilution of the commissioner's powers. Having plenty of cash to throw around in the free agent market each year, the Mets ownership was not interested in supporting the other clubs in their threat to lock out the players in order to curb the rapid escalation of salaries. McMullen, always one of the most militant owners, had his club on the market for sale and needed Vincent's support. Suddenly McMullen's allegiance shifted from the other members of the PRC to the commissioner, even though he privately confided to several that he was behind the hard-liners.

For the fourth time in less than a week, Vincent told the owners—his employers—that he would not agree to their request. Later that afternoon accounts of the private meetings were "leaked" to the press. Several owners accused the commissioner of waging a public relations battle against them by using the media for his own self-serving purposes. "It's ridiculous. He works for us, but whenever he doesn't get his way he calls a press conference to justify his decision," one owner said.

USA Today and the *New York Times* both leapt to the commissioner's defense. The next day, two story lines emerged. The first was that Vincent had survived a surprise coup and was now in total control. The *New York Times* headline read: "Vincent Repels Move to Cut His Power on Labor." The other was that Vincent had somehow saved the game for 1993: "Vincent Saves the Game Again," *USA Today* proclaimed.

While some owners were furious, others could only laugh. "I kept wondering if I had been at the same meetings I read about," one owner said. Contrary to the *USA Today* story that only a "small fraction" of owners had been involved, twenty-two to twenty-five owners had backed the PRC recommendation to keep Vincent out of the labor process. "We eventually have to confront the union on the matter of the structure of the game, as more and more teams simply are not making money," said one ownership representative. "The way it is now, the commissioner has the ability, at whim, to undermine the authority of three-quarters of the clubs. The eighteen or nineteen small-market teams have met and have a definite agenda, and the lack of attention from the commissioner regarding economic issues is upsetting to many of us in small markets. This isn't a league issue, it's a market issue."

Even though much of the media, including the *New York Times*, reported that a lockout of the 1993 season was all but certain, the PRC and its president, Ravitch, had not decided whether or not to reopen talks on the labor agreement. One reason for waiting until

1994 involved the commissioner, of course. Since Vincent's contract expired on March 31, 1994, the clubs could wait until then, not rehire Vincent, and turn the powers of his office over to the Executive Council (i.e., Reinsdorf and Selig). Ravitch wouldn't have to worry about a meddling commissioner under that scenario. But Ravitch still would have preferred to get the commissioner's agreement to just stay out of negotiations. As one owner said, "We have to have some bargaining strength, just as the players always have their war chest." The owners were concerned that if Vincent was allowed to exert himself in the labor process, with the power to open camps and undermine a lockout, they would lose their leverage. They were incensed at his refusal to back off. By Thursday, the commissioner realized that his support consisted of only Fred Wilpon, Eli Jacobs of the Orioles, maybe John McMullen of the Astros, and George Bush, Jr., of the Rangers, whose father was an old friend of Vincent's.

Vincent called the owners together and tried to downplay the rift. He explained to his bosses that he understood the role of the PRC and that Ravitch had been hired to handle the negotiations. According to many owners who attended the meeting, the tenor of his remarks was conciliatory as he emphasized his awareness that the PRC had a job to do and that Ravitch would be handling all the negotiations and that he would not interfere. He also said that he agreed it was important for one voice to speak for management. The owners left the meeting more united than ever to take a hard stand against the players. They also assumed that when Vincent said that management should be represented by only one voice, he was referring to Ravitch. They were in for a surprise.

As the owners were checking out of the hotel, Vincent quickly returned to his office across the street. Within the hour, he had Levin summon columnist Hal Bodley of *USA Today* and reporters Murray Chass and Claire Smith of the *New York Times* to his office. He then gave his spin to the series of events that had occurred during the week. He informed the writers that he had been responsible for the successful sale of the Mariners by summoning Reinsdorf and Kuhlmann to Washington and telling them to get the deal done. He then "revealed" that he had successfully fought

off a palace coup, led by Reinsdorf, Selig, and Ravitch and including only a small group of owners. Finally, he mentioned that he
had held a meeting of the owners earlier that day in which "I
made it clear that I have no intention of changing my authority
under the Major League Agreement." Friday's papers presented
to the public the image of a strong commissioner rapping the
knuckles of a small group of subservient owners.

Bodley's column ran under the headline, "Owners Heed Vincent's Stern Message." According to Bodley, "The owners had
been lectured, shocked, and embarrassed, but Vincent rebuffed
the attempted power play." Bodley then went on to say that
Wednesday night at the owners' dinner, "One owner after another approached Vincent, shook his hand, and congratulated him
on his leadership of the past ten days. Owners who had been on
the fence were now proudly in his corner." Bill Giles, owner of the
Philadelphia Phillies, could only laugh.

"That was a private dinner," Giles said. "Bodley wasn't there,
and I sure don't remember a row of owners coming up to the
commissioner and congratulating him," Giles continued. "As a
matter of fact, the events that occurred that week were about a
hundred eighty degrees different than was reported. Except for
two or three clubs, we all came away convinced more than ever
that the commissioner has to be removed from the upcoming
player negotiations."

And so the month of June ended with Howe out (maybe) and
Steinbrenner back in (shortly), to the chagrin of many Yankee
fans, who felt that their team had lost out in the exchange. The
Japanese were finally allowed in, but only to pay the bills. Once
again, St. Petersburg was left out. After six months on the job,
Dick Ravitch was settling in, while Commissioner Fay Vincent was
under attack to get out. The Detroit Tigers were tapped out, while
the Baltimore Orioles in their new ballpark were cashing in. At
least the game played between the white lines was more predict-
able: The Blue Jays and Twins were still in, while Cleveland was
still out.

Donald Fehr and Marvin Miller were amused by it all. By strength-
ening the commissioner's powers, the owners had helped

strengthen the bargaining power of their most bitter adversaries. It was all so ironic. While the commissioner is supposedly the highest authority in the game, he works for the owners and can only exert his power in labor negotiations over them, and not over the players. If the clubs decide to lock the players out, the commissioner—swayed by public sentiment—could invoke his "best interests of the game" powers to force the clubs to open up their gates. On the other hand, he could never force the players to accept a labor proposal based on the "preservation of the integrity of, or the maintenance of public confidence in, the game of baseball." No commissioner ever has, and no commissioner ever will.

When Judge Landis was granted his powers by the owners, there was no agreement with the players. It was not necessary back then—the players did whatever the clubs wanted them to do. While all commissioners over the years have invoked their authority, they have never dared to use it against the players' union. If a commissioner ever ordered the union, for instance, not to go out on strike, Fehr and his colleagues would wake George Nicolau out of a deep sleep to get their grievance heard before sunup. They know that the commissioner's mystical power over them would be shown once and for all to be an illusory force. As a result, they want the commissioner involved in labor negotiations. He can only weaken the owners' position, by pretending to be neutral.

During the 1990 negotiations the owners had inserted into the collective-bargaining agreement language that supposedly gave the commissioner the power to be the final arbiter in any dispute between the clubs and the players over issues involving "the integrity of, or the maintenance of public confidence in, the game of baseball." However, the players reserved the right to renegotiate the agreement if the commissioner were to ever inject himself in a dispute between the owners and the players. Fehr then had Vincent write a personal letter to him, which was attached to the agreement, in which the commissioner said that he would never take any action that would "negate rights of the players under the new Basic Agreement."

The owners had been checkmated once again, because the Basic Agreement between the players and the owners also says that no major league rule can be unilaterally changed by the clubs if the change would detrimentally affect the players. So even if the owners were able to persuade Vincent to give up his power, the Players' Association would probably file a grievance against the owners, because keeping the commissioner out of labor negotiations is clearly detrimental to the players' best interests. The owners were stuck with their loose cannon unless they could force him out of office.

The game was on the brink, and the inevitable showdown between the owners and the players was only months away. The rhetoric was all too familiar. Selig and his colleagues warned of failed franchises, players out of jobs, reduced revenues from television, and the end to "The Greater Fool Theory." "There will be no waiting line of wealthy entrepreneurs clamoring for the chance to buy a baseball franchise," Selig warned. "The economics of the game are disastrous. As Paul Volcker told me, 'The business of baseball is an economic anachronism,' " Selig bemoaned. Volcker, the former chairman of the Federal Reserve Board, was an appointed member of the Joint Economic Study Committee, which was set up by both the owners and players to study the problems facing baseball.

According to Selig, franchise values have not only peaked, but are now declining. "More than a third of the clubs would sell if they could find a buyer. And this notion about cities without major league baseball longing for an expansion franchise or encouraging an existing team to relocate is nonexistent. The cities that have been discussed—St. Petersburg, Phoenix, Orlando, Indianapolis, Washington, Vancouver, and the Carolinas—are all comparable to the smaller cities already in baseball. The present economics wouldn't work in these cities either."

The Milwaukee owner then fired a volley at the union. "The Players Association refuses to believe several clubs are in financial difficulties, and most of the owners are convinced that the union will only open its eyes when a club or two goes into bankruptcy. However, that would have a disastrous impact on our sponsors. The chairman of the Miller Brewing Company warned me that advertisers don't want to be associated with sick industries." Selig would make sure that Ravitch got all the support he needed.

Here we go again, Fehr retorted. The Nintendo people just

bought the weakest franchise in baseball for $125 million, $117 million more than the original cost of the franchise fifteen years before, he exclaimed. If the industry-wide problems are so bad, why don't the big-market teams share more of their local TV money with the smaller markets? Fehr wondered. And just last year, Fehr added, cities were crawling all over themselves to pony up and pay $95 million to get an expansion franchise in the National League, *before* paying even one player's salary.

The 1992 season was approaching the halfway mark. Fehr and his chief lieutenants, former Orioles shortstop Mark Belanger and union counsel Gene Orza, huddled in their offices at 805 Third Avenue. It was time to start the preparations. The first bulletin was ready to go out. Fehr issued a memo to all the players informing them that the initial distributions from the collusion settlements would probably be made in early 1993. It was a not-so-subtle reminder of the union's past victory over the owners for trying to control salaries. It was also the first wake-up call to the troops. As in past campaigns, many more would follow. Ravitch was rallying his forces also. He now knew that he had the commissioner on the run.

Meanwhile, a tired Fay Vincent completed his annual visit to all the ballparks and returned to his summer home on Cape Cod for a vacation over the Fourth of July. He did not send George Steinbrenner a birthday card. The fireworks exploding in the distance were a reminder of the combustible state of affairs engulfing the national pastime. Looking across the bay, the commissioner focused on the menacing clouds forming on the horizon. A northeaster was approaching. Unless the weatherman was wrong, it was going to be a particularly long and nasty one.

CHAPTER FIFTEEN

THE FINAL THREAD

THE ALL-STAR BREAK, JULY 1992

Each year major league baseball shuts down for three days in July to showcase its stars in the annual All-Star Game. A festive atmosphere surrounds the break as summer vacationers tune in from the mountains and shores while backyard grills are still warm from the Fourth of July celebrations. Coming as it does so close to the most patriotic of holidays, the All-Star Game has always been symbolic of baseball's heritage as the national pastime. And major league baseball makes sure that the red, white, and blue bunting is prominently displayed for the national television audience. Those chosen by the fans to play in the game are being rewarded for their great performances over the first half of the season. Those not so lucky get to spend the three days at home relaxing with their families. Because the World Series is the only other time that players from the American and National leagues compete against each other, the July contest is a rare opportunity for each league to promote its "brand of baseball" against the other's. For all these reasons, "The Midsummer Classic" always receives high television ratings and the networks consider it, along with the playoffs and World Series, among the "crown jewels" of the sport.

The 1992 All-Star Game in San Diego was shaping up as another public relations winner for major league baseball. The weather forecast for the game was perfect, President Bush was planning to attend, and San Diego's favorite son, Hall of Famer Ted Williams, was lined up to throw out the first pitch. Even CBS was buoyant: The projected ratings for the game would keep it in first place for the week against ABC and NBC. The network told the Democrats in New York that they could forget about coverage of their national convention that night.

Unfortunately for Commissioner Vincent, the 1992 All-Star Game was only a momentary stop on his downhill run. Shortly before the game, he announced that it was in "the best interests of baseball" for Chicago and St. Louis to move to the National League West and Atlanta and Cincinnati to the National League East, under a realignment proposal to begin in 1993, when the Florida Marlins were to join the National League East and the Colorado Rockies the National League West.

Vincent thought he was safe on this one. Even his most diehard opponents had to agree that it made little geographic sense for the Braves and the Reds to be in the Western Division while the Cubs and the Cardinals, two teams closer to the Pacific Ocean, played in the East. He assumed that the National League clubs would applaud his decision since all of them, except the Cubs and the Mets, had voted in favor of realignment. In fact, five National League clubs—San Diego, Montreal, San Francisco, Pittsburgh, and Atlanta—had encouraged him to get involved. But no sooner had he announced his decision than the rest of his bosses from the National League became more infuriated than ever with him. By forcing the realignment on the National League without their approval, Vincent managed to turn the wrath of the league owners away from the Tribune Company, whose selfish motives in opposition to the realignment were being denounced by the press, to the commissioner himself.

Outgoing National League president Bill White, who had been trying for months to persuade the Cubs to change their position, was the most vocal opponent of Vincent's decision. With pressure from the other National League owners, he thought he was making some headway with the Cubs. His office was putting the finishing touches on a flexible schedule for the 1993 season that would allow WGN-TV to continue to broadcast most of the Cubs games early enough to lead into the station's lucrative late-evening news. By ordering realignment, Vincent had cut the legs out from under the league president, and White feared that the commissioner's decision was a potential knockout blow to the independence of the two leagues. Why have separate leagues with their own constitutions if the commissioner can overrule them? the National League president wondered.

The Tribune Company did not sit idly by. Once again, another test of the commissioner's "best interests of baseball" powers was being launched. The Chicago Cubs quickly sought an injunction in federal court to block Vincent's realignment order. The Cubs contended that they were suing on behalf of their "inconvenienced" fans, who would suffer a hardship if the majority of their games were to start later because of the West Coast matchups. The public didn't buy it. The Tribune, as owner of both the Cubs and superstation WGN-TV, was really concerned that it would lose viewers, and therefore revenues, because of the delayed telecasts. On a more technical charge, its suit also contended that the National League's constitution forbids the transfer of a team to another division without the club's approval. Although the Major League Agreement between the clubs gives the commissioner broad discretionary powers to take punitive as well as legal action in case of any conduct by clubs that he believes is not in the best interests of baseball, the Cubs argued that the agreement also says that the clubs are not subject to the commissioner's jurisdiction if the constitution of either major league expressly provides for a resolution by other means. And the National League constitution addressed the procedure for its member clubs to follow regarding realignment.

Vincent looked around for support, but none was to be found. Even the clubs that favored realignment wanted the league to resolve its differences internally. Sure, some old-fashioned arm-twisting by the commissioner would be appreciated, but not an all-out confrontation pitting his "best interests of the game" powers versus the league's own procedures for handling the matter. Vincent arrived in San Diego to find out that a fax was circulating among the owners to get him to resign. Peter O'Malley, the instigator, had joined the bandwagon. Realizing that the O'Malley power broker days were over, the Dodgers owner was trying to get active again. As the owners pressed for his resignation, Vincent said he wouldn't quit.

Reinsdorf then told the press that before Vincent was hired, Kansas City Royals owner Ewing Kauffman reminded the other American League owners that Peter Ueberroth had taken pleasure in saying that he couldn't be fired. "Can't we do something about that?" Kauffman asked his fellow owners before they voted on Vincent's appointment. According to Reinsdorf, he then went to Vincent's hotel room and asked the then deputy commissioner whether he would agree to resign if he lost the support of a majority of the owners. Reinsdorf remembers Vincent saying that since the owners were about to vote on his nomination, he didn't think it was appropriate to change the Major League Agreement. However, "I can assure you that if I ever lost the support of a clear majority of the owners, I would have to resign; no commissioner could operate under those circumstances," Reinsdorf quoted Vincent as saying. Vincent told the media that he didn't remember the conversation.

The issue of realignment was a relatively minor one in the scheme of things. But the battle over the commissioner's power to overrule league constitutions was and is a fundamental reason why the Major League Agreement between the clubs, the independence of the two leagues, and the future role of the commissioner has to be completely overhauled if the club owners and Richard Ravitch and his successors are to have any chance of reaching some kind of lasting agreement with the players. And Vincent was making matters worse.

Another use of his "best interests of the game" power had backfired as well. During arbitrator Nicolau's hearing on the grievance filed by the Players Association to reinstate Steve Howe, three Yankees officials, including general manager Gene Michael and field manager Buck Showalter, had been called as character witnesses by the Players Association. Ironically, the third Yankees official, Vice President Jack Lawn, had headed up the federal Drug Enforcement Agency under President Ronald Reagan.

The Yankees' testimony was what one would expect. They told the arbitrator that Howe was a fine baseball player, a good teammate, a fierce competitor, and that the Yankees were a better team with him than without him. They obviously would have preferred to have Howe continue playing, and their bias was understandable. The lawyers representing the commissioner's office should have left well enough alone. Normally, the PRC's lawyers, well versed in labor law, handle all grievance issues between the league and the Players Association. But because of the growing rift between Vincent and Ravitch, the commissioner hired a couple of criminal lawyers instead.

On cross-examination they asked the Yankees officials whether they agreed or disagreed with the lifetime suspension given to Howe. Showalter said that he guessed he disagreed with the severity of the suspension, but added that it was not his role to make these kinds of judgments; he was having a hard enough time trying to stay out of the Eastern Division cellar. His boss, Gene Michael, said that he used to be much more conservative about drug offenders, but by being around Howe, he had become more sensitive to the view that drug abuse is a sickness in many cases. He now questioned whether someone should be permanently banned from his or her employment because of a sickness. The commissioner's lawyers refused to let up. Would Michael feel the same way if the player had been banned for gambling? Michael wasn't sure of the relevance of the question, but answered that he still felt society should try to help sick people, and not just punish them.

Michael Weiner, a lawyer for the Players Association at the time, never really thought that the Yankees executives would help their case much. He knew that under the best of circumstances it was an uphill climb to have a arbitrator reduce the suspension of a player convicted of a substance abuse violation, and that in Howe's case the climb was akin to scaling Mount Everest. Even though the three Yankees officials had mentioned that they were not in total agreement with the commissioner over lifetime suspensions, Weiner felt that their testimony would carry very little weight with arbitrator Nicolau. The case soon took a very different direction.

Deputy commissioner Stephen Greenberg reported back to Vincent with his notes regarding the testimony given by Michael and

Showalter. The next day Vincent summoned the three Yankees officials to his office at 11:00 A.M., two hours before the Yankees were to play the Kansas City Royals. They were told that they could not bring a lawyer. Michael was particularly upset. Only two weeks before, the commissioner had called him in to interrogate him regarding George Steinbrenner's involvement in running the club during his exile. On that occasion Vincent wouldn't let Michael bring the attorney he had chosen because Vincent thought the lawyer was too friendly with Steinbrenner. Now, Michael was being reprimanded for personal views that had been pried out of him by the commissioner's own lawyers.

When the Yankees game started without Showalter in the dugout, the press knew something was up. The media quickly scurried to the commissioner's office for his briefing. Suddenly, the press reported that the commissioner was considering suspending Michael and Showalter for having testified as character witnesses for Steve Howe. The Players Association was indignant. Was this an attempt by Vincent to intimidate other witnesses they might call?

Union chief Don Fehr was further outraged when he heard that not only had the commissioner reprimanded the two Yankees officials, but he had relied on Greenberg's notes and not on the official transcript of the hearing for his conclusions.

"We'll subpoena people if necessary to find out what went on between the commissioner and the Yankees people," Fehr said. "I'm at a loss to explain what is going on over there at the commissioner's office. Things are getting a little weird," Fehr said. The commissioner's actions now gave the Players Association a new angle to pursue in the hearings. It would make the commissioner's motive the focus of its defense. Was there some secret agenda to enhance his power that had led him to permanently ban Howe? they wondered.

George Nicolau postponed the hearing for a few days and told both sides to cool down. He then announced that he would not reopen the case to hear evidence of possible pressure put on the three witnesses by Vincent. But he also ordered that Howe be evaluated by medical specialists to see if he had a medical disorder that contributed to his habit. The Players Association then went on the attack. It filed a charge with the National Labor Relations Board (NLRB) accusing Vincent of using his office to intimidate witnesses against testifying on behalf of the players' union. It also filed another grievance with Nicolau.

The documents sent by the Players Association to the NLRB really embarrassed Vincent's bosses. Lawn told the NLRB that at Howe's grievance hearing he was "sworn to tell the truth and I only testified in accordance with my conscience and my principles." Vincent was incensed at his testimony, and according to Lawn, the commissioner barked at him: "You should have left your conscience and your principles outside the room."

Suddenly Vincent, and not Howe, was under attack for the whole incident. Realizing that he had made a mistake, the commissioner sent a memorandum to the owners saying he would be more prudent in the future before jumping into the middle of a grievance hearing, but by then it was too late.

The commissioner himself put an interesting spin on the matter in an interview with *Newsweek*'s David Kaplan just before the All-Star Game. In response to Kaplan's question of whether he had miscalculated in hauling in the Yankees officials, Vincent responded, "We all have to be aware that taking views that are matters of conscience—that are in conflict with our employers—might cost us our employment in a rare case." Vincent's employers were in agreement. They were making plans for his retirement.

The Major League Agreement states that the question of reelection of a commissioner can be considered by the owners fifteen months before his term is up. Since Vincent's contract was to expire on March 31, 1994, the earliest the owners could vote on his future was December 31, 1992. They were hoping that he would resign before then. If not, they were already planning to take their "no-confidence vote" and then fire him before his term was up. They knew he would probably fight it, but they were prepared to take their chances. They did not want Vincent to be involved in the negotiations regarding the new television contract, much less the upcoming labor confrontation.

The All-Star Game had barely ended with the American League routing the National League 13–6, when Nicolau handed down his decision regarding the owner's new plan for the June Amateur Free Agent Draft: He threw it out. The owners, by trying to unilaterally change the system without getting the players' approval, had lost again. Nicolau's ruling was another blow to the owners' attempt to run their business without the players' involvement.

The owners had voted to change the draft rules in March. During spring training, Vincent had told Bill Conlin of the *Philadelphia Daily News* that the draft plan wasn't his idea and, according to Conlin, strongly implied that the scheme had been drawn up by the PRC and Ravitch.

"That's a damn lie!" Ravitch exclaimed. "I told the owners at the March meeting that at best they had a fifty-fifty chance to win a challenge to the change. It was my advice to put it on the table as part of the next collective-bargaining package."

Ravitch's outburst was understandable. Now that Nicolau had ruled that the changes could not be made, the Player Relations Committee president had lost a bargaining chip with the union in the upcoming negotiations. There would be no way that the players would agree to change now. And, as Ravitch knew too well, Nicolau was still deciding what penalty to impose on the owners for their actions. He might even abolish the draft completely, which would really make Ravitch's job tough.

White Sox owner Jerry Reinsdorf admitted that Ravitch had tried to persuade the owners not to unilaterally change the draft at the March meeting. Reinsdorf had agreed. It wasn't because he opposed the plan. But he knew that the union would file a grievance and was concerned that Nicolau would side with the owners. "If we had won the grievance, we would have left ourselves open to an antitrust lawsuit. Even though we had three top law firms give us the same opinion—that the players wouldn't win—why take the chance?" Reinsdorf said.

An unlikely source corroborated Ravitch's protest that he wasn't responsible for the rule change. "It came from Steve Greenberg and Bill Murray, who worked out of the commissioner's office," the Players Association's Gene Orza revealed. "Of course, Vincent and Greenberg are the perfect stalking horses for the owners. With their academic backgrounds, they honestly believe that it looks bad for baseball to compete against the colleges to get kids to turn their backs on a college education to play baseball. The owners, naturally, only care about taking the leverage away from the kids to go to college. So they hide behind the commissioner's rationale for changing the draft because it sounds good to the public. But, no, neither Ravitch nor anyone else from his office was behind it," Orza confirmed.

A week later U. S. District Judge Suzanne Conlon dropped a bigger bombshell on the commissioner: She granted the Cubs' request for an injunction. "It is clear the broad authority granted the commissioner by Article One of the Major League Agreement is not as boundless as he suggests," Judge Conlon wrote in supporting her decision. Furthermore, she added that the provisions of the National League constitution are clearly intended "to protect the substantial interest of an individual club in its divisional assignment from adverse action by the majority."

The commissioner quickly appealed her decision, and it seemed likely that the case would end up in the Supreme Court. Since Bowie Kuhn had prevailed over both Charley Finley and Ted Turner when they'd challenged his powers, Vincent was confident that Conlon's decision would be overturned. But if his gamble was wrong, the limitation on the commissioner's most cherished power would be a devastating erosion of the office's authority to act as an unbridled judge, jury, and prosecutor in the future. On the other hand, if the commissioner won, the integrity of each league to run its own business was in jeopardy. Vincent had succeeded in creating a greater than ever rift between the commissioner's office, the leagues, and the various club owners. The confusion over management's ability to conduct its business would only make the upcoming negotiations with labor more difficult.

And so the second half of the season started with Mark McGwire chasing Roger Maris's home run record, Robin Yount and George Brett closing in on 3,000 hits, Nolan Ryan adding to his strikeout total, and Carlton Fisk throwing runners out as he chased Bob Boone's record for most games caught by a catcher during a major league career.

Meanwhile, off the field the owners were fighting among themselves while trying to get their designated leader to quit because he couldn't be fired. As bad as their internal squabbles were, they were having even less success in letting the independent arbitrator and a federal judge resolve their differences for them.

The news from their broadcasting partners wasn't any better: CBS wanted a refund from Major League Baseball and ESPN was about to tell them that it was not going to pick up its option for 1994.

On the most important problem affecting the future, Richard Ravitch was trying to decide whether to confront the players over salaries now or wait for a year. At the same time, dozens of the game's top players did not have a contract for the 1993 season. Then again, there was no assurance that anybody would be playing in 1993.

If anyone was counting on the Joint Economic Study Committee to develop a consensus on how to straighten out the mess, all he or she had to do was to call up the executive director of the Players Association.

"I wouldn't hold my breath," Fehr said about the committee's chances. "The owners have basically told us that they won't agree with us on anything until we acknowledge that the clubs are all going under." Bud Selig, of course, saw the problem as just the opposite. "The players won't even consider a change to the system until a club or clubs go broke." The Milwaukee owner then announced that once again the report from the Joint Study Committee was being delayed. It might be ready by the end of the year, he hoped.

While the committee representing the owners and players was agreeing not to agree, Vincent called together a committee made up of other conflicting interests. Four representatives from the big market teams and four from their smaller counterparts were trying to figure out, in the words of the Red Sox's John Harrington, "how to fit one shoe into another" regarding revenue sharing of local broadcast rights. Unlike Selig, Harrington was at least realistic: He wasn't setting any date for his committee's report. It was just as well. Harrington's committee would be the last one appointed by Commissioner Francis T. Vincent.

On September 7, 1992, three years after Bart Giamatti and Fay

Vincent went to Cape Cod for a Labor Day vacation from which Giamatti never returned, Vincent informed the owners from his summer retreat on the Cape that he was resigning immediately "in the best interests" of baseball.

In the end it had been swifter than they had planned. At the urging of Jerry Reinsdorf and Bud Selig from the American and Bill Giles and Peter O'Malley from the National leagues, the two league presidents called a special meeting of all the owners in Chicago on September 3 to consider the powers and term of the commissioner and to hold a debate on whether Vincent should be asked to resign. They also asked the commissioner to join in the discussions.

Vincent refused the invitation, denounced the meeting in a five-page letter as illegal under the Major League Agreement, and hired Brendan Sullivan, a prominent Washington lawyer, to represent him.

Defying Vincent's threats, the owners met in Chicago and passed a resolution that was supported by eighteen of the clubs stating that there was a lack of confidence in Vincent and asking for his immediate resignation.

Vincent immediately informed the press that he would never resign and would fight the owners' actions all the way to the Supreme Court, if necessary. The issue was clear cut. Did the owners, who hired him, have the right to fire a commissioner whose broad powers could not be diminished while he was in office? The majority of owners felt they could, while Vincent publicly stated that a firing is the ultimate diminution of power.

But over the Labor Day weekend Vincent realized the inevitable: He might win the battle, but clearly he would lose the war. While the lawyers on both sides would be collecting their hefty fees, March 31, 1994 would arrive long before Clarence Thomas and his colleagues would get their opportunity to decide the commissioner's right to stay in office. Vincent realized that once his term expired the owners would completely overhaul the Major League Agreement and radically change the powers of the commissioner to oversee the game in the future. And so Vincent quit, and for the first time in seventy-two years baseball no longer had a commissioner. One owner, in particular, thought it was about time.

Walking unrecognized down Chicago's Michigan Avenue, Jerry Reinsdorf doesn't appear to be the most prominent sports figure in Chicago, and probably the most powerful figure in both major league baseball and the National Basketball Association, but he is. Who else has his phone calls returned by Bo Jackson, Michael Jordan, and NBA commissioner David Stern? They do so because he is their boss.

Besides owning the White Sox, Reinsdorf, along with several other investors, purchased the Chicago Bulls in 1985. Having made his fortune in real estate syndication, Reinsdorf knows how to negotiate a deal involving bricks and mortar, and in 1988 he used the leverage of moving the White Sox to Florida to persuade Chicago to build his club a new Comiskey Park. A new Chicago Stadium for his Bulls, financed by a consortium of Japanese banks, is in the works.

Reinsdorf, along with Bud Selig, is the most influential owner in baseball. He has been actively involved on the three key committees that run the game: the Ownership Committee, the Executive Council of Major League Baseball, and the Player Relations Committee. He was one of the new kids on the block when Ueberroth came in as commissioner, but he quickly immersed himself in all facets of the game. Because he and Selig are the only owners who spend the majority of their time focused on their sports businesses, Reinsdorf has achieved the respect of his peers—even George Steinbrenner. Since he also happens to own a franchise in one of the major markets, Reinsdorf, unlike Selig, has power as well as influence.

Reinsdorf's main interests are the Bulls and the White Sox, and not necessarily in that order. Even though he owns two of the premier franchises in sports today, his all-time favorite team is still the old Brooklyn Dodgers, whom he idolized as a young boy growing up in New York. Memorabilia from the Brooklyn team adorns his office high above Michigan Avenue. One gets the feeling that he doesn't like the O'Malley family very much, in large part because of Walter's uprooting of the Bums during Reinsdorf's childhood.

While respecting their business acumen and the success that Walter and his son Peter have had with their franchise out west, Reinsdorf is convinced that the O'Malleys have always placed the Dodgers' best interests above the collective interests of the industry. In Reinsdorf's mind, whether it was propping up a weak commissioner like Bowie Kuhn or signing Kirk Gibson after the collusion decisions, the Dodgers owners, instead of helping to solve baseball's problems, have contributed to them. Having controlled the commissioner's office for so many years, the Dodgers were reluctant to support any attempt to centralize baseball's business operations. Reinsdorf agrees that Ueberroth went too far, but he is no fan of Vincent either.

The ever-present cigar, dark-rimmed glasses, and noticeable trace of a Brooklyn accent are what one notices first on meeting Reinsdorf. His accessibility and even temperament leave more lasting impressions. Both friends and rivals marvel at his capacity to shrug off public criticism, some of which has been downright vicious. He keeps several of the more irate hate letters from fans, including one in which his life was threatened when he proposed to move the White Sox to Florida. While the leaders of the players' union consider him to be the most militant owner in attempting to control player salaries, they begrudgingly admit that he'll give you his candid opinion on a subject, whether you agree with him or not. His opinion of Fay Vincent is one example:

"We rushed too fast in naming Fay as commissioner after Bart died. But we were in the middle of the season, Bart had been everyone's choice, and no one wanted to go through the lengthy process that led to Ueberroth's appointment. Looking back, we should have named Fay as interim commissioner and taken our time."

Reinsdorf feels that NBA commissioner David Stern is the perfect commissioner for the times. "Stern makes no apologies for what his job is, which is to make as much money as possible for the owners. Vincent, on the other hand, spends too much of his time talking to the press. He's obsessed with his public image."

Reinsdorf admits that the institution itself may be partially at fault. Because its traditional interpretation conflicts with the practical demands of a changing game, the baseball commissioner's job has become impossible for one man to fill.

Reinsdorf and many other owners feel that Bowie Kuhn, besides lacking management skills, was too tied to the O'Malley camp to have been an effective leader. Ueberroth, a strong manager, was brought in primarily to generate more revenue for the owners. But while he succeeded in filling the clubs' coffers, he had little sensitivity to the other nuances of the job. When he resigned suddenly, Giamatti was hired quickly. The consummate intellectual, Giamatti realized that his strengths were not in business and administration, and he reached out to Vincent to be his "nuts and bolts" man.

The job of chief executive officer was perfect for Vincent; but according to many owners he was a failure as baseball's commissioner because he did not show the one personality trait they felt baseball desperately needed: leadership. The circumstances under which he expelled George Steinbrenner, his attempt to resolve the impasse between the players and the owners during the last collective-bargaining agreement, his failed attempt to generate humor at the expense of one of baseball's television partners, his statements regarding Japanese ownership, his handling of the Steve Howe case, his fight with the Cubs over realignment, and his opposition to the broadcasting of games by superstations were cited as examples of his lack of leadership.

As usual, Reinsdorf's partner, Eddie Einhorn, has his own opinion of the office of the commissioner. "Look, the role of the commissioner is outdated. Landis was brought in to clean up the game and deal with the scandals that existed. The 'integrity' issues were there long before the union organized or the big economic issues came about." In Einhorn's view, Vincent was not the problem—the role of the commissioner is. "The game hasn't changed, but the world has. Just because records go back one hundred years doesn't mean you don't change to keep up," Einhorn argues. The commissioner's office as presently structured, he feels "slows the process down."

Vincent may have believed that he was different from all the other commissioners, but he was not. His preoccupation with taking polls, talking to the press, and visiting every ballpark during the course of the season all come with the territory, and always have. When Einhorn refers to "the process being slowed down," he is referring to the time constraints on the commissioner to both act as a public ambassador and also perform his duties as the "protector of the integrity of the game." Neither function brings any added value to the bottom line.

Reinsdorf believes that Vincent was as much to blame for the state of things as the structure of the office is. "Fay takes great pride in the fact that he visited every club last year during the season. Do you know how many man-hours that amounted to? Those hours could have been better served concentrated on other matters." Other owners have also suggested that Vincent's health has been a drain on his ability to perform the tasks expected of him. As one owner said, "He spent all day on administrative matters that should have been delegated, and then he would go home every night at five o'clock exhausted." The process was not slowing down; many felt that it had come to a grinding halt.

Giamatti's untimely death may have actually accelerated the inevitable demise of the commissioner's role as baseball's leader. A charismatic figure, Giamatti was ideally suited to play the role of the Sun King. He could overpower the owners with his intellect while convincing the public that he was, after all, like them, just an ordinary fan. Kuhn could do neither, while Ueberroth had no desire to try.

Giamatti enjoyed the role of conciliator. It reminded him of chairing a faculty meeting at Yale. "Baseball people are no different than members of a faculty. They both spend a large amount of time talking to colleagues on the phone. They defend their own departments religiously; they argue passionately for hours on the most minute matters; and they both are ultimately concerned about their own tenure and perpetuating their institutions."

As the head of a major university, Giamatti understood his role as the chief fund-raiser for the institution. Placating egos of prominent alumni while asking for capital contributions was no different than responding to the whims of self-made millionaires who own baseball teams. Likewise, chairing faculty meetings where professors complain out of frustration about the lack of funding for programs is very similar to overseeing two baseball deans (presidents of the American and National leagues) and twenty-eight department heads (general managers) who also vent their frustrations over economic issues beyond their control. And, of course, the continued survival of the institution depended on his ability to keep the students (or in this case the players) in the classroom and not out on strike.

Giamatti was astute enough to know that he had the perfect background to fulfill the traditional role of commissioner—indeed, it would be his mission to raise it to a higher level—but he also knew that he lacked both the training or desire to run the business side of the game. Fund-raising had been the least enjoyable part of his tenure at Yale. He was convinced that Fay Vincent would be the perfect person to assist him in this area.

Besides appointing Vincent to be baseball's first deputy commissioner, Giamatti continued to restructure the office of commissioner after taking over from Ueberroth. While Ueberroth had forced the owners into agreeing to consolidate many of their powers under the commissioner's domain, Giamatti decided to expand the office itself. He would personally oversee baseball operations, public relations, and player issues. Vincent would run the business side, and a holdover from Ueberroth's and Kuhn's administrations, Ed Durso, would be responsible for legal, financial, and security affairs.

Giamatti's plan to restructure the commissioner's office would have worked for a while because of the sheer magnitude of his personality and his great communicative skills, but the twin economic tornadoes of spiraling player salaries and disproportionate revenue sharing among the clubs would have eventually blown him away. With Vincent's help, Giamatti probably would have delayed the inevitable, although the institution would still have had fundamental problems. Vincent on his own had no chance.

Two weeks after Giamatti's death, Durso left to join the ESPN cable network as its senior vice president and legal counsel. Vincent then chose Steve Greenberg to fill what amounted to both

Durso's and Vincent's prior jobs. Vincent would oversee everything. But the political infighting among the owners and the overriding importance of structuring a new financial partnership with the players sealed Vincent's fate.

Einhorn's comments are accurate: It was not Vincent's fault. The owners allowed the role of commissioner to develop the way it has. The fundamental problem is that while he is supposed to represent some higher interest and act as prosecutor, judge, jury, and executioner over his employers, he is also supposed to take orders as their chief executive officer and provide leadership in putting their financial house in order. But since the commissioner has no economic stake in the business he runs (he is paid as a salaried employee only), he instead grasps at the power with which he has been endowed. Faced with the problem of choosing where to focus the majority of his time, he will always gravitate toward the public prestige associated with being the Almighty Protector of the Game.

Kuhn became a symbol of the owners' malaise and had to be removed. Ueberroth realized that the owners would not reelect him after he grabbed, consolidated, and used the power of the office to chasten them, so he decided to quit, especially when he realized he could make a lot more money doing something else. Giamatti, with his background in academics, considered personal financial gain secondary and had an understanding of how to use power to satisfy his personal needs without being destroyed by it. He, perhaps, would have survived.

Vincent was doomed to fail because he lacked Ueberroth's forceful style or Giamatti's powers of persuasion. As a result, he was unable to forge a consensus of owners behind him. While he relished his role as the traditional protector of the game's heritage, whether, in his eyes, George Steinbrenner or the Japanese were the threat, in the end he was considered by the owners to be their greatest liability. Likewise, he defended his accomplishments as baseball's chief executive officer, supervising the day-to-day running of baseball's central office as well as the various departments in charge of developing new marketing opportunities. But a majority of the owners felt that he was partially to blame for the declining revenue projections of the sport because of his focus on other matters. And in spite of the owners' urging, Vincent couldn't resist meddling in labor negotiations, since he understood that resolving the labor impasse is the most important issue facing the game today.

As Vincent returned to New York to clean out his desk the owners headed to St. Louis for their quarterly meetings. The owners quickly stripped the commissioner's office of the various functions that had been consolidated there during the Ueberroth and Giamatti reigns.

To the surprise of no one, Bud Selig was affirmed as the de facto commissioner in his new role as chairman of the Executive Council. A ten-member Restructuring Committee was formed to redraft the Major League Agreement, so that a new commissioner, similar to the NBA's David Stern, could be selected within a few months. Naturally, Jerry Reinsdorf would play a key role on this committee.

Boston's John Harrington, Bill Giles of Philadelphia, and Tom Werner of San Diego were named to a three-man committee to negotiate the national television agreements. And Richard Ravitch was in full command to run the Player Relations Committee without a meddling commissioner.

As the twenty-eight owners returned to their businesses around the country and Canada, time was running out for the sport that prides itself on not having a clock. The games on the field might be played without a watch, but the games contested outside the white lines are ruled by it. The business of baseball is controlled by deadlines. And the most important one in its history was approaching fast with neither side having a clue what to do about it. If they had, they would have seen that even with all of its problems, baseball's next hundred years held the promise of being even more entertaining—and profitable—than its first.

PART III

FUTURE ENCOUNTERS

CHAPTER SIXTEEN

FREEING UP THE MARKET

W hen the baseball all-stars left San Diego to rejoin their teammates around the country, another group of talented athletes was making its way across the Atlantic. Basketball fans from
around the world were eagerly waiting for the European debut of
the United States Olympic team.

But the "Dream Team" of NBA superstars had another port of
call to make before it docked in Barcelona for the 1992 Summer
Olympiad. As part of the inducement to persuade Michael Jordan
and company to leave their golf courses for two weeks during July
and August, the NBA had arranged with the basketball players'
union for the team to train in Monte Carlo before the Olympics. As
the players were wined and dined by Prince Rainier and his royal
family, held free public clinics, and attended the famous casinos in
their fashionable tuxedos, the league received unprecedented media coverage from an adoring international audience.

Six months before, the Spaniards had thought another team
was coming to Barcelona. Major league baseball announced that
the St. Louis Cardinals would spend a week in Barcelona during
spring training, playing exhibition games against a Japanese all-
star team as a prelude to the Summer Games, where baseball
would be an official medal sport for the first time. The trip was all
arranged, and the European sports community was anxious to see
the game of baseball played by a top professional team. But the
commissioner's office and the Cardinals had forgotten one small
detail: They never got official approval from the players before

announcing the games. Two weeks before the team was to leave St. Petersburg, Florida, the games were canceled.

The Cardinals and the league had "assumed" that the players would be thrilled to leave Florida in March for a trip to Spain, and had left the details to the lawyers to work out. In baseball, that usually means trouble. The Players Association said "sorry, no deal" when the league refused to reveal the financial arrangements, leaving the Cardinals and baseball with a self-inflicted black eye to explain to their foreign promoters. Of course, they immediately blamed the greedy ballplayers. Meanwhile, huge Michael Jordan murals were being plastered all over Barcelona, and on every street corner it seemed that a fan was wearing an NBA-licensed product. Things had improved quite a bit for the National Basketball Association in ten years.

In 1982 several NBA teams were on the brink of collapse. The sport was rocked by a series of drug scandals. The league had no marketing strategy and the public was turning its back on a game played predominantly by blacks from the inner cities. Sure, Magic Johnson and Larry Bird arriving on the scene at the same time in 1980 had helped. And in 1984, Michael Jordan's grand entrance completed the triumvirate. But what really rescued the NBA was a novel revenue-sharing agreement entered into between the clubs and the players in 1983 to save the league from bankruptcy.

In return for the clubs agreeing to pay the players 53 percent of the league's gross revenues, the players agreed to a salary cap whereby no club could spend more than $2,640,000 on its payroll, or an average of $220,000 per player. Over the years, there has been some tinkering with the formulas, and while sometimes the clubs are as confused as their fans as to the interpretation of the rules, the system has been a financial success for both sides. Today, the average player in the NBA makes over $1 million a year. Besides the lucrative financial rewards of the agreement, the NBA and its players are true partners, so that when Commissioner David Stern announced a new TV contract with NBC a few years back, a beaming Charles Grantham, the head of the players' union, sat at his side.

In the summer of 1990, shortly after the NBA announced its new TV package, Michael Jordan's agents were lining up a million-dollar promotion that would involve the Chicago superstar competing one-on-one against another NBA star, supposedly Magic Johnson, at a Las Vegas casino as part of a made-for-TV special. Almost immediately, the NBA, in tandem with the union, including several prominent players such as Larry Bird and Isiah Thomas, denounced the contest. Bird was quoted in the Boston papers as saying that it would not be good for the NBA's image to have two of its top players competing in a contest to take place in the gambling capital of the United States. The public applauded Bird's reaction; the NBA and its union successfully squelched the idea; and the league and its plays won high marks for their concerns about the integrity of the sport.

Chicago Bulls owner Jerry Reinsdorf, someone who is quite familiar with Michael Jordan and the NBA way of doing things, gives a more accurate interpretation of the story. "We convinced Michael that his one-on-one promotion would potentially detract from our television contract and licensing agreements with our exclusive sponsors. Since the players benefit more than we do, peer pressure certainly played a role in convincing Jordan to drop the idea."

When Magic Johnson suddenly announced in 1991 that he had tested positive for the AIDS virus, the entire league came to his support. At the press conference at which he made his stunning public revelation, Commissioner David Stern was at his side to announce that the league would give Magic all the support he needed. It is hard to imagine anyone from baseball's ownership doing that for one of its players under the same circumstances.

The NBA and its union have a joint drug program that is very specific in how it treats an offender. The agreement calls for different levels of discipline based on whether the player turns himself in or is caught, whether it is his first or second offense, and so on. Contrast this to major league baseball—the Steve Howe case, as an example—where disciplinary action is unilaterally handed out by the commissioner and is automatically followed by the union filing a grievance, thus forcing an independent arbitrator to decide if the suspension should be allowed. It's been this way since Bowie Kuhn, and it is no different now than it was then.

Having the perspective of owning franchises in both leagues,

Reinsdorf calls the relationship between owners and players in basketball "refreshing." Naturally, he would like to see a revenue-sharing formula, coupled with a cap on salaries, implemented in baseball.

"Why fix the system if it isn't broken?" Gene Orza from the Players Association asks. Orza and the rest of the union's leadership have become laissez-faire economists. "Let the free market work. Salaries respond to revenues. If revenues come down, salaries will come down."

The pendulum has definitely swung in the other direction. Up until 1990 the union was always more anxious than the owners to commence negotiations on a new agreement, as the players were seeking changes to the old ways of doing things. In particular, the players were looking for additional benefits to their pension plan, the removal of restrictions that prevented them from freely moving from one club to another, and the negotiation of salaries for younger players through binding arbitration. But in 1990 the players changed positions with the clubs—the teams sought concessions and major changes to the system while the players were satisfied with the status quo. Fehr's comment about the difficulties facing the Joint Economic Study Committee graphically points out the predicament faced by the owners in convincing the players that economic chaos is around the bend. The athletes have heard this tune before, and it has always been followed by greater prosperity through larger television contracts and franchise appreciations.

The PRC's Richard Ravitch shares Reinsdorf's views regarding the need for baseball to take a page from the NBA. He also warns Fehr and the union that if they are waiting for an NBA scenario to occur before they agree to a major rehauling of the system, it will be too late. "The NBA was at the bottom of the curve when they struck their deal with the players. The upside potential was all there. Franchises were going for a song and the national television contract was relatively small," the PRC chief explains. "Now look: Clubs in baseball aren't going to go under—someone will always put up the seed money to see if the dog will talk. But the amount they are willing to spend is going to come down," Ravitch argues. Fehr and Orza, however, point to the recent sale of the Mariners,

Tigers, and Astros for higher-than-expected amounts to refute Ravitch's prophesy.

Around and around it goes. Enough.

Baseball needs to do three things to resolve its messy affairs and get on with a strategy to compete with basketball and soccer on the international stage. First, the owners need to remove all business and labor issues from the commissioner's office. Second, they should restructure the central office under a chief executive officer who is not the commissioner. And third, with one unified voice, the owners need to strike a meaningful partnership arrangement with the players.

Before they take on the players, the clubs must first resolve their own internal problems. Baseball's central office now has five major executives with different roles and responsibilities: the commissioner, the vice commissioner, the president of the Player Relations Committee, and the presidents of both leagues. In their place, the office of vice commissioner and the two league presidents should be abolished, and a new corporation should be established to run the business side of baseball, headed up by a chief executive officer chosen by a board of directors that includes a representative of the players.

The primary function of the CEO of Major League Baseball, Inc. should be similar to that of any other head of a Fortune 500 company. The day-to-day operations of the sport, all agreements affecting revenues, and all major decisions that affect the collective interests of the clubs should be under his control, subject to the board's approval. One of his major areas of responsibility should be long-range planning, with the primary focus on the international arena. There is no need for a deputy commissioner, whose present job is to be the chief operating officer of baseball. A chief executive officer with a strong background in business—unlike Steve Greenberg, with his legal background—would run the day-to-day operations of the central office. The CEO of the industry must be a dealmaker with political instincts whose job would be to bring added value to the bottom line.

The commissioner, whose domain has included these duties in the past, would be hired by both the owners and the players to

perform two specific tasks: first, he would be the public spokesman for the game; and second, he would act as the final arbiter on
issues affecting the integrity of the game. While these duties would
be similar to his present powers, he would have no active involvement in either the financial or labor matters of the sport. The
present system does not work; one man cannot do all these jobs.
The commissioner, like Caesar's wife, must be above suspicion,
but unlike Caesar, he should not be all-powerful. George Nicolau,
who in essence is the present final arbiter on all issues, would be
the perfect commissioner of the future. Peter Ueberroth, or perhaps Richard Ravitch, would be ideally suited to run the corporation. Fay Vincent himself was qualified for that job when he was
brought in by Bart Giamatti to be the first deputy commissioner.
Giamatti's instincts were correct: Baseball needed a capable businessman to run the shop. But the shop was just too big for one
man.

In conjunction with the reorganization of baseball's central office, the tradition of having two league presidents should be done
away with. Certainly it is important to maintain the autonomy of
each league, both for historical and business reasons. As Phillies
owner Bill Giles points out, baseball is the only sport that remembers a team for being the runner-up. Who can recall who the
Boston Celtics beat in the 1960 NBA playoffs? But every baseball
fan knows that the New York Yankees won the American League
pennant in 1960 and lost in a dramatic seven-game series to the
Pittsburgh Pirates. Eddie Einhorn and several other owners, primarily from the American League, have proposed the elimination
of the two leagues and the creation of separate conferences, à la
the National Football League. Peter O'Malley, Bill Giles, and Atlanta's Bill Bartholomay—all National League executives—wish
the league presidents would spend more time selling the game
and visiting the various cities to promote their leagues instead of
focusing the majority of their attention on scheduling and dealing
with umpire issues. But the leagues should not compete with each
other off the field. Only the commissioner should be a spokesman
for the game.

While the league presidents are no longer necessary, the leagues
should remain independent; but there is no reason for the leagues

to continue with their own archaic rules, which are often in conflict with the other league's rules. As an example, umpires from the two leagues should call balls and strikes the same way and should be under the auspices of the commissioner and not under a supervisor who is a former umpire as is the case now. The controversy over the use of the designated hitter should be resolved, one way or the other. For the fan, the rivalry between the leagues would continue. But behind the scenes, the central office of the game would be far more efficient. Issues such as realignment and expansion would be decided by the corporation, representing the majority's interests, and not, as now, by the leagues, who have their own self-interests to promote.

Finally, the PRC should continue as a separate corporation under the jurisdiction of the owners, with the sole authority to negotiate all collective-bargaining issues with the Players Association. Neither the commissioner nor the chief executive officer of Major League Baseball, Inc. should have any control over or say in labor-related matters. Kuhn, Ueberroth, and Vincent contributed to the friction that has developed between the players and the owners by becoming active participants in the labor process.

When the owners and the players get around to sitting across from each other, the first thing they should do is shake hands and acknowledge that they are partners. They then must agree on what the industry really earns. All sources of revenue should be on the table, including national television contracts; local broadcasting revenues; gate receipts; concession incomes; licensing agreements; and international income from licensing rights and broadcasting fees sold abroad. Ideally, the Joint Economic Study Committee will have done much of the number crunching and the union will be able to find its own economists to verify the accuracy of the numbers.

Once the revenue numbers are agreed on, it is imperative that players and owners settle on the percentage of revenues that will be put aside to cover the following: the players' pension; funds needed for other player benefits; and a deferred-compensation fund to pay a player, after he retires, an annuity accrued out of a percentage of his earnings withheld while he played. By establishing a deferred-compensation plan on a league-wide basis, Major League Baseball and the Players Association will address a problem that has existed since the first professional player received a paycheck: how to insure that no player leaves the game broke once his playing days are over. Too often players have had to strip out their pensions before they were even scheduled to start kicking in. The recent public revelations of slugger Jack Clark's bankruptcy filing is only the latest example of the financial disaster that has left many players destitute.

Once the owners and the players come to an agreement as to what the total revenues are and what percentage of them should be applied to the fixed player expenses, they both must let a free market system determine salaries. Up until now, both sides have been reluctant to let it work. Marvin Miller once told Jerry Reuss, a key member of the union's leadership during his days with the Los Angeles Dodgers, that his fear was that the owners would agree that all players could become free agents at the same time. Miller felt that with a flooded market of talent, the bidding process would be limited and overall salaries would come down. Don Fehr admitted the same concern to the Joint Study Committee. Except during the period of collusion, the one-two punch of free agency and arbitration has worked its magic for the players: A few key free agents drive up the market each year, and then, based on those new salary plateaus, arbitrators award even higher salaries to arbitration-eligible players than were granted the prior year.

The owners have also always feared a true open market. According to the union's Gene Orza, "The owners are in favor of a competitive market when they are the sellers of the commodity, but not when they are the buyers. If Miller Beer and Budweiser offered the same deal to a club, the owners would scream 'anti-trust!' as loud as they could." Major league baseball clearly cherishes the order and stability that a monopoly brings, as the owners have repeatedly argued that unrestricted free agency would destroy the competitive balance between the clubs by allowing the big-market teams to horde all the top players. But the reduction of the reserve clause through free agency has shown the opposite to be the case. George Steinbrenner and Gene Autry have proven over the years that an open checkbook does not lead to a full trophy case.

There seems to be only one negotiated settlement under which the marketplace can be trusted by both sides to set players' salaries. What if the players were willing to give up salary arbitration in return for unrestricted free agency? In other words, what if every player could negotiate with whomever he pleased whenever his contract was up? While a club might lose a budding superstar after one season, at least it wouldn't be forced to pay its other young players salaries that an arbitrator forced on it based on the salaries that other clubs paid their players.

One of baseball's most powerful owners has considered the trade-off. "We'd have to think about it," Reinsdorf says.

"We owe it to our players to consider it," Orza responds. "I know of Marvin's past concerns, but how could we not take that to our players? All we've ever asked is that ballplayers be treated like everyone else is in society and have the right to choose where they want to work."

The solution seems clear: Let the free market dictate salaries. If the players are right and revenues continue to go up, then salaries will follow. If, on the other hand, the television-contract and other revenue streams slow down, salaries will come down. If any player could sign with whatever club he chose when his contract was up, there would be no need to have an arbitration system. Eliminating the arbitration process would be a victory for Bud Selig and the small-market owners. The big-market clubs could afford to bid for free agents. The smaller-market teams could take a tip from the Cleveland Indians and tie up their young talent with long-term contracts.

For almost twenty years, the players have fought to remove all the restrictions that have been placed on free agency through prior collective-bargaining agreements. Likewise, the clubs have always tried to lessen the worth of a free agent by attaching some form of compensation to him. In the early days, there was a free agent draft and the clubs could only sign a certain number of players. The present encumbrance on a free agent is the amateur draft pick that the club who signs the free agent must give to his prior club. If the players are finally allowed to negotiate at any point in their careers as unrestricted free agents, the arbitration process—the owners' main complaint—would be eliminated. With the collusion decisions handed down by the independent arbitrators, and the agreement by clubs to be liable for treble damages in the future, the players now have the protection they need in the future in case an open market suddenly shuts up again. Under the changes proposed, baseball's future labor problems would be greatly reduced.

The clubs' payrolls, and success on the field, would be more dependent on front office talent than on some part-time arbitrator. This is the way it should be. Minnesota's Andy MacPhail, Atlanta's John Schuerholz, and Oakland's Sandy Alderson have succeeded in bringing championships to their communities despite the market size of their cities. The small-market teams have nothing to fear by opening up the market completely.

A highly respected commissioner, chosen by both the owners and the players, would emerge as the spokesman for the game, assuring the public that its traditions and integrity will be preserved. And a chief executive officer would insure that the process, in Eddie Einhorn's words, does not "slow down." Major league baseball could then get on with the rest of its business and try to catch up with other sports. Its television partners are waiting in the on-deck circle.

CHAPTER SEVENTEEN

PAY YOUR MONEY AND TAKE YOUR CHOICE

Perched above the mostly silent crowd in his luxury box overlooking the new Comiskey Park, Eddie Einhorn sighed, "There's no excitement in the air. This series means nothing. The fans are already more interested in Notre Dame's upcoming football game against Michigan."

There were two weeks left in the 1991 season when the Oakland Athletics traveled to Chicago for a two-game series with the White Sox. Both teams had been mathematically eliminated from the race in the Western Division of the American League. When the schedule makers had announced the series early in the year, it had been assumed by most that the two games would play a key role in determining the divisional winner, as the teams were preseason favorites to win the American League pennant. Instead, the game had no bearing on the outcome of the race.

"Baseball is the only professional sport that practically shuts down before its season is over. Except for a couple of clubs that still have a chance of winning their division, the public is already thinking about football," Einhorn said. At the time, the White Sox and A's were battling with Texas to see who would end up in second behind the Twins. "This place would be rocking," Einhorn continued, "if the winner stood a good chance of making the first round of the playoffs."

Ever the promoter, Einhorn was thinking about two extra tiers of playoffs to generate additional revenues for baseball. This was important to the owners, because their broadcasting partners had already announced that the rights fees paid to major league baseball would be coming down at the conclusion of the highly lucrative contracts negotiated by Peter Ueberroth.

Before he resigned, Vincent had told the clubs that they should expect about a third less, or $5 million per club. But based on the expected losses of $700 million by CBS and ESPN on their combined $1.46 billion, four-year deal, many in the industry predicted that the new agreements would be cut in half. Since Florida and Colorado would be sharing in the future contracts as well, the clubs were potentially looking at a drop of $8 million apiece in annual revenues.

Jon Mandel was a voice in the dark. Peter Ueberroth had not even yet negotiated the record-breaking contracts with CBS and ESPN when Mandel of Grey Advertising was quoted in a *Sports, Inc.* October 17, 1988 article as being concerned that whichever network got the package, it would probably lose money, and it would not be a good deal for either the network or Major League Baseball. At the time he made his prediction, Mandel's firm represented forty-two national accounts, including Mitsubishi Motors, Quaker State Oil, and Domino's Pizza. He was proven right.

Yes, the recession has hurt. But the viewing public has consistently turned off the national game as more and more local games are made available on cable. There has been a steady decline in CBS's ratings since it captured the contract from NBC in 1990. Einhorn candidly admitted what a lot of fans would second: "The dollars we have received are the highest ever while the quality of the game being played is the lowest."

When ESPN bid for the baseball contract, it wanted to do two things: first, increase its visibility as a big-time network, making *SportsCenter*, its evening studio broadcast, the one show people would watch for all sports news, especially baseball; and second, get high ratings. Steve Bornstein, ESPN's president, says it was a terrific idea, only the ratings weren't there. By the middle of 1992, the third year of the contract, ESPN had only been able to draw approximately half the ratings it thought it would.

CBS and ESPN did derive some benefits. ESPN's universe certainly grew, and it became perceived as the baseball channel, so if anything happened in the sport, baseball viewers turned to ESPN.

Meanwhile, CBS enhanced its image as the sports network, the playoffs and World Series were of tremendous value with its affiliates, and it regained the number one rating among the major networks.

CBS and ESPN decided that they wanted baseball in the future, but at a lower cost. ESPN was not interested in picking up the option for the 1994–1995 seasons, and instead tried to negotiate a new deal that would extend through 1999, which was rejected by baseball. One thing Major League Baseball made clear from the beginning with ESPN was that it didn't want too long a contract because eventually it planned to go in-house, either with a baseball channel or as some sort of package with other sports. There is no question that by the end of the decade, major league baseball will broadcast some of its games in-house, with the public being able to choose between two, three, or four daily games.

Both NBC and CBS lobbied baseball to remove ESPN from the equation as they told Vincent that if major league baseball would dump ESPN, they would ante up more money. However, because of the low ratings during the season, the two networks were unwilling to put baseball on during prime-time night hours. So, for the time being, the owners stood with ESPN. As Bill Giles said, "Baseball needs ESPN and ESPN needs baseball."

The first problem faced by the owners was deciding who was going to negotiate the agreements this time around. Most of the owners did not want Vincent to handle it, and his forced resignation was partially caused by the owners' fears that he would enter into new agreements while he still had the power. The options for broadcasting games in the future had become as varied and complicated as a Chinese menu. Besides the three major networks and the ever-expanding cable broadcasters, baseball's plans for an in-house network where it would sell its own ad time and create its own pay-per-view alternative was a viable concept. But before any negotiations with the networks could commence, baseball would have to figure out how to limit the growing appeal of the super-stations.

As CBS's and ESPN's financial woes continued to mount, the superstations from Chicago, New York, and Atlanta were attracting more and more viewers as new cable operators picked up the free programming. Peter Ueberroth had seen the menace that the superstations represented as soon as he was hired as commissioner. Not only were they a threat to the local monopoly that each team had in broadcasting its own games, but by saturating the country with free games, superstations were diluting the value of the national radio and television contracts as a whole.

Ueberroth's solution had been a practical one: Make the superstations pay a royalty fee into a central fund divided equally among all the clubs. As their audiences grew, so would the amounts collected by the central fund.

Ten years later, Vincent wanted Congress to pass a bill that would require local cable operators to black out superstation cablecasts whenever they competed with the games being shown on local broadcasts or cable TV. Bill Giles, an active member of baseball's television committee, opposed Vincent's proposal. "The superstations have been good for baseball. Since the superstations started broadcasting games several years ago, more people have been watching games on cable, and at the same time attendance at the parks has risen," Giles argued. "Besides, the superstations are now providing about fifty million dollars to the central fund each year. Are we going to be able to replace that from our other television partners? I don't think so. Also, aren't we better off handling these problems ourselves and not getting the government involved?" Giles warned.

There is no question that baseball will be going to an extra level of playoff games in the near future to expand its broadcasting revenues. Einhorn and Giles are behind it, and if the players are shown that it will generate more revenues for them to share in, they will be in favor of it too. There has been some movement afoot to divide the two leagues into three divisions, in a 5-5-4 format, with the best second-place team added to the playoff mix. More likely, the leagues will stay with two divisions and the team with the best overall record in each league would get a bye into that league's championship finals. The traditionalists would like this, since it would reward the team with the best record in each league, regardless of whether it plays in the Western or Eastern Division.

The non-division-winning team with the best record, whether it was from the East or West, would play the other divisional champion in the first tier of playoffs. The first round of playoffs would be a three-out-of-five format, with all the games held at the home park of the team that won the division. (The divisional winner should be given the home field advantage in the series as a reward for being the best in its division.)

By adding a new tier of playoffs, major league baseball would accomplish several things. Traditionalists have always argued that any inclusion of more teams in the playoffs would cheapen the importance of the regular season, but under the proposed format, the team with the overall best record in the entire league would be rewarded to a greater extent than it is now. Also, the new system would create additional excitement in the fall.

The playoff format would be as follows:

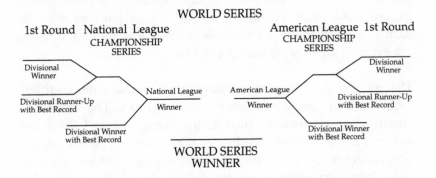

In 1991, Toronto and Minnesota won their divisions in the American League by comfortable margins as the rest of the league sighed the familiar refrain, "Wait till next year." However, if the non-division-winning team with the best record had also made the playoffs, seven other American League clubs would have been in contention going into the last weekend. In addition, Toronto and Minnesota would have had to continue to play hard after they clinched their divisions, in order to avoid the first series. Finally, as currently structured, the four-out-of-seven series between the divisional champs is rotated each year between leagues to determine who gets the extra home game. Under the proposed format, the team with the best overall record in the league would get it, as it should.

Baseball will probably offer an extra tier of playoffs initially to ESPN. This will undoubtedly be unpopular with the public, as many homes still do not have cable. The public will be even more upset a few years later. By 1997–98, most of the country will be sufficiently cabled so that not only will the first round of playoffs not be on a national network, it will be on baseball's in-house channel, which probably will broadcast the first level of playoffs on a pay-per-view basis. NBC and CBS would then split the league championship series, as in football, with NBC getting the American League and CBS the National League and the networks trading the All-Star Game and World Series in alternate years. The cable partner would continue to carry games during the week, but the pay-per-view option of the baseball channel would allow the fan, wherever he or she lives, to view his or her favorite team's games—for a price. For instance, if a Dodger fan was living in Asheville, North Carolina, there would be a way for him or her to get every Dodger game that is televised.

The owners are about to make another break with tradition: regular-season games between the two leagues will be introduced shortly. Natural rivalries such as the White Sox and Cubs will attract a huge audience, leading to higher ratings and additional advertising revenue for the networks, which in return will spell more money to major league baseball for the rights. Advertising executive Jon Mandel concurs that a limited number of interleague games would get great ratings. The Philadelphia Phillies recently polled their fans, and according to Giles, discovered that 80 percent of them would like to see interleague games, but not the creation of three divisions within each league.

Mandel feels that the networks should review once again a prime-time slot for "Monday Night Game of the Week," which was dropped by ABC in 1988 because only 6 percent of the public was tuning in. At the same time, its other prime-time shows were being watched by 15 to 20 percent of the viewing audience during the summer. But the networks' prime-time shows are now down to a 10 percent rating, and a 6 percent audience doesn't look so bad. If major league baseball were to present one interleague game a week, and hype it as a Monday night special, the package would be very lucrative, Mandel speculates.

The major problem that both networks and owners see is the decline in overall viewers of the major networks. A new generation is growing up with the fifty-seven-channel mentality—not the three channels that the older generation grew up understanding. The audience base is smaller and smaller and the competition for the entertainment dollar gets greater and greater. Five years ago there were fans of thirty-five to forty-five who were thrilled that they could see one, two, or three baseball games a night. In five years the twenty-year-olds of today will find it hard imagining a world without all of the new options—including being able to see just about any major league game being played, anytime.

Television viewing has already become highly fragmentized. Sports in general, and baseball in particular, will continue to offer more and more choices to a demanding public—at a steep price, of course.

More teams in the playoffs, regular-season interleague games, and pay-per-view will all come about before the year 2000. It is doubtful that Congress will allow major league baseball to put the crown jewels—the All-Star Game and the World Series—on a pay-per-view basis, but if a fan wants to watch anything else, it will probably be available to him only if he is willing to pay for it. What he will be paying to watch in the future will also include games originating from other parts of the world. Nippon TV may soon join the three major networks in bidding for World Series rights, particularly if it included a real "world series" between the winner of the Japanese title and the American champion. The Japanese baseball contingent is not the only foreign baseball promotor looking for a crack at beating the U.S. in a real World Series. America's national pastime is now being played throughout the world, and in some highly unusual places.

CHAPTER EIGHTEEN

THE INTERNATIONAL PASTIME

O n a warm summer's January evening a couple of years ago in a Fremantle, Australia restaurant, an American was reading aloud a story about the World Series of cricket. "How can it be the World Series of cricket?" exclaimed the American. "The only countries in it are Australia, New Zealand, and Sri Lanka."

"You're one to talk," said the waiter, slamming a platter of sizzling prawns down on the table. "You guys have a World Series of baseball and you're the *only* bloody country involved. My kid's playing t-ball in Perth. I can't wait for the day when there really is a World Series and the Yanks finally lose."

"That's the way people in Brooklyn used to feel," replied the American. "So keep your chin up, sport."

There will be a global World Series, sometime, somewhere; there's too much money to be had by television for there not to be. Eventually, the Americanized Pacific Rim and the Caribbean will be wired for cable and there will be a true world championship. How far off? In 1984, the U.S. Olympic team was composed of Will Clark, Barry Bonds, Barry Larkin, B. J. Surhoff, and Mark Mc-Gwire, among others. *Sports Illustrated*, ESPN and *Baseball America* all saluted that all-time illustrious team six years later, with one small detail often forgotten: It didn't finish first. First Taiwan knocked off the Americans, and then Japan beat them 6–3 in the medal game for the championship, despite the fact that thirteen of the U.S. players had a month earlier been selected in the first round of the amateur draft. Then in September 1991, when it came time for the Japanese to go through what they thought was the formality of finishing first or second in the Asian Games and getting one of the two qualifying berths for the 1992 Olympics, they almost didn't make it. Japan lost to the Australians, and had the Aussies not blown a lead against Taiwan with two out in the bottom of the ninth inning, they would have qualified with Taiwan, not Japan.

While major league baseball is bogged down in its own internal problems here at home, the rest of the world is catching up. True, the commissioner's office does have an international division, but its success will be limited until the players are included in developing long-term strategies. It was not NBA Commissioner David Stern who the fans came to see in Barcelona.

While the National Basketball Association All-Stars were demolishing the competition in Spain, the group of collegians representing the U.S. in baseball lost twice to Cuba and Japan, and went home without even a medal, as Taiwan took the bronze. Major league baseball, of course, would never shut down its season for two weeks in the summer to send its best professional players to the Olympics, but neither do the Japanese, who rely on players from club teams sponsored by Japanese conglomerates like Nippon Oil, Takugin Bank, and Mitsubishi Electronics. The U.S. fields only the third- or fourth-best amateur team in international competition.

There were already professional baseball leagues in Japan, Korea, and Taiwan by the 1990s. By the winter of 1991–92, a dozen major league teams were sending players to the summer (our winter) league in Australia, and beginning in '92, major league baseball was televising a U.S. "Game of the Week" over Australia's National Channel Nine. The Blue Jays' Wayne Morgan, probably the best-traveled scout in the game, says that despite some slowdown due to political unrest, mainland China is also making extraordinary strides. "They have the numbers, obviously," says Morgan, who attended the Asian Games in Peking. "But they also have a lot of good athletes with perhaps the best instincts of any of the Pacific countries except maybe the Australians. There's a lot of potential there down the road."

Baseball has always been one of the sports of choice in Puerto

Rico, the Dominican Republic, Venezuela, Mexico, and Nicaragua. Its popularity has grown in Europe, albeit slowly. Even the Soviet Union has begun sprouting teams.

When Peter Ueberroth opened everyone's eyes to the riches of licensing dollars, some ingenious marketing sorts figured out that licensed products could be sold anywhere and everywhere in the world. Go to Bangkok: There's an A's hat. Tune into Desert Storm: Saudi officers are seen wearing Mets and Dodgers caps. During the 1991 American League Championship Series, a Toronto cab-driver told his passengers that he had sent a dozen Blue Jays caps to his relatives in Pakistan. While the National Basketball Association has a clearly thought out marketing plan in place to license its products around the world, baseball apparel primarily makes it way to foreign lands by haphazard means. If major league baseball does not soon take the lead in promoting its licensed products around the world, the Japanese will get there first with their team logos.

By 2000, much of the world will be wired for television. The problem will be how to construct a World Series; how often to play it; and how to layer the different levels of countries—like the World Cup in soccer—so that there will still be a minimum of interest in second-tier countries like Italy, France, and mainland China.

By then, there will likely be an annual series played between the American World Series champion and the Japanese champion. In the month between the end of the Japanese and American seasons, there could be a tournament played between the champions of the Korean, Japanese, and Taiwanese leagues, with that champion playing a home-and-home series with the American champion.

The National Basketball Association brilliantly used the Olympics to showcase its talent and its glamour while promoting itself worldwide by its very entry into the 1992 Games, right down to naming the team on national television. Baseball cannot do that, for two reasons: First, baseball may lose its official Olympic status because not enough countries around the world play; and second, unlike basketball, to go headlong into the Olympics would require virtually closing down the regular season for three weeks, something the major league teams are not going to do, for obvious TV-dollar reasons.

Major league baseball will have to come up with a format that is a cross between World Cup soccer and the Canada Cup in ice hockey. In the year 2000, there will probably be a two-tiered world tournament in February and March. In Group A, there will be the U.S., Japan, Korea, Taiwan, Venezuela, the Dominican Republic, Cuba, Puerto Rico, Canada, and Australia. All the other countries will be in Group B, with nations eventually moving up and down according to performance. In 2000, the Puerto Rican team might still have Ruben Sierra, Pudge Rodriguez, and the Brothers Alomar, who'll all be in their early or mid thirties. The Dominican Nationals might have all three Martinez brothers of Dodger fame. Cuba could use some of its native sons in their late thirties like Jose Canseco, Danny Tartabull, and Rafael Palmeiro, as well as the dozens of Cuban players who'll be playing in the majors by the mid-nineties.

All it would really take is three weeks in March after a two-and-a-half-week training period, and while the owners may wail about the players not being in shape, they didn't worry about too little time once the lockout was ended in 1990. The best from each of the participating countries would compete, and while in 2000 it may not be a huge television success, it will be a growing television event. For instance, there could be the Western Division (the U.S., Canada, Cuba, Puerto Rico, the Dominican Republic, and Venezuela) and the Eastern Division (Japan, Taiwan, Korea, Australia). Each country's all-star team would play the others; then, after the initial nine games, played over two weeks, there would be the final round-robin, with the Eastern and Western champions plus the wild-card club playing in the final week. The various sponsors would promote the games worldwide, and it would be a fascinating lead-in to the regular season. Ask the participating players if they'd miss all they got out of in spring training. Tim Raines killed those training theories when collusion forced him to sit out spring training in 1987: He went on a tear his first week back in May, including the game-winning home run he hit against the Mets in his first game back.

*   *   *

As baseball begins to take hold around the world, major league clubs have started to open their eyes to the talent elsewhere. The Blue Jays tried to pay a Korean pitcher named Dong Wong Choi nearly $400,000 in the early eighties, but that nation's baseball officials wouldn't let him out. Toronto also offered a Taiwanese pitcher more than a quarter of a million dollars in 1984, but he opted for Japan. And look at Australia: By the end of the 1991 season, not only was Sydney shortstop Craig Shipley playing for the Padres, but the Yankees' best pitching prospect was a six-foot-seven fireballer from Adelaide named Mark Hutton and the Brewers are making plans to replace B. J. Surhoff with a Brisbane catcher named David Nilsson.

In addition, the Japanese have built the most expensive twenty-first-century complex in the Dominican Republic outside of San Pedro de Marcos, miles from the Dodger Academy that was considered state-of-the-art. The Baltimore Orioles have built a small complex in Perth. Ted Williams has held hitting clinics in the Soviet Union.

Outside of a few clinics and trips to Japan, major league baseball has not directly exposed the world to baseball. What has brought its game to a curious world audience is the proliferation of satellite communications. While the American public has been exposed to global conflicts, the world's sporting community has been able to witness our leisure-time activities. In 1980, 5 percent of American households were wired for cable; little more than a decade later, nearly 70 percent of American homes were wired for cable, and the U.S. public thought nothing of watching live SCUD missile attacks, or riots in Tiananmen Square. Meanwhile, foreigners could pick up baseball games for free by just looking up at the stars. In 1991, Andy Messersmith's cousin John—who lives on the Tropic of Capricorn in a town of five hundred on the Great Barrier Reef called Emu Park, Queensland, Australia—watched every game of ESPN's "Baseball Tonight" on his dish. "I feel like I'm back living in Chatham, Massachusetts," says John Messersmith. Little did his Cousin Andy know when he won perhaps the greatest arbitration victory in sports history in 1976 that fifteen years later, baseball would be the fastest-growing sport in Australia.

No Pacific Rim culture is more geared to Americanization than Australia, from television to music to clothing. Almost all Aussies live within an hour and a half of the ocean, in what is the California life-style redux. The outdoors and sports are every bit as much part of the culture there as they are in California.

But while in the States the catcher takes a strikeout and fires the ball down to third to begin the around-the-horn toss, in Australia the catcher throws to first. "The water goes down the drain in the opposite direction in the Southern Hemisphere," says Toronto scout Morgan. "So does the baseball."

Australia is roughly the same size as the United States; its population is the same (16.5 million) as New York City and Long Island combined. The travel posters capture the romantic Wild West Outback, but, in reality, it is a beach country, and two-thirds of the population live in five cities: Brisbane, sophisticated and wealthy Sydney, traditional Melbourne, Adelaide, and Perth. While Brisbane is baseball's melting pot for the Aussies who live in the east, nearly three thousand miles to the west, Perth is the real baseball capital of Australia.

There are fewer than a quarter of a million people living between Brisbane and Perth, for Perth is the most isolated city in the world, 1,750 miles from Adelaide and closer to Singapore than to Sydney or Brisbane. It is a city that shines, with the brashness of a young Dallas, the climate of La Jolla and, fueled by the recent influx of Hong Kong businessmen fleeing the future takeover of their country by China, the potential to be the hub of the Indian Ocean looking north to Bangkok, northwest to India, and west to Africa. It was here that nearly a century after baseball was introduced by American gold miners in the late 1860s the sport began to change from Australian to international. It was also here that a week before traveling to Brisbane, Mets scouts Roland Johnson and Joe Mason, as well as Toronto's Morgan and a couple of other American scouts, were exposed to the strain between two baseball cultures.

Johnson and Mason found out that Australia is not like the Dominican Republic, Venezuela, or Puerto Rico, where scouts are often begged to sign youngsters. The Americans had gotten a taste of the Australian uneasiness one afternoon when a youngster asked Toronto's Morgan, "Are you one of the American spies?" Then, the Mets scouts walked out of the park because of remarks by Australian Baseball Federation Vice President Neville Pratt during the opening ceremonies of the national under-18 tournament. Pratt offered a warning in his speech. "We have a number of major league scouts here. The ABF has no objection to a player signing a professional contract; however, there has been a spate of signings for paltry amounts of money without the player or his parents being fully advised of the ramifications. . . . Apart from the Los Angeles Dodgers, who have regularly made their coaches available to this country and hosted our Australian youth teams, the other American clubs have done nothing to advance baseball in Australia." Out walked Johnson and Mason.

Sport in Australia is recreation, whereas in America it is an avocation and business. Baseball Down Under is still a minor sport, like soccer in the U.S. "Baseball is starting to take off, but Americans had better move slowly, because Australians are wary of the pros," says the Aussie national junior coach Steve Gilmore, a transplanted Floridian. "They still play under an entirely different, British system with different motivations, attuned to the Pacific and international baseball, and they laugh at the American presumption of holding *the* World Series."

"The last two Australian cricket team captains, Greg Chappell and Alan Border, are baseball players who've said that if the rewards were the same, they'd be playing baseball instead of cricket," says Jon Brown, whose JFB Sport operates both the Queensland Rams and the Brisbane Bullets, a basketball team. "There is an enormous shift toward American sports. This isn't going to be a British sporting country for much longer. In 1987, we couldn't get four hundred people in a two thousand-seat arena to see basketball in Brisbane. Now we sell out a twelve thousand five hundred-seat arena, tickets for the finals are scalped for a hundred and fifty dollars, we got them televised, and now several big sponsors have come in for this season. NASCAR is taking off. In Queensland—which is being called 'The Future'—and Western Australia, the baseball and economic boon states, we're seeing a tremendous growth in Hong Kong, Chinese, Japanese, and American investment. Some wealthy Asian nations are looking at all the untapped land in this country and are dying to get in here."

One or two Japanese major league teams have even explored building spring training facilities in Queensland. The Yomiyuri Giants vacation at the Yeppoon resort of Iwasaki, which in turn is building a baseball facility for the locals. "Asia and America are looking," says Brown. "Baseball is going to reap huge benefits from this emerging economic shift in sponsorship, equipment, and media coverage. Remember, now we only have two or three television channels in most of our major cities. Cable hasn't hit yet. But all that will be changing."

By the time the 1990s started, several major league clubs had already moved into Australia. The Orioles had their winter farm club set up in Perth. They were sending four to six players there, and had made peace with Pratt and the other Australian officials. The Dodgers and Angels were among the dozen teams to send players to the winter league there, and Los Angeles and Baltimore got into bidding wars on two young Australian players.

Meanwhile, in the Caribbean, while economic problems cloud the future of Dominican Republic baseball, Puerto Rico, Venezuela, Mexico, and Nicaragua baseball all continue to grow. Even when the Sandinistas were in control, baseball was a major part of Nicaragua's culture. "It was the ultimate pressure," said Brant Alyea, Jr., the son of a former major leaguer (who played in that country in the winter of 1966 and fathered the boy there), who grew up in Managua and was smuggled out by the Blue Jays in a scene right out of the film *El Norte*. "Every level you reached, if you didn't make the next level, you had to go into the army. Talk about players playing for their lives . . ."

Mexico's economy may begin to boom as the century turns, and economists feel that South America could be the Pacific Rim of the year 2000. Start with caps for Caracas, then think about baseball cards in Buenos Aires. By the year 2000 in Perth, they're going to know Robbie Alomar. In Hong Kong—or whatever it will be—they'll know Steve Avery. In Yorkshire, Great Britain, they might even know Juan Gonzalez. Think back to 1980 and our country's television habits. Then spin the technology worldwide.

Eddie Einhorn's fears may prove correct: While the owners fight among themselves and with the players, the rest of the world is catching up. They're not only buying into the national pastime, they may soon beat major league baseball at its own game. As the public chooses the game that it wishes to see, it will also find that besides competition between international teams that it didn't even know knew the rules of baseball, it will see games played in stadiums that only existed on drawing boards in the early 1990s.

CHAPTER NINETEEN

TEMPLES OF THE FUTURE

The Los Angeles Dodgers and the Boston Red Sox are two of the most lucrative franchises in baseball. They also own their own ballparks, free and clear. But most of the other teams have successfully convinced their respective communities that they are a civic treasure and should have their ballparks financed partially, or even completely, by public funds. In some cases, the public can come out ahead, too. The additional income from luxury boxes, concessionaire revenues, and parking fees may help the team sign free agents. The city might also receive lease payments to defray the stadium's cost, as well as tax and tourist dollars, that would more than offset the windfall given to the club.

A city and team that are made for each other are Baltimore and the Orioles. Baltimore's Memorial Stadium was a neighborhood park, with little white houses out beyond center field. It was home for the first game the Orioles played when they left St. Louis in April 1954, and when it came time for its final Orioles game there were six employees who had been there all thirty-eight seasons. Ernie Tyler had been working there since 1957, sitting on a chair beside the backstop screen, retrieving foul balls. Over the years he'd missed only a couple dozen games. He raised one son, Jimmy, who was the home clubhouse attendant, and another, Fred, who was the visiting clubhouse man. His wife used to prepare the postgame clubhouse spreads, including what players throughout the American League referred to as "those legendary crab cakes." The Tylers *were* Memorial Stadium, and Memorial Stadium was baseball the way it used to be in "We Like Ike" days.

237

When Earl Weaver managed and Pat Santarone was the grounds-keeper, they raised a tomato garden in foul territory down the left field line.

Memorial Stadium had housed great players and great teams. The Orioles stunned the Dodgers in the 1966 World Series with Frank and Brooks Robinson and some kid pitchers named Jim Palmer, Dave McNally, and Wally Bunker. They were the best team in baseball from 1969 through 1971, although, like the 1988–90 Athletics, they lost two World Series. They came back to another World Series in 1979 but lost, then won it again in 1983.

There was always a sense that the players from those years were spirits in a material world, possessed of rare senses of humor. When Steve Stone was pitching his way toward the Cy Young Award in 1980, he was the center of considerable media attention. He liked to sit in front of his locker with books that impressed the Eastern media. His teammates, Mike Flanagan and Jim Palmer, would often change his bookmarks, and once even cut the book from its binding and substituted another one. Flanagan later noted, "Stone never realized—but then, he never knew that his bookmarks were changed, either."

After the first game of the (then five-game) 1983 playoffs against the Chicago White Sox, the Orioles were down a game and faced a difficult task: Start a rookie, Mike Boddicker, in Game Two, then go to Comiskey Park for three games. They also needed to win three out of four. When the Baltimore players failed to come out to the dugout on time for the National Anthem, many press box experts were convinced that the Orioles had finally begun to be daunted by the pressure. Boddicker shut out the White Sox 5–0. Afterward, Flanagan explained, "We were watching 'People's Court,' and there was no way anyone could leave the clubhouse before Judge Wapner made his decision." "Nervous?" Flanagan later recounted. "Most of us were at least tense, because the plaintiff had one heckuva claim." They won three straight, and buzzed through the Phillies in five games to win the Series.

It could have happened nowhere else.

But on October 6, 1991, Memorial Stadium finally came to its final day. Former and active players came out by position (yes, even Lenny Sakata, who caught one inning in his entire career but in that one inning saw Tippy Martinez pick three straight runners off first base, took his place behind the plate), and because everyone in Memorial Stadium's neighborhood knew everyone else, including the players, they didn't introduce them by name. The faces and the builds were enough. Dennis Martinez flew in from Montreal. Rick Dempsey flew in from Milwaukee, and acted as cheerleader as the fans started their famous "O-R-I-O-L-E-S" chant. Jim Palmer stepped on the mound, and began crying, uncontrollably. Weaver was to be the last to come out, but as he stood in the runway he began mumbling, "I cannot go out there. I can't do this." Baltimore public relations director Rick Vaughn put his hand on his shoulder to tell him it was all in fun, but Weaver couldn't look up at him: He was already crying too hard.

Finally, in the top of the ninth inning they brought the thirty-nine-year-old Flanagan—who began with the Orioles in 1975 and was in many ways the personal symbol of the franchise—in from the bullpen to throw the last pitches any Oriole pitcher would ever throw in Memorial Stadium. As he walked in from the bullpen, every fan was on his feet, cheering and crying and applauding. On the message board, there was an announcement that Flanagan had been signed to a new two-year contract, and when he got the final Tiger hitter, he too wiped his eyes as he walked off the field for the final time.

So ended Memorial Stadium. Weeks later, they took home plate and transplanted it across town in the new Orioles Park at Camden Yards. Thirty-eight seasons and a lot of feelings had been left behind up at 33rd Street, but it was 1991, and Memorial Stadium had outlived its usefulness to the business of baseball. In 1992, the Baltimore Orioles were moving crosstown to become the Washington Orioles, or perhaps the Baltimore-Washington Beltway Orioles.

Orioles Park at Camden Yards is not the Toronto Skydome. It is the Orioles' vision of Baltimore at the turn of the century. The city that was once (in)famous for The Block and crab cakes has moved on to Harborplace and the economic viability that makes it an attractive place for tourists and businesses. The park is carved out of a neighborhood, a block from brick row houses and three blocks from Harborplace, with a warehouse-turned-condominium past right field. It has modern nostalgia; it is asymmetrical, with a short right field fence, and its entryways look like Franklin Field or Harvard Stadium. It has the feel of the cloudy tradition of the Grande Olde Game, yet is modern and so perfectly set that when Oriole President Larry Lucchino was trying to sell free agents Glenn Davis and Dwight Evans on returning for the 1992 season, he offered to fly each into town for a tour of the new park. Davis was so impressed that when he signed a two-year deal with the O's rather than hit the free agent market, he said that the thrill of playing in the new park was a factor in his decision.

But art and nostalgia aside, the new Orioles Park is baseball as it is played now: a dollar and cents proposition. The team got Maryland Governor Donald Schaefer, who when he was mayor of Baltimore had turned "Orioles Pride" into civic pride and had masterminded the Harborplace and downtown renovation, to float bonds to build the park, which is located on the Beltway to Washington. Even though it was a nightmare to get to Memorial Stadium from Washington (one had to linger in traffic going cross-town)—nearly 30 percent of the Orioles attendance came from Washington. Because of the new park's closer proximity to the nation's capital, luxury boxes are an easier sell; 4,400 of them have full bar and restaurant services, which provide additional revenues to the club. In Memorial Stadium 31 percent of the park's configuration were box seats; in Orioles Park at Camden Yards, 53 percent are box seats selling for up to $14 a pop, which significantly increases the club's take. Three million attendance? Three and quarter? Three and a half? "If you want to sign free agents like the Davises and to keep the Gregg Olsons, Ben McDonalds, and Cal Ripkens, you have to be able to compete," said Lucchino.

Ballparks themselves have become an essential element of the business. Walter O'Malley understood that from the beginning. If he were to remain in Brooklyn, he wanted a domed stadium. (Yes, Walter O'Malley was looking for a domed stadium in the fifties.) Then when he beat the rest of the baseball world and moved the Dodgers to Los Angeles in 1962, he built the prototype clean, scenic, accessible, and service-filled baseball theatre. Over little more than a decade, between 1965 and 1977, eight of the National

League's twelve current parks were built (Wrigley Field, the league's oldest, was built in 1916; Montreal's Olympic Stadium, the league's youngest, made its baseball debut in 1977). Houston opened its futuristic Astrodome in 1965. Candlestick Park—that miserable construction that sits out on the dock of the bay— opened in 1960. The rest are the cookie-cutter parks. If one were to be awakened in an elevator at 3:00 P.M., he would have a hard time figuring out if he were in Veterans Stadium in Philadelphia, Three Rivers in Pittsburgh, Jack Murphy in San Diego, or Riverfront in Cincinnati. They're virtually all the same: built with baseball and football in mind, symmetrical, and usually without any discernible personality—although the planes going out of La-Guardia and the smell of garbage do combine to give Shea Stadium, which was built in 1964, a unique flavor. It was as if the fellow who designed Ramada Inn motels was contracted to do eight of the twelve National League parks.

O'Malley has constantly upgraded and improved Dodger Stadium so that at the age of thirty, it looks as if it were three. The California Angels and Kansas City Royals each learned from O'Malley. Each club hired longtime minor league executive Cedric Tallis to put together its ballpark, and the results are two other parks from the same era that produced the majority of the National League parks that are still entertainment palaces. Anaheim Stadium has been enlarged and improved, while Royals Stadium—adjacent to Arrowhead Stadium as part of a two-stadium complex outside of Kansas City that was finished in 1973—is a near-perfect atmosphere for the small town of Kansas City. "It's a different crowd in Kansas City, and people want it to be *family entertainment,*" says John Schuerholz, who worked for the Royals for more than two decades before leaving to run the Atlanta Braves. The park is kept spotless. The clubhouses look as if they were built over the previous winter. Abusive language is simply not tolerated in the stadium; curse, and thou shalt be hauled off.

As the Orioles tried to sell their potential free agents on their new stadium, so one of Ted Turner's selling points in luring Schuerholz away from the Royals was the prospect of a new ballpark in Atlanta. Turner and the club president, Stan Kasten, guaranteed Schuerholz that he would have significant input in the planning and development of their new stadium in the 1996 Olympic complex. Fulton County Stadium, the prototype cookie-cutter park, has outlived its usefulness.

The Oakland Coliseum may have been one of the dullest, dankest ballparks ever constructed. With enough foul territory to fit in the state of Rhode Island, fans are too far from the field of play. The stadium was built primarily for Al Davis and the Raiders, and when Charley Finley moved the Athletics out to the East Bay from Kansas City in 1968, it appeared to be a disastrous move. The population of the East Bay had yet to explode, Finley did little to make fans want to come to the park, and not only were there plenty of good seats available for playoff and World Series games in Oakland's great 1972–73–74 run, but by the late seventies pitcher Matt Keough was calling the A's "the team baseball left behind." But when the Haas family bought the club, the team's innovative president, Roy Eisenhardt—Walter Haas's son-in-law—started to turn the Coliseum into the most fun-filled park in the Major Leagues.

Eisenhardt hired a marketing whiz named Andy Dolich, who not only creatively promoted the Athletics (his "BillyBall" T-shirts are still collectors' items), but made innovations at the stadium that remain unique. The concessions vary from nachos grande, with outstanding guacamole, to five different types of international sausages to french fries that easily whip those at McDonald's to a number of international beers. The A's were way ahead of the creative T-shirt craze. They put in a Dolby stereo system that was state-of-the-art; not only did they understand baseball's curious bond with rock 'n' roll, but they capitalized on the Bay Area's eclectic musical background. Huey Lewis and the News were doing anthems in 1984, back when they were workin' for a living. They had classical night. They had between-inning videos. Eisenhardt combined his romantic vision of baseball with entertainment, and he and Dolich came up with three different scoreboards—the message board with its traditional electronic information in left field, a mammoth screen in center (where, until thirty minutes before game time, they show the best out-of-town game of the day, right off their satellite dish), and an old-time, hand-changed, inning-by-inning wooden scoreboard in right, à la Wrigley. The Rolling Stones' Steel Wheels tour played the Coliseum days after the earthquake in 1989 because "the sound and video systems are always great here," according to Laurie Lachemann, wife of the former Oakland third base coach who now manages the Marlins.

In contrast, playing in the Kingdome in Seattle, a wash of bored concrete, is like playing in a garage. The Mariners' electronic board looked like a Philco until 1990, when it was finally updated—but given the budget, it was outdated before it was completed.

By the end of the eighties, most clubs understood that new stadiums were vital to upgrading the game as entertainment. Ueberroth's insistence that new parks be designed as "baseball-only stadia" came not only out of nightmares concerning leases and conditions (baseball is hard to play after football players have turned over the fields like Rototillers), but out of his instinctive feeling that fans need to be on top of the game, the way they are in the romanticist's icons, Wrigley and Fenway. This was especially difficult in the American League, where so many of the parks had become outdated. Memorial Stadium was rushed into action in 1954, Milwaukee's County Stadium in 1953, and Arlington (Texas) Stadium was upgraded from a minor league park for the move of the Washington Senators in 1972. Chicago's Comiskey Park had been opened in 1910, and two years later, on the same April day, Fenway Park and Tiger Stadium opened. A decade later, Yankee Stadium arose in the South Bronx; it was upgraded in 1974–75 (when the Yankees played at Shea Stadium). Cleveland's Municipal Stadium opened in 1932; it looked like a WPA project then, and still does today. The Metrodome was built as a quick answer to what seemed to be the inevitability of the Twins moving to Tampa; much of the team's audience comes long distances, and since the clouds roll in almost daily, it was impossible to get the RVs and vans rolling in from Clear Lake, Iowa, and Rapid City, South Dakota, unless you could guarantee a game.

Fenway and Comiskey parks and Tiger, Memorial, Municipal, and Yankee stadiums were built for the demands of their times: in the city, on the trolley lines. Until after World War II, how much of an audience did one expect to get from outside a fifteen-to-twenty-mile belt? But by the eighties, with more than 90 percent of baseball's audience drawn from outside city limits, the necessities had changed. When the Tigers culminated their World Championship 1984 season, in which they started off 35–5 and swept through the postseason by winning seven of eight games, a post-game "celebration" turned into an ugly street riot. Cars were over-turned and set on fire and many members of the club and the media were trapped in the park for hours.

In late 1983, Hudson's, Detroit's largest and most prominent department store, announced it was closing down, making Detroit the largest city in the country without a department store. The downtown area was economically dead, the byproduct of what is one of the worst cases of urban development in United States history as the business center of Detroit has moved out to Dear-born, Southfield, and other suburban locations. By 1991, the Ti-gers were desperately trying to get a new park. With a team that hit home runs and was, at the least, interesting, they were third in the majors in road attendance for the 1991 season—and twenty-first in home attendance. "We cannot compete in this stadium," the club president, Bo Schembechler, repeatedly stated at the time. "It's unfair to think that you can shackle us to a rusted girder in Tiger Stadium."

Purists organized the "Save Tiger Stadium" movement, but the fact remained that it was downtown, had 2,500 obstructed-view seats, and was saddled with cramped, outdated facilities, from its concession stands to its rest rooms. Schembechler lobbied for a stadium outside the city, in the financial district. The state legis-lature argued that it must be in the city, which Schembechler realized was not the answer.

By the late 1980s, the White Sox could not compete with the Cubs. The Cubs were the favorite team (a local comedian's line is, "Do you know what it's like to be a South Sider in a world of North Siders?") to start with. Then the Cubs had WGN-TV. Comiskey wasn't romantic, like Wrigley; it was old, rickety, and tough to get around and through. So Reinsdorf and Einhorn ar-gued for a new ballpark, until they finally gave up and agreed to move to St. Petersburg, where they would have bathed in a potentially golden market, complete with a staggering cable television contract. At the last moment, the State of Illinois gave Reinsdorf and Einhorn the stadium deal they wanted, and they stayed, with a stadium built across the street from the old Comiskey. Their marketing people found that American sport fans are obsessed with black and silver or black and gold as team colors, and chose the black and silver hats and uniforms. Not only did they draw nearly three million in 1991 when the park opened, but by the end of the year the White Sox hats had shot past Cubs hats in nationwide sales and were the third-largest-selling caps in the majors.

The new Comiskey fits Chicago, the White Sox tradition, and the Illinois state budget. It also fits Reinsdorf's needs, with its luxury boxes and state-of-the-art facilities, while allowing him to keep some of the old touches, such as a glass case with the suit Roland Hemond wore the day the Sox clinched the division in 1983. And, according to Eddie Einhorn, one year after the new park opened, the club did not receive one irate letter attacking the demolition of the old park, a sharp contrast to the thousands the owners received during the discussions over the construction of a new Comiskey Park.

North of Chicago, the Skydome fits Toronto, which, since the Jays were only twelve years old when it opened, didn't have to worry about tradition. And, in wealthy Toronto with its ten million people in the metropolitan area, they didn't have to worry about cost. Skydome has $3.75 Big Macs, a hotel, a Hard Rock Cafe, a retractable roof, and the sense that if the crew of the space shuttle wanted to see a game, they'd land in Toronto.

The Skydome, the new Comiskey Park, and Orioles Park at Camden Yards became tourist attractions as soon as they opened. The Cleveland Indians needed something to attract customers back into the downtown area, with their 1994 park part of that effort. The Indians are in a unique situation, because the members of the Jacobs family are among the biggest real estate developers in the city. After rebuilding a stretch of empty warehouses and mills and turning them into the chic Flats area, the family had become the symbols of the regeneration of another Rust Belt city where the population base had moved to the 'burbs. The Indians had been trapped in the damp, dark grasp of a 77,000-seat stadium—where if you drew 30,000, it seemed as if it were empty—and Browns owner Art Modell was hardly a model landlord.

John Hart, another of the breed of young, talented general managers, explains some of the problems with Cleveland Stadium. "Because the park is so big, there is a sense that there is no urgency to buy a ticket in advance. The lack of parking compounds the problem, and the lease is very unfavorable to us." The new park will seat somewhere between 40,000 and 45,000 and will have parks, walkways, and shopping areas adjacent. And as important to the Jacobs family, it will also have luxury suites.

"The idea is that the ballpark is part of one's day," says Blue Jays President Paul Beeston. "In Toronto, you can shop, eat, and then see the game in a spectacular setting that's clean and modern enough for the family. The romanticists don't like these modern parks, but they'll come to the park anyway. You're always trying to reach a new audience."

No new ballpark more perfectly suits its environs than the Texas Ranger's 1994 complex in Arlington. When George Bush and his group bought the club, he soon realized that his medium market could not compete unless he got a new stadium with luxury boxes, a higher percentage of box seats, better concessions and parking deals, etc. The City of Arlington passed a referendum for a half-cent increase in the sales tax to back $135 million in bonds for the complex, with the Rangers contributing $30 million up front and more than $60 million over the next thirty years. It is, like Camden Yards, a baseball park, pure and simple. It is asymmetrical, based on what club attorney and Vice President Tom Schiffer calls "the best instincts of baseball." Schiffer told the architects that "Wrigley Field is the doughnut hole from which all future parks should be developed, if you think of all around it as the doughnut," which meant something with a seating capacity of under 45,000, with little foul territory, and offering a feeling to the fan that he is part of the show. Schiffer attended a 1990 playoff game in Fenway Park and sat in a box that juts out in foul territory down the left field line. "I felt as if I were sitting in back of the shortstop," says

Schiffer. There will be a similar feeling in the Rangers' new park as well.

But the Texas ballpark is simply a part of a 177-acre complex, one with a river flowing through it. Little Johnson Creek actually becomes a significant waterway, widening and narrowing at appropriate spots. The landscape is designed in curves modeled after the work of Frederick Law Olmsted, who created Central Park in New York and Boston's Emerald Necklace, perhaps the finest example of nineteenth-century urban planning in the country. There are boat houses, a baseball-shaped promenade, an apartment complex, a Little League field, the Texas Hall of Fame, an amphitheater, a river walk with an expensive retail area and restaurants, and a mass-transit station. When the Rangers are on the road, the old DiamondVision board that sat in Arlington Stadium will be at the Little League park, so the kids can watch their heroes. "It also is purely Texas when you enter the park," says Schiffer. "When you look at the brick arches, the columns, and the red brick and pink granite, there's no question you're in Texas."

Oh yes: You get there on the Nolan Ryan Expressway.

Next, new stadiums will go up in Atlanta and Milwaukee. By the end of the decade, however, not only will baseball face stadium crises in Pittsburgh, Detroit, Cincinnati, and both Shea and Yankee stadiums, but the Cubs and Red Sox will be physically and fiscally unable to compete in their tiny neighborhoods. The problem in both cities is tradition, although now that the White Sox have wrung money out of the people, the Cubs can more easily move. Wrigley and Fenway are both tourist attractions that draw 300,000 to 500,000 a year in out-of-towners, both have been upgraded with luxury boxes while having the advantage of forcing customers to buy their seats early—and neither will work in the future.

While Fenway Park is charming, quaint, and historic, it also has dreadful drawbacks. First, there is the access. Boston is a traffic nightmare to begin with, but the streets leading into the Fens/ Kenmore Square area are narrow, angular, and overly congested. Second, there is virtually no parking; much of it is controlled by

independent lot and gas station owners who in the heat of pennant races charge anywhere from $10 to $20 a vehicle. Third, there
are a number of obstructed seats. Fourth, the seats and aisles are
obsolete, uncomfortable, and built for the average-sized person at
the turn of the century. Fifth, there is very little room in the area
underneath the stands, which makes passage difficult and dramatically cuts back concessions. Sixth, while the rest room facilities have been upgraded, they are still antiquated and often
disgusting. Finally, despite an $11 million reconstruction, the park
constantly has to be repaired and rebuilt. With every year, the
danger factor increases. After all, it does sit on land reclaimed
from the Back Bay.

The Cubs can move north. But land in the Boston area is so
tough to come by that the Red Sox are severely restricted. Unlike
those in other cities, Boston voters know that the Sox wouldn't
move, because New England institutions just don't, and it's contrary to New Englanders' consciences to even *think* about voting
for public funds for an athletic team. So somehow the Red Sox
have to take the appealing characteristics of Fenway and find a
nearby site to build their own complex with modern conveniences.
Since there is a movement to bring the 2016 Summer Olympics to
Boston, and the National Football League is trying to get the
Patriots to move into the small, condensed city limits of Boston, the most plausible plan is for the city, the state, and the two
teams to work together and take land either at the University of
Massachusetts-Boston or Forest Hills sites and develop a two-
stadium complex, similar to Kansas City's, with a roof that slides
back and forth between the structures. In a thin local economy
with no public support, it is a monumental task. But the alternative is the realization that Fenway Park may collapse or become
completely obsolete, and that both of those scenarios are possible
before the turn of the century. If only Frederick Law Olmsted were
still alive and a big Roger Clemens fan.

Interleague baseball. Another round of playoffs. Australians
winning the World Series. All are hard enough for the traditionalists to swallow. But move the Green Monster out of Fenway?
Never!

It will happen.

CHAPTER TWENTY

A NIGHT
AT THE PARK

⚾

"BUY ME SOME PEANUTS AND CRACKER JACKS."

Ever since the National League was formed in 1876, baseball has always been about business. Likewise, racism, gambling, litigation, and drug addiction are not newcomers to the sport. But for its first hundred years major league baseball was always able to eventually divert public attention away from its off-the-field problems, because the owners had total control over the game. The economics, however, changed on a chilly October night in 1975, when television discovered the game's popularity with 62 million prime-time viewers. The battle for control of the benefits from television started one year later when the players won the right to negotiate their salaries in an open market as free agents. And the game hasn't been the same since the owners were forced to become partners with the players.

It has been written by many that a true baseball fan neither wants to know nor cares about the business of baseball. Indeed, such an awareness only arouses contempt for the game played off the field. Just give us the game between the white lines, please. Baseball has always been viewed as an escape from society's problems, not as a mirror of them. We derive comfort, so it goes, from the familiarity of an institution that has resisted all but the most minor tinkering since its inception. This perception of baseball is touched on briefly by George Will in his best-seller *Men at Work*. He quotes the legendary club owner Bill Veeck as saying "Dugout to dugout, the game happily remains unchanged in our changing world."

But Veeck, ever the promoter, understood better than most that events off the field over the past twenty years have dramatically affected the game as it is played between the dugouts. Indeed, he was forced to sell the Chicago White Sox to Jerry Reinsdorf because of his inability to compete under the new ground rules. As the stakes have grown dramatically higher, the business of baseball now appears in bold type on page one, while box scores are buried in the back.

If the owners and the players are able to end their battle for control by devising a free market system that does not pit city against city and teammate against teammate, the opportunities for continued prosperity and international growth are limitless. Of course, if they don't, financial decisions will continue to change the way the game is played on the field for the worse. A team might deliberately prevent a player with performance incentives from achieving individual success to keep his salary down, affecting the outcome of the game, and possibly a pennant race. The Players Association has already raised this concern with the independent arbitrator. Likewise, a player who is eligible to file for arbitration after the season might fake an injury to maintain a .300 batting average in September. More and more, players are reluctant to chance further injury by playing with relatively minor aches and pains. As pointed out in the August 19, 1991 issue of the *Sporting News*, more major leaguers went on the disabled list in the month of June 1991 than during the entire 1970 season. If baseball follows its present course, the public will soon cry out "A pox on both your houses" as the networks dramatically reduce their fees. Cities passed over for expansion will look elsewhere and sue baseball to have its antitrust exemption removed. A third league will emerge, statistics will become meaningless, and Japan will play Cuba in the real World Series.

It is to be hoped that self-preservation will win out over greed. But if the game on the field continues to be overshadowed by the money game played off it, the simple confrontation between pitcher and hitter will become meaningless and boring to the fan. Boredom is what baseball has most to fear. The public may put up with—and even be interested in—debates over whether Pete Rose should be allowed into the Hall of Fame or whether Steve Howe should be reinstated. But its patience is running out with both management's and labor's public posturing over who deserves more of the pie. The owners' public outcry about players' salaries being out of control falls on deaf ears when it is also pointed out that several clubs generate huge profits at the expense of their rivals without whom there would be no league. Likewise, the players derive no sympathy from the public when they argue that they are indentured employees. As player agent Alan Hendricks once told the founder of the Players Association: "Marvin, the slaves are free and their grandchildren are driving BMWs." Getting the owners and players to allow a free market system to operate without salary arbitration will be the first big step. A more permanent partnership built on trust and mutual respect is even more important.

Besides resolving its labor problems, baseball must mesh its past with its future. The game's history and its attachments to traditions, to storytelling and to lore must be preserved. As important, experts in modern marketing principles, behavioral sciences, and creative business practices must be allowed to coexist with the traditionalists.

But who are the traditionalists? Since Carlton Fisk broke in with the Boston Red Sox in the early 1970s, twenty-two of the twenty-six clubs, including the Red Sox, have changed hands. Six different presidents of the Player Relations Committee have negotiated with the players. Over his playing years, Fisk has listened to four different commissioners and three American League presidents preach on the need for baseball to return to its traditional roots. He is about to hear from two new ones. Baseball's only links with the past are its retired players and its middle management, its "civil servants"—general managers, farm directors, and other baseball people—who have no control over the game's future.

The quintessential nineteenth-century American game played between cities will in the twenty-first century become an international contest between countries. And while the commissioner's office, the twenty-eight major league clubs, the Players Association, and the networks have derived their powers through different and often conflicting means, never has the need for a unified course of action been more critical.

In a rare moment of self-reflection during the heated arguments over the most recent expansion by the National League, Commissioner Fay Vincent pointed out that "squabbling within baseball, the finger-pointing, the tendency to see economic issues as moral ones . . . all of these are contributing to our joint fall from grace."

Vincent should have heeded his own warning. Of course, he was right. The game of baseball played at the professional level is meant to be about entertainment, and should be fun for everyone—the participants, the public, and the promoters. But if those who run the game continue to justify their economic motives as based on "what is morally right," paradise—assuming that it ever existed in baseball in the first place—will never be regained.

Likewise, the public should not confuse the professional game with the sport itself. They have very little in common aside from the fact that neither can answer the question that Carlton Fisk—always the catcher—is prone to ask: "Why can't pitchers learn to throw strikes?" Certainly the amateur game of baseball—whether it be a local American Legion game or a backyard pickup game—will continue to provide comfort to all who enjoy baseball as a way of passing time and forgetting economic worries on a hot summer evening. However, once a fan pays admission to a professional game—or subscribes to a cable telecast of his favorite team—he has made a choice about how he wishes to spend his entertainment dollar, and certainly has the right to question whether he is getting his money's worth. If he is upset either with the cost of the product or with the level of play in the big leagues, he can always stay home, read a good novel, and cancel his cable package.

Baseball purists constantly talk about the "good old days." But the commercialization of the professional game has had some positive side effects. Major league baseball is certainly far more competitive today than it was before 1976. Despite the fears of the owners that free agency would allow the New York and California teams to dominate the World Series by hoarding all the stars, the reverse has been the result. Over the sixteen-year span between 1976 and 1991, twelve different teams have claimed the title of world champions, and during the first decade of free agency only Cleveland, Seattle, and Texas did not win a divisional championship.

It is much harder to create a dynasty today than it was twenty years ago. With more young players being rushed to the majors to counteract teams' losses of free agents, clubs can go through rapid cycles of winning and losing, and some seem to happen at the same time. Andy MacPhail and the Minnesota Twins certainly have lived through a roller coaster cycle. In 1987 they were world champions. Three years later they landed in their division's cellar. The following year, 1991, they were world champions again. Their opponent in the World Series that year, the Atlanta Braves, were a perennial last-place team. The Twins and Braves got to the World Series in the same way: Both clubs developed a strong farm system and supplemented it with key free agent purchases. Adding a touch of symmetry to the matchup, the Braves are one of the superstation teams and the Twins are one of the leaders of the small-market clubs. Each year on any warm spring day baseball fans know that their team—even the Cleveland Indians—has a legitimate chance of winning a pennant seven months later on a cold night in October.

Another benefit of the riches that flow to the sport is that players today are much better-conditioned athletes than they were in the past. Even the legendary Ted Williams, the last player to hit .400, agrees. The huge incomes that players now make allow them the luxury of dedicating themselves to their craft year-round. Players arrive at spring training in far better shape than their counterparts did twenty years ago. And as more all-around athletes follow Bo Jackson's lead, the athletic skills of the players coming into the game will only get better. Many of the most exciting players in the game today are from Latin America, a fairly recent development, and Cuba will soon allow its best to join the majors. Australia has already sent players up north, and other countries will follow suit as their national programs develop, driven partially by aspirations for an Olympic medal.

Green-grass and open-air stadia are returning to the game. The success of the new ballparks bodes well for the construction of more "user-friendly" parks in the future. Oakland and St. Louis (and of course the Chicago Cubs) have proven that weekday matinee games can sell out. Fans will become more interactive as more and more communities are wired for cable. The rapidly developing hardware will allow fans the opportunity to watch the games they want to watch. Satellite dishes will soon replace antennas on rooftops, and an Oakland fan in Miami will be able to support the A's, and not the upstart Marlins, if he buys the Oakland feed.

In the future, major league baseball will have to listen to what the fans want, because it will be in its best interests to do so. And a day at the ballpark (as well as a night) will continue to offer an entertainment experience that no inside arena or air-conditioned movie house can offer.

MILWAUKEE, 2000

The trip into the ballpark in Milwaukee had become an easy one. The couple and their eleven-year-old daughter only had to drive ten miles to the local train stop, hop on the B train, and get off at the ballpark. By the time then Brewers owner Bud Selig finally overcame all the political, historical, ritualistic, and financial obstacles to replacing aging County Stadium with a new park in 1996, the delay in some ways had become a blessing. It allowed Selig and his daughter, Wendy Selig Prieb, who succeeded him, to enact a tie-in with the public transportation system to lower traffic on local highways and avoid parking lot delays. The three fans from the suburbs had left their house at five for the seven o'clock game, caught the five-twenty train, and were left at a platform thirty yards from the stadium entrance at five-forty, with ample time to spare to see the last few minutes of the Red Sox batting practice.

Like the stadia built in the nineties in Baltimore, Cleveland, Texas, and Denver, the Milwaukee park has a traditional design, baseball's answer to the hip roof colonial. The facade is predominantly brick, the walls low enough so that every long fly ball offers the suspense of a home run or an above-the-fence catch—baseball had had to come up with something to challenge the slam dunk—and a clearing had been left open in center field to reveal the Milwaukee skyline and the old brewery and sausage factories.

Like their nineties counterparts, the Seligs built their park with virtually no foul territory, so that fans are on top of the players, which was part of the young girl's fascination. For her parents, a baseball game is enough, but she is eleven, and when she was born even her grandparents had laptops. She loves to watch the players as people, this day especially, for Brewers superstar Kenny Felder was horsing around with the fans as he played catch in preparation for the pregame infield practice. Also, she knew, between BP and infield practice, about forty minutes before game time, there would be the daily home run derby, featuring one player from each team.

As the fans sat down in their seats along the third base line, the father prepared the video screens. For no cost, one got the screen and its in-house telecast of the game, complete with statistical information, replays, and, of course, commercials. For this night-at-the-ballpark service, the father punched his credit card number, first into his daughter's system, then into his wife's, and finally into his own.

The video systems are not available in the grandstands or bleachers. However, there is plenty of information and color available on the three scoreboards. There is a hand-held traditional scoreboard, a high-tech message board with replays, plus cut-ins of highlights from out-of-town games and information on those other games—such as, this night, Travis Fryman hitting his 300th career homer for the Marlins. The other message board includes all Brewers game information, such as batting averages, hitting streaks, etc.

The father attends about ten games a year on business, dining in the Brewers' private restaurant and watching the game from one of his company boxes. His wife's law firm also owns a box that is used for client entertaining. But this had become their daughter's favorite night out, beginning with the video system.

Once the credit card was entered, the process of ordering supper began. Many of the other fans chose from the cluster arrangement of the various food counters with so many specialized options—bratwurst, Taco Bell, Burger King, Pizza Hut, Wok-Inn, Brewer Chicken—that choosing a meal only took a few minutes. The Brewers had installed the french fry machines that became so popular in airports in the late nineties, and from beer to bottled water to Washington State wines, one could get almost anything in the guaranteed ten minutes or the meal was compliments of the club.

But for the young girl, it was more fun to watch the players and order from her seat, and her father wanted to watch the Red Sox up close. So he

*punched in the selections—a piece of chicken, a cup of pasta, and Adiron-
dack water for her, sweet and sour pork, an egg roll, and a glass of Chablis
for his wife, and a steak burrito, nachos grande, and Dos Equis for himself. He punched in the order, tapped the credit card acknowledgment
arrow, and sat back.*

*Ten minutes later, the vendor arrived with his order, only about $10
more expensive than waiting in line. "I knew the computer age would tie
in with civilization in some way," he told his daughter, knowing she
wouldn't understand what he was talking about—but then, she never had
been hungry and thirsty and sitting in the bleachers while a boisterous
crowd spilled beer on top of her. Box seat shopping includes hats, bats, and
all the memorabilia items; push the right button, MasterCard is billed,
and within the half hour your officially licensed Brewers jacket arrives like
duty-free goods.*

*The video system offers a dozen possibilities besides being able to order
food and "officially licensed products." Included is the capacity to flip to
any other game on The Baseball Channel. There is a tie-in to Stats, Inc.,
so that by typing in the right code, one can find out every possible statistic
concerning any player, as well as the Stats, Inc. leaders and trailers in
such obscure categories as number of pickoff throws per batter. There is an
electronic encyclopedia, which the fan can use to check where Robin Yount
stands, age-of-accomplishment-wise, among players with 3,000 hits.
There is SportsTicker, for all updated scores, current player statistics,
transactions, and news. There are the headline sports and news channels.*

*One of the most popular features is the manager game, where between
pitches one can punch in what strategy one would like; there are a number
of strategic options, and after the mother suggested a hit-and-run for the
Red Sox in the third inning, the screen showed that 11 percent responding
favored the same play. This night the Brewers jumped out to a 6–1 lead in
the fourth inning, and had it up to 11–3 in the sixth. The young girl,
losing interest in the players, finished playing baseball Nintendo games
and went for a walk to the stadium museums, which include the Milwaukee Baseball Hall of Fame, the Great Diamond Moments video room, and
the Milwaukee Personality Room, featuring videos and exhibits focusing
on Milwaukee-born celebrities, from Harvey Kuenn to Harold Stassen.*

*By the bottom of the seventh, the father became frustrated that he was
one of the 87 percent of the playing customers who'd wanted Red Sox
manager Rick Burleson to take out reliever Craig Bush, who instead had*

been batted around for six runs in two and a third innings as Milwaukee upped its lead to 14–4. The fan now knew he had no chance of seeing Boston's star closer, Frankie Rodriguez, so he punched the train schedule up on his screen, saw that they had seventeen minutes until the next scheduled one, rounded up his wife and daughter, and began heading home. His team was in first place, his daughter had caught a foul ball, and the World Champion Pittsburgh Pirates would be arriving tomorrow for the Pirates' and Brewers' annual afternoon interleague game. The client's proposal could wait another day.

INDEX